Foundations for the Renewal of the Diaconate

David Bourke
Karl H. Kruger
William F. Schmitz

Translators

Bishops' Committee on the Permanent Diaconate
National Conference of Catholic Bishops

In its planning document, as approved by the general membership of the National Conference of Catholic Bishops in November 1986, the Bishops' Committee on the Permanent Diaconate was authorized to prepare a series of monographs as part of a structured catechesis on the permanent diaconate. The third document in the series, *Foundations for the Renewal of the Diaconate*, was approved by Bishop Dale J. Melczek, chairman of the committee, and by Deacon Samuel M. Taub, executive director of Secretariat of the BCPD, and is authorized for publication by the undersigned.

Fordham University

LIBRARY

May 27, 1993   AT

Monsignor Robert N. Lynch
General Secretary
NCCB/USCC

LINCOLN CENTER

New York, N. Y.

ISBN 1-55586-185-7

"The Genesis and Growth of the Proposal," by Josef Hornef; "The Spiritual Life of the Deacon," by Hannes Kramer; "The Deacon and the Lay Person," by Paul Winniger; "From the History of the Diaconate," by Walter Croce, SJ; and "The Theology of the Diaconate," by Augustinus Kerkvoorde, OSB, translated from the German by Deacon William F. Schmitz of the Diocese of Rochester, New York. "The Theology of the Restoration of the Diaconate," by Karl Rahner, SJ, translated from the German by Karl H. Kruger; "The Teaching of the Second Vatican Council on the Diaconate," and "On the Diaconate," by Karl Rahner, SJ, translated from the German by David Bourke.

Dedication

To *Karl Rahner,* a giant among the theologians of this century, whose interest in the possibilities in renewing the diaconate helped lead to its restoration.

To *Hannes Kramer,* who first heard the call to be a deacon in 1947 and in his positive response initiated a movement which culminated in the restoration of this servant ministry to the Church Universal.

Acknowledgments

We are especially indebted to the publishing houses of Herder Verlag and the Crossroad Publishing Company for permission to publish the articles that are included in this volume. Next after that is citing the work of translating the five articles that have been excerpted from *Diaconia in Christo* by Deacon Bill Schmitz for whom this was a labor of love, a service freely given in true diaconal fashion. Without his service this project would not have been initiated. We shall always be grateful to him.

I should also like to express gratitude to the executives of the International Centre for the Diaconate and especially to the Centre's executive director, Margret Morche, who has given such full-hearted cooperation in researching and reproducing materials from the early post-war period, many of which are no longer in print.

And, finally, heartfelt thanks to Dan Juday, director of USCC Publishing and Promotion Services; Linda D. Hersey, editor and project manager; and Dottie Titman of our committee support staff, without whose encouragement and, above all, patience, this volume may never have come to completion.

Contents

Foreword / 1

Introduction / 3

The Genesis and Growth of the Proposal
by Josef Hornef / 5

The Spiritual Life of the Deacon
by Hannes Kramer / 28

The Deacon and the Lay Person
by Paul Winninger / 51

From the History of the Diaconate
by Walter Croce, SJ / 61

The Theology of the Diaconate
by Augustinus Kerkvoorde, OSB / 90

The Theology of the Restoration of the Diaconate
by Karl Rahner, SJ / 139

The Teaching of the Second Vatican Council on the Diaconate
by Karl Rahner, SJ / 182

On the Diaconate
by Karl Rahner, SJ / 193

Foreword

Over the period of the last five years the works collected in this volume have been assembled, translated, and arranged to give the reader a deeper appreciation of the development of a theology of the diaconate as a lifetime commitment to the service of the Church, open to married as well as celibate men. Authors represented here are all of a western european background: German, French, and Belgian. These are but several essays that were published during the Second Vatican Ecumenical Council and circulated among the council fathers in a single volume, *Diaconia in Christo*. Included are three works of the late Jesuit theologian Karl Rahner, published in those years that followed the closing of the council. These writings constitute a part of the patrimony of all deacons of the Church. It is for them, of this generation and those that are to follow, that this project has been undertaken and now brought to completion.

Most Reverend Dale J. Melczek
Apostolic Administrator
Diocese of Gary
Chairman, Bishops' Committee
on the Permanent Diaconate

Introduction

The proposal made to the fathers of the Second Vatican Ecumenical Council to restore the diaconate as a permanent order in the threefold ordained ministry in the Latin Rite of the Catholic Church has a longer history than has been previously supposed. Most of that history has been written in languages other than English. This present work is a project that, undertaken more than five years ago, had its genesis in a conversation in Jefferson City, Missouri, with Fr. Joseph Starmann in 1984. Fr. Starmann alluded to a book that was published in Germany by Herder Verlag, which contained a number of articles about the permanent diaconate and expressed the hope that he would be able to translate this work into English. I learned more about this book, titled *Diaconia in Christo,* when visiting the International Centre for the Diaconate in Freiburg, Germany, in 1986. The following year, at Herder Verlag, permission was requested to translate and publish five of the thirty-nine pieces that are included in this volume. When permission was granted, a brother deacon, William F. Schmitz of the Diocese of Rochester, was contacted to ask if he would undertake the necessary translations from German to English. This he agreed to do. When it was suggested that three theological works on the diaconate by Jesuit Fr. Karl Rahner be included in this volume, the necessary permissions were obtained and the work went forward.

If one were to gather the seminal documents on the present-day renewal of the diaconate (these would include Paul VI's apostolic letters *Sacrum Diaconatus Ordinem* and *Ad Pascendum, Lumen Gentium,* no. 29, and the 1971 and 1984 revisions of the *Guidelines for the Formation and Ministry of Permanent Deacons*) and have them available as reference while reading through this volume, it would become apparent the part that *Diaconia in Christo* and Rahner's theological investigations have played.

We shall always be indebted to the persons of Rahner, to whom we must give first place, Croce, Hornef, Kerkvoorde, Kramer, and Winninger, and others associated with them, for the diaconate that is evolving in our day.

It is hoped that this volume will be a useful contribution to the English-language literature on the renewed diaconate. May it provide those who are called to this Ordo, or who bear a responsibility for the continuing growth and development of this servant ministry, an increased awareness of and appreciation for the rootedness of the proposal that resulted in the vote of the council fathers on October 3, 1963, when 1,588 of the fathers voted to include the diaconate and its restoration in the *Constitution on the Church.*

"Digitus Dei (the Finger of God)," are the opening words by Josef Hornef in the first piece of these collected works. So we continue to believe that we see the finger (or the hand) of God at work in the Church as the restored diaconate continues to be renewed in our time.

Samuel M. Taub
Director, Secretariat for
the Bishops' Committee on
the Permanent Diaconate

Dr. Josef Hornef was born in 1896 in Germany. He studied in Germany at the Universities of Freiburg im Breisgau, Bonn, and Giessen. He received doctorates in both Civil as well as Canon Law.

Dr. Hornef, a lifelong jurist, became attracted to the notion of a restored diaconate in the 1930s. A devoted and active Catholic, he observed how the National Socialist regime was wresting the diakonia from the Church and making it the sole monopoly of state welfare organization under regime control. Suspect by the regime, Dr. Hornef and his family were relocated to a village where he spent thirteen years in "forced exile." After the war, he was established in Fulda as Chief Provincial Court Judge. There he continued to pursue his interest in the diaconate. In 1947, he began writing articles about the renewed diaconate as part of the ongoing reordering of the life of the Church. In these writings, Dr. Hornef has provided invaluable service as a perceptive observer of the signs of the times and as an able chronicler as well. The following article was written circa 1961.

Samuel M. Taub

The Genesis and Growth of the Proposal

by Josef Hornef

"*Digitus Dei* [The Finger of God]?"

"Despite many initial difficulties and problems that groping search that is underway in various parts of the Church, and which is moving forward in a common direction, is undoubtedly the genuine expression of a proposal, which points to the inner working of the Holy Spirit in the Church and, therefore, calls for an open and loving evaluation" (Hermann Seiler in *Der grosse Entschluss* [*The Great Decision*] Vienna, September 1959, p. 503; following the thought of Robert Rouquette, SJ, in *Etudes* [Paris, May 1959]).[1]

This attempt to trace the lines of development, followed by the proposal to restore the diaconate over the last three decades, cannot claim to be complete, especially where its earliest beginnings are concerned. The thought certainly existed in some heads long before it ever took written shape. On April 20, 1840, Frankfurt physician and author J. K. Passavant wrote the following to Melchior von Diepenbrock:

> The priestly state is too sharply separated from that of the laity; the cause is in part celibacy, in part the ways things developed in earlier centuries, when only the clergy were scholars and, therefore, the contrast between priest and laity was almost always that of the lettered and unlettered. Celibacy has its good sides. They are so well-known that they require no further explanation. The disadvantages, however, can hardly be denied and, in particular, that specific one whereby many exemplary people disqualify themselves for ecclesiastical service, who because of their youth are not confident that they can completely measure up to the task. Here, it occurs to me, there are two alternative remedies: the Church can either permit priests to marry in the manner in which the Greek Uniates are permitted to do, or she can expand the sphere of activity of deacons, so that these men, who would be allowed to be married, could carry out in part the teaching office and other ecclesiastical functions, while the priest (who would therefore have to be senior) would exclusively administer the sacraments, especially confession. If in the considered opinion of the bishops, then, several deacons (archdeacons) could be drawn from the best educated ranks of the so-called laity, then the Church would have excellent ministers at her disposal. These deacons, should they become widowers, would, as a rule, then move on to the priesthood. The first alternative would only be carried out if entire communities would work together within the Catholic Church . . .; the second, however, could be implemented *right now via a council.* . . . Individual communities would have to have some say in the selection of the bishops. . . . Just think about a bishop starting off, going forward with the mandate of an entire diocese (papal approval would always be essential), surrounded not only by the ranking clergy but also by the most qualified men (as archdeacons of their diocese). What institutions could be started up, set in motion. . . . what tremendous possibilities!

Diepenbrock, who was later to become Cardinal and Prince-Bishop of Breslau, responded to his friend concerning the above on April 23, 1840:

> All open-minded, thinking people perceive the need to restructure the Church, but only the very few grasp the way to do it as clearly as you have done. I consider the fact that such ideas are being publicly expressed as an act of love toward mankind (A. Erb, *Gelebtes Christenum* [*Living Christianity*] Freiburg, 1938, pp. 59ff).

Reflections such as these were not limited to Germany. It has only recently become known, that the well-known French priest Dom A. Grea, using an exposition of the theology of the diaconate based on the patristic tradition, proposed the restoration of an ordained diaconate having an expressly charitable character (in the spirit of St. Vincent de Paul) in his 1885 work, *De l'Eglise et sa divine Consitution* [*The Church and Her Divine Constitution*] (J. Presle, *"Dom Gréa et le diaconat"* in *Bulletin des Chanoines reguliers de l'Immaculee Conception* [*Bulletin of the Canons Regular of the Immaculate Conception*], New Series no. 72, Canisy-Manche, January/February 1962). Refer also to what A. Marranzini, SJ, had to report in this volume about V. Marchese's 1912 proposal. Others certainly might be able to provide additional supplemental information either from their own personal memory or even from the literature.[2] Since the author of this article has been bound up in the proposal since 1948, it is hoped that it would not be held against him, if he shares his own personal experiences in the course of the article.

It is significant that the first, albeit vague, emergence of the idea of restoration of the diaconate in Germany can be found in the periodical *Caritas* (Freiburg im Breisgau). *Caritas* Director G. von Mann of Freiburg im Breisgau published in the July/August 1934 issue of the above-mentioned periodical an article, *"Der Caritasdiakonat und seine Erneuerung"* ["The Diaconate of Charity and Its Restoration"]. He deals with the nature of charity, grounded in the mystery of the Body of Christ, with "the stimulation of charitable activities by the parish community." The diaconate of charity, rooted in the liturgical, sacrificial community, should arise anew from the deepened Christ-consciousness of the community. He welcomes the efforts to "shape the diaconate, *as a first step to the priesthood,* into a diaconate of charity" and mentions the fact that theology students should even be engaged in charitable works during their vacations. For the ministry of the *laity* in charitable service, he recommends a liturgical form of "missioning by the Church." Even though the "diaconate" being promoted is limited to charitable service, neither is there as of yet any mention of ordination to deacon (to the extent that there is no intended reference to the charitable service of future priests). The thought being put forward suggests more the idea of a "fraternity," as a organizational form. But these are to be sure only the first steps along the way.

Two years later, in August 1936, an article by Hanns Schuetz of Koblenz entitled *"Diakonie der Liebe"* ["Diaconia of Love"] appears in the same periodical. Schuetz is a graduate (1931) of the Aachen Social Service Worker School. The social service workers trained in the Aachen and Freiburg institutions wanted to form an appropriate professional association. The

Freiburg "alumni" had already met in Cologne in 1934. It had been hoped that a solution might be found in some kind of "Charitable Service Fraternity." On the 22nd and 23rd of September 1935, a meeting of Freiburg and Aachen "alumni" was held in CologneHohenlind with the support of the national headquarters of the German *Caritas* Society. For one of the speakers there, Dr. Schraeder—the director of the Aachen School—there was, practically speaking, only *one* concrete possibility for closer bonding—both to the Church and among professional associates: the restoration of the (male) diaconate according to the early Christian understanding thereof, with a threefold mission—liturgy, charity, and catechesis. The restoration of this office was at that time a necessity, if charitable service was to survive in both the deeds and consciousness [of the people], given the current maelstrom of national events ("The Third Reich" and the domination of the National-Socialist People's Welfare Organization). The speaker [Dr. Schraeder] envisioned a need for an ecclesiastical training institute, the formation of an ascetical community and a missioning (*missio*) by the bishop. Schraeder believed that the restoration should be tied to the still active ministry of sacristan, which in turn should be elevated to the ministry of deacon.

Schuetz, who already had previously been working with these ideas (and had also been in communication with Dr. Schraeder concerning them), sends a letter dated December 1935[3] to those who had attended the [September 1935] meeting. In it, he is seeking to lay the conceptual and material foundation for a profession of social-charitable service, which he would like to see exercised as church-affiliated service. He asks those professional colleagues, who share his common interest and common objective, to sign a "statement of commitment":

> I wish to carry out my professional service and form my life in the spirit of the love of God. I wish to serve the Church faithfully. . . . To the extent possible, I will cooperate with my parish as the appropriate sacrificial community. . . . I wish to be associated with the community of those, who, with me, are committed to a common professional objective.

With one's signature, one was obligated to say a certain prayer each day, to receive communion once a year for the intentions of the association, and to attend the annual meeting of the association. Even if these were only preliminary steps, it is certainly worth noting that the path leading to an association that will one day converge with the diaconate must be a path of personal sanctification.

Approximately twenty social workers responded to the invitation. Unfortunately, the effort came to nought. No official ecclesiastical support was forthcoming, even though such a diaconate was probably the final opportunity to retain church-affiliated charitable work [in light of the situation in Nazi Germany].

In the August 1936 article mentioned above, Schuetz published the ideas discussed in *CologneLindenthal* [sic]; however, he has now separated the proposal from the efforts of the social-charitable group to form a professional association. He sees the question of the restoration of the diaconate henceforth as a parish problem. It is also an extension of the altar as the common sacrificial table. "With the restoration of the diaconate, the pastor could have at his disposal professional assistance, both for the planned expansion of his ministry, as well as for pastoral care in homes." Further activities could include all kinds of catechesis and youth leadership. He holds fast to the idea, that the office of sacristan could serve as the point of departure. Schuetz speaks of a "missioning" by the bishop; he cautiously avoids any reference to diaconal ordination. He sees those charitable activities carried out in the diaconate of priest-aspirants as insufficient to cope with the urgent tasks at hand. He envisions a full-time "deacon," who exercises his office in church-affiliated service and who serves as a bridge between clergy and laity. Schuetz's initiative, however, elicited no response.

The war comes. Priests interned for years in the Dachau concentration camp, including Fr. Otto Pies, SJ, and Vicar Wilhelm Schamoni, are spiritually awakened and engage in extensive discussions about the sufferings of the priests in the concentration camp. Based on their observations and experiences, they reach conclusions (pertaining largely to the future education and formation of priests), survey the possibilities of reorganizing ecclesial work, and so forth. In conjunction with the anticipated critical shortage of priests, they exchange ideas concerning a possible restoration of the diaconate. W. Schamoni recorded the results of these discussions at the end of 1944 while he was still interned in the concentration camp. He succeeded in saving his notes in the aftermath of the collapse [total defeat] of the Third Reich. It is therefore possible—despite the shocking circumstances in which it was given—to share here the testimony of his efforts.

It is clear that access to the priesthood should definitely not be rendered easier. To the contrary, the goal should be to strive for the 100 percent religious cleric. The question then arises:

> . . . as to whether or not it is right to leave pastoral care in the hands of a relatively small number of priests and their lay assistants. Archbishop Constantini had suggested that the work of a handful of missionary

priests could be rendered more fruitful by ordaining an army of lay catechists to the ecclesial office of the diaconate. This suggestion needs to be examined to see if it is also applicable to our [present] European circumstances. Such a diaconate of married, employed, capable assistants, especially from the teaching profession—but also from all other professions and fields, and of course not bound to pray the daily office—would offer the following advantages:

1. Overworked and overburdened pastoral priests could be relieved of the catechesis of children and adults, which could then be entrusted to specially qualified individuals. Ecclesial office would lend a special sacredness and dignity to the missioning of these individuals.

2. Communities, deprived of Mass despite [officially authorized] bination and trination would be afforded the opportunity for prayer services, liturgies of the word and communion services. The establishment of new communities and actual community life would be possible even with the most serious shortage of priests.

3. The preaching of these deacons, who would be involved in the work-a-day world, would be particularly persuasive and down-to-earth. One perceives in current preaching that it is being done by individuals who are *"segregati a populo"* ["separated from the people"].

4. The Church has largely become a Church of authorities and officials. The feudal state and the civil servant state have rubbed off on her. The diaconate would be an effective means to return Holy Mother the Church to a Church of the people.

5. The Church has not succeeded in holding its ground among either the leading intellectual classes nor among those classes most easily led astray, the proletariat. In their own *milieu,* deacons *from* these classes *for* these classes could gain influence incomparably deeper than could any priest, since priests would never develop within this *milieu* the kind of rapport that deacons would have already established. One could develop the diaconate into a means to win back the de-Christianized *milieu.* An intelligent deacon from the working-class would, without any special theological training, be able to touch the heart of his worker colleagues with just the right words.

6. Many vocations to the priesthood would result from the exemplary family life [of married deacons].

7. Deacons could hardly do any harm. If they do not keep their promise, the Church does not need to keep them, as opposed to what it unfortu-

10

nately must try to do when dealing with priests. The Church does not have to give much, only a measure of trust, and she realizes an enormous gain.

8. Converted protestant pastors could as full-time deacons be given a new, important range of activities.

9. The diaconate could be a bridge to the eastern churches.

It is gratifying to see, dating even back to that period, a wealth of ideas, which we later (1953) find again extensively in Schamoni's monograph and which even today play such an important role in our organization. (Schamoni has definitively confirmed to this author, that he was in fact addressing the subject of an *ordained* diaconate—see the remark cited earlier about praying the office.)

In the October 1947 issue of *Stimmen der Zeit*, Fr. Pies, who was seriously ill when released from the concentration camp, publishes an article entitled "Cellblock 26—Experiences of the Priestly Life in Dachau," dealing with the sufferings of priests interned there. He also reports about those topics that were the subject of many discussions among priests who were ready to discharge their responsibilities in the face of death. In conjunction with the increasingly more serious shortage of priests, he poses the question as to "whether or not it was time to act upon those nudges that were—apparently— being initiated by the Holy Spirit" and to permit the diaconate to rise again. The reference here is also to a diaconate of married, employed, and proven men (i.e., to a part-time diaconate). Fr. Pies in so doing refers back to those notes, which were recorded by his friend W. Schamoni in conjunction with their discussion in Dachau.

At the time this author first saw the article by Fr. Pies in *Stimmen der Zeit*, he had been living for more than thirteen years in forced exile, having been relocated by the Nazis as a judge from a Catholic area to Upper Hesse. He had endured with his family the sorrows of this *diaspora,* doubly sorrowful because of the hostility of the regime to Church, and strove with his loved ones to fulfill the duties of sacristan, lector, and organist in a mission church community twenty kilometers distant from the main parish community. It is understandable, then, that the idea of a rebirth of the diaconate would touch the depths of his soul. In vain, he begged Fr. Pies to publish further information about the suggestions developed in Dachau; Pies was unable to do so because he was inundated with work.[4]

This author himself then in 1948 wrote an article entitled "On the Restoration of the Diaconate"—having no knowledge whatsoever about any

11

other publications on the topic (with the exception of the article by A. Schuchert, see below) or any information about the diaconate among the evangelical Lutheran Christians. With his manuscript in hand he had to go from one periodical publisher to another, until it was finally accepted and published in the November/December 1949 issue (no. 6) of *Die Besinnung* [*Reflections*] (Nuremberg, publisher Karl Borromäus Glock).

The goal of his efforts is to propose an ordained diaconate as a lifetime profession in the sense of a vocation, with pastoral priestly duties (liturgy, charitable works, catechesis, pastoral care in homes, youth work), without the obligation of celibacy, but in its place exemplary family life. However, a part-time diaconate ("voluntary" diaconate) with the minor orders as prerequisites is also proposed. Both forms would exist side by side. The pastoral perspective is heavily influenced by the *diaspora* experience. Neither life enriched by liturgy nor the great importance of charitable activities is as of yet sufficiently well appreciated. The fact that the very first written acknowledgement received was from the Evangelical Lutheran Relief Organization (Stuttgart) should not go unmentioned. On Pentecost 1950, this author read a paper on the proposal at the convention of the Society of Catholic University Professors in Eichstaett. Further papers and numerous articles followed (from the viewpoints of ministry, the missions, liturgy, and so forth).

In 1948, the *Woerterbuch der Religion* [*Dictionary of Religion*] by Anton Anwander is published. Under "Clergy and Laity" is found the following:

> It would be in the most appropriate accordance with the principle of tradition in the Catholic Church ... if the most religious, most upstanding and most capable laymen, as in earlier times, but naturally with a different type of formation and training, were admitted to the clerical state via the transformation of the diaconate.

It is presumed that the reference here is to a part-time diaconate.

We find another recommendation in *Glauben und Leben* [*Faith and Life*], the Mainz diocesan newspaper, on August 1, 1948. A. Schuchert (the former rector at Campo Santo in Rome, who died in 1962) publishes in an article entitled "Youth and the Diaconate," which mentions recommendations "that have been made by the best of our youth themselves." He speaks about an apparently celibate, ordained deacon as a special vocational status:

> The official [ordained] deacon could perform valuable work in the large *diaspora* communities. By sharing the rectory residence with the appointed pastor live with him in a model spiritual community, which

would take on a different form of community perhaps than that of pastor and associate pastor. In many places today, we are familiar with the female pastoral assistant. The deacon as pastoral assistant could work in close collaboration with the overburdened pastor on a much broader scale.

In May 1949, *Deutsche Volkschaft* [*German Society*] carries an article by H. H. Gehle, "The Diaconate, the Lay Office of the Church." He is concerned with the activation of the work of the laity, particularly in the area of charitable works. "Charity is the lay office of the Church." He is speaking here about the activation of the mystical Body of Christ, not in societies or organizations, but about the activation in former or new orders, about carrying out official ecclesial tasks in the name of the bishop within a distinct diaconal lay order, in addition to and separate from the priestly order in dioceses. What is lacking here is a clear-cut delineation between the ordained cleric and the layman, who by virtue of baptism and confirmation is missioned.

According to the July 2, 1950 issue of *Glauben und Leben,* the "possibility of a diaconate as a permanent state" is also mentioned at the First German Liturgical Congress in Frankfurt am Main in the summer of 1950. In the same year, the director of the Zürich *Caritas* Headquarters, Vicar General Prelate A. Teobaldi, speaks out in favor of (even if only in passing) a restoration of the diaconate at a *Caritas* conference in Freiburg im Breisgau. He would like to see the inception of new professional status, the ordained deacon. In the *Neue Zürcher Nachrichten* [*New Zurich News*] dated October 3, 1950 (in a supplement, "Charity and Social Service"), he can say of himself that he has been speaking out in favor of this proposal for a long time. "We are convinced that it must one day become a reality, since the complete development of Catholic life in these times is moving in that direction." Responses to his statement included both enthusiastic letters and skeptical opinions.

In the November 1951 issue of *Der Seelsorger* [*The Pastor*] (Vienna, publisher and editor-in-chief, Prelate Karl Rudolph), there is an article on the rebirth of the diaconate, "The Modern Official Diaconate" by F. Gstaltmeyer. This individual believes that a point of departure for a multifaceted, official diaconate is sacristan service. The place of the deacon in ministry would be roughly analogous to that of a "lay brother (in the best sense of the word) in a monastery."

During the same fall 1947 time-frame in which Fr. Pies published his work in *Stimmen der Zeit* [*Voices of the Times*], a young man, who was a passionate forest ranger in a mountainous region of the Allgäu, gave up his profession. Hannes Kramer knew that he had been called by God to diaconal service. He believed (on the basis of other church-related involvement) that he could best answer his call by pursuing the appropriate social service training. In his hope to achieve in this way the high ideal of the diaconate—no matter how utopian this objective may have seemed from a human standpoint—he attended the 1950 Freiburg Social Workers' Seminar of the German *Caritas* Society. In the spring of 1951, he showed up there [as a student] for the first time with his professional image of the deacon, which had been stamped with the love of the Good Shepherd. Other fellow students of his had also been silently carrying around this image within themselves. So a "diaconate circle" was formed; for a long time it remained limited to seven young people. The small group met frequently to work out the basic concepts for the restoration of the diaconate. Not until a half year after the circle had been formed did Kramer learn about the article by Fr. Pies in *Stimmen der Zeit* as well as about this author's publications. The first "Diaconate Circle Working Paper" appeared on May 1, 1952, with Hannes Kramer as the responsible signatory. It was intended to maintain the sense of community among the circle members who had now been separated because of their professional jobs, to serve to deepen the idea of the diaconate, and to the extent possible, to put the idea into practice in the workplace of that time. The first issue contained a basic program, which was extensively expanded in issue no. 2. The young men were concerned with a full-time diaconate—a profession as a vocation—with primarily charitable activities. What is important here is that from the outset there is clear focus on an ordained diaconate. Thorough social service training (with certain supplemental aspects) . . . ascetical formation . . . education for a simple life-style . . . community life for those to become deacons and of those already in active ministry as deacons in accordance with methods similar to those followed by evangelical Lutheran deacons . . . and a practical period of internship upon completion of the training—all of these would be required. The deacon would not have the obligation of celibacy. What is also important is that these young men are already striving for holiness, in pursuit of their future goal, by means of a serious prayer-life and appropriate behavior in their professions. They are also encouraging their wives and fiancees to join them on their journey to the diaconate. From the outset, the working paper was also intended to inform and win over to the idea of diaconate a broader circle of interested parties—clergy and laity. The number of subscribers increased steadily, its content became deeper, and the proposal began to grow towards maturity.

The beginnings, the early voices speaking out for the rebirth of the diaconate, have intentionally been set forth here in detail. For one thing, the 'sources are widely scattered. For another, this closer examination shows that things were already happening before the last war, and that after the war they started up again on a broad basis and in many various ways. An overview of available literature proves that these initiatives continually occurred in different locations and were independent of each other. Despite the multiplicity of the individual concepts, it is clear that the single objective is the rebirth of the office of deacon. In this spontaneous, continuous recurrence of initiatives, one can see a sign of the governance of the Holy Spirit, as had been already noted in Dachau and acknowledged by Rouquette and Seiler (see the "Foreword"). In conjunction therewith, one must call special attention to the strong participation of laymen right from the outset in the efforts to bring about the rebirth of the diaconate. It can also be clearly seen and will become even clearer in what follows—that men of the *Caritas* Society and in charitable service positions have been heavily involved in its development from the beginning. That is completely understandable, given the current situation at *Caritas,* which is earnestly struggling with the danger of an overemphasis on the organizational aspects and which would like to see charitable services renewed from the altar outward [*Translator's note:* flow from a eucharistic source].

We cannot fail to mention here an experiment that could be treated as a point of departure for the diaconate. After the director of the Social Service Seminar in Freiburg, Hans Wollasch, in a March/April 1952 article in *Caritas* had examined and affirmed the possibility of a male *charitable-social service* pastoral assistant, a *catechetically* trained pastoral assistant immediately became a reality: The Archdiocese of Cologne in the fall of 1952 created for young men a "seminar for catechists and pastoral assistants" who in service of the Church wanted to become "lay workers, catechists, and church youth ministers." After an auspicious beginning, the institute came to nought within a few years. The reasons cannot be gone into here; in any case one cannot, according to things as they then stood, deduce an argument against the diaconate. Rather, the facts could support the case, that the ordained deacon would have his rightful and clearly delineated place in the parish community, rather than the lay pastoral assistant.

The first monograph about the renewal of the diaconate appears in 1953. It bears the noteworthy title *Familienvaeter als geweihte Diakonen* [*Family Fathers as Ordained Deacons*] (Schöningh, Paderborn) and is intended to be a response to the "monologue of the laity" relative to our topic.[*Translator's note:* An English translation, *Married Men as Ordained Deacons,* was published in London by Burns and Oates in 1955.] The author is the already-mentioned Vicar Wilhelm Schamoni, who had not forgotten the conversations in Dachau and was encouraged by Fr. Pies in this work. He had used a sabbatical in Rome to delve into historical questions especially. Schamoni advocates above all the part-time married deacon and would like to see mature men who have proven themselves in work and family life ordained. He has definite reservations about the full-time diaconate. He fears it could become a refuge for those unsuccessful in life, but more to the point, that the institution of a full-time diaconate will lead to further "clericalization" and "officiousness." Therefore, he regards the full-time diaconate more as an exception. In certain special situations, exceptional part-time deacons could be given full-time assignments. Lay brothers in the mission societies could be called to this vocation; theology students who at least know themselves not called to priesthood could, in light of their completed theological training, work as deacons. The diaconate opens an avenue here for converted married ministers to serve the Church. Schamoni refers especially to the resident deacon as the leader of a mission church or an out-station of the missions. He emphasizes the great importance of the diaconal liturgical service in places where no priest visits or which are only rarely visited by a priest. The deacon could play a pioneering role in setting up new communities. He further speaks out about the deacon in the missions and recommends that experienced catechists be ordained to the diaconate.

If *Die Besinnung* (Nürnberg) in 1949 was the first publication to address the matter of the diaconate, the *Werkhefte für Katholische Laienarbeit* [*Notes for Catholic Lay Work*] quickly generated lively interest about the question. The November 1950 issue contained the first indication: John Manuel's "How Did It Get This Far?" Over the years, there followed a series of publications. *Begegnung* [*Encounter*] (editor, W. Peuler) and the *Allgemeine Sonntagszeitung* [*The General Sunday Newspaper*] (earlier called *Michael*) also came out for the rebirth of the diaconate. After *Caritas* (Freiburg) published three articles by Wollasch (see above) and Hornef in the spring of 1952, *Caritas* (Lucerne) dedicated its entire 1953 publication to the proposal on the diaconate. Following Pius Parsch's train of thought, publisher Hugo Wyss, initially sought to mobilize the laity for charitable service (May 1952). He placed the "universal diaconate" to which everyone is called alongside the "universal priesthood" of all Christians. Moreover, in the 1/1953 issue ("The Restoration of the Diaconate"), he is already discussing the two possibilities: the official diaconate of ordained deacons and the "diaconal" activity of the laity, which should likewise originate at the altar and as much as possible be linked/joined to a certain service at the altar. In numerous articles in 1953 and thereafter, the proposal will be discussed again and again in *Caritas*.

16

In its October 1953 issue, *Der Seelsorger* [*The Pastor*] (Vienna) publishes an article: "Lay Assistants or Ordained Deacons?" by Karl Böhmerle of the Vienna Catholic Action organization. The answer that Böhmerle provides to the question is clear: lay assistants *and* deacons! (Böhmerle mentions that these thoughts stem from his own reflections; he had only become aware of Hornef's articles, which were in surprising agreement with his own ideas, after having committed his first essay to writing). At the beginning of 1957, there follows a special issue of *Der Seelsorger,* "Educated, Trained, Ordained," in which Böhmerle further extends his thoughts. He complains that although in Vienna rather good opportunities exist for the religious training of the laity (Theological Year for Lay Studies and Adult Education), men involved in Catholic Action (a well-known european Catholic laymen's service organization roughly comparable to the Knights of Columbus or St. Vincent de Paul Society directed by european clergy, unlike the two above-mentioned U.S. organizations, which carry out their work with their own lay leadership structure) lack fundamental religious knowledge and, above all, ascetical formation. He also mentions the lack of necessary certification. He urgently calls for the availability of good religious education joined with spiritual formation and, indeed, on a broader scale. Suitable deacons would be found among the young men prepared in this way.

Böhmerle affirms the full-time deacon who would be chiefly active in the ministries of pastoral care and charitable works, whereas he assigns to the part-time deacon the task of preparing the laity for their apostolic role and supporting them in it ("Co-Workers of Catholic Action"). Furthermore, he sees the part-time diaconate in (perhaps *too*) close association with Catholic Action. In principle, he is completely clear on this point: the deacon is in the hierarchical order subordinate to the priest, but Catholic Action by its very nature remains lay activity. Prelate Rudolf writes in the foreword:

> Today, pastoral care cries out unrelentingly for a stronger infusion of ordained personnel. It is gratifying to see that the newly awakened community-consciousness is calling for a more effective organizational integration of the community. . . . Lay assistance alone does not suffice. . . . The most energetic members of the laity are already asking to be endowed with the grace and authority that comes with ordination.

That special issue engenders lively discussions in subsequent issues of *Der Seelsorger* (vols. 6, 7, and 12, 1957).

More and more professional theological periodicals make their pages available for these discussions. More and more theologians offered their opinions although at first incidentally: Yves Congar, OP; D. Zähringer, OSB; Prof. F. X. Arnold (Tübingen); Joseph Löw, CSSR (lecturer at the Austrian Theology Week in Linz, 1953); P. Brockmöller, SJ; and Prof. Fleckenstein (Würzburg), among others. In his essay "The Universal Apostolate" (in *Der grosse Entschluss* [*The Great Decision*] (Vienna, June 1954), Prof. Karl Rahner explains:

> The idea of the married deacon has nothing to do with relaxing the rule of celibacy. It is basically a matter of the renewal of the diaconate as a hierarchical office with a real, defined sphere of activities, with a field of apostolic work (which has practically died out), and the conferring of ordination for such work. As soon as this office is recognized as permanent, standing independently on its own and not as a stepping stone to ordination (that is, not as a transition to the celibate priesthood—the author), no one need think any longer, that it necessarily would have to be administered by one who is unmarried. It would, therefore, have a ranking in the hierarchical apostolate and not in the lay apostolate.

Even outside Germany the question was taken up—in Switzerland, Austria, France, even Holland and Denmark. Schamoni's book appeared in English in 1955 as *Married Men as Ordained Deacons* (Burns and Oates, London). It is understandable, that depending on background and location, things are seen from different viewpoints by individual proponents of the diaconate. Böhmerle approaches it from his leadership role in Vienna's Catholic Action group, Hornef from his *diaspora* experience. He has an image of the deacon as a pastoral assistant engaged in a wide range of tasks. The people within the Diaconate Circle and the evangelical Lutheran approach (Prof. Krimm of the Institute for the Scientific Study of the Diaconate, Heidelberg) will expressly call attention to the essential importance of the charitable service aspect of diaconal ministry. If Kramer and his men incline more strongly to a diaconal ministry of charity, it is to the credit of Prof. Rahner to have struck a balance: One diaconate with a wide range of tasks but which affords the possibility of specialization so that an individual—depending upon his preference or specialized education, can be engaged either (primarily) in charitable work or specialize in catechesis or even in youth ministry. Whatever the situation, in each case liturgical involvement is necessary. Even for the deacon, liturgy should be the center of his life. In support of this, the article by Raphael Hombach, ODB, "History and the Revival of the Mass with a Deacon," was a big help (*Liturgie und Moenchtum*, Folge, Heft XIV, 1954). He points out the possibility that the deacon (at least insofar as he resides in a parish) can proceed to the altar daily with the priest for the celebration of the Holy Sacrifice of the Mass.[5]

Prof. Rahner presented his above-mentioned balanced ideas in a lecture to the Deacon Circle in February 1956. His considerations appeared in "Deacon Circle Working Paper" no. 5, 1956. They formed the basis for his essay "Preliminary Dogmatic Remarks for Correctly Framing the Question about the Restoration of the Diaconate." Now for the first time there is a theological foundation for the efforts to restore the diaconate. Rahner summarizes the basis for the restoration in the following way:

> The Church has functions to perform which in fact—above all, in our own situation—cannot be adequately carried out by priests, even though in the office of priesthood there are interior elements of a perduring nature which will always be essential to the Church. From the testimony of Scripture and Tradition the diaconate is not simply a mere stepping stone by which a man attains priestly ordination, only to have his diaconal role end upon completion of this transition to the priesthood. Rather, in its essence the diaconate is a distinct office sharing in the one Order, an office which can and even should represent a permanent and lifelong *commission for a man.*

The proposal was given world-wide exposure for the first time during the International Pastoral Liturgical Congress at Assisi in September 1956. In his lecture "The Liturgical Renewal in Service of the Missions," Missionary Bishop W. van Bekkum of Ruteng, Flores, Indonesia spoke out urgently in favor of the renewal of both minor orders and the diaconate as independent offices. Here the question was taken up from the point of view of missionary liturgy and as a significant possibility for missionary adaptation. The presentation was "one of the most impressive and the most noteworthy of the Congress because of the concreteness of his message and the openness of his speech."

Bishop van Bekkum brought with him recommendations from the Chinese and Indonesian bishops that pointed in the same direction. These efforts were also welcomed at the educational meeting of missionaries that was taking place at the same time at Assisi. Here, the conferring of ordination upon lectors was strongly proposed as a first step. Prof. Johannes Hofinger, SJ, of Manila had already spoken out in favor of this at the International Liturgical Meeting in Louvain in 1954. Following the conclusion of the Congress in Assisi, Hofinger in *Zeitschrift fuer Missionswissenschaft und Religionswissenschaft* [*Missions and Religious Studies Magazine*] 3/1957 made his position perfectly clear in response to our question: "In the Missions Should There Be a Separate Status of Deacons?" He affirmed the official deacon for the better unfolding of the liturgy, especially for "worship services without a priest" in the distant outstations, as well as his importance in the field of charity and his value as a connecting link between the people and the priest. He would require thorough formation (academic standards). Today, as a rule, the training of the catechist does not yet suffice to enable him to be ordained a lector. Hofinger's chief hesitation was that the institution of the married deacon would be falsely interpreted: "Today married deacons, tomorrow married priests." He even underscored the economic difficulties. He did not want part-time deacons in the missions. Instead, the minor orders should be conferred for part-time activity.

An event of the greatest significance deserves to be recounted. It occurred during the Second World Congress for the Lay Apostolate at Rome in 1957. Pope Pius XII himself happened to speak about the proposal. He had become acquainted with it through P. M-D Epagnuel, who had presented him with his essay in the *Nouvelle Revue Theologique* (see below). The pope passed it along to the Holy Office to study the question. The Holy Father desired at an appropriate place in his talk to clarify wherein the distinction between priest and laity lay. Decidedly, it lay in ordination! The proposal for the rebirth of the diaconate was not yet, at least not today, ripe. But when the time is ripe, the deacon stands alongside the priest (that is, through ordination the deacon is a cleric, no longer a layman—the author). There was no doubt about it: these words from the Holy Father were a great opportunity for the proposal. We may and should assist in bringing the proposal to maturity.

It was a great day on the way to the revival of the diaconate, when at the International Congress for Mission and Liturgy in Nijmegen-Uden (September 1959), the Archbishop of Nagpur, Eugene D'Souza, declared himself emphatically in favor of deacons both in the missions and in already Christianized lands. Under no circumstances did he want to stop at the minor orders; for him it must be the ordained deacon! For the same reason a missionary employs only a married catechist, so too should the deacon be married. Without a doubt, marriage offers greater stability. At the same time, the institution of the married deacon preserves the world from unhappy priests. Of course, the remarks of Archbishop D'Souza did not go unchallenged. Could it be otherwise? An African bishop who took part in the meeting remarked to this author that so little was known about these things, that one could not have expected everyone to agree right down the line.

Meanwhile, more monographs appear. In 1958, the book by Fr. Prof. Paul Winninger of St. Thomas Seminary in Strassburg, *Vers un renouveau du diaconat* [*Toward a Renewal of the Diaconate*] (Desclee de Brouwer, Paris), is published. Winninger gives an overview of the various views of the individual advocates of the proposal, who had made their position known for the most part in German-speaking countries. Extensive agreement is apparent, even though specific differences cannot be denied. Finally, Winninger presents his own ideas in a "Conclusion." In it, he is particularly concerned with the relationship of the diaconate to the place and tasks of the laity, as well as to the priesthood and to celibacy. The deacon should be involved in Catholic Action as a chaplain (spiritual advisor). The diaconate offers to the elite from Catholic Action and to the layman involved in missionary work the possibility of dedicating themselves to God in a religious state of life (to which every apostolic movement tends in a special way). If, in this regard, Winninger maintains that the lay apostolate, especially Catholic Action, is at its present stage of development incomplete, that it lacks a crowning [as a sign of full maturity] (which is clearly seen in the possibility of access to the diaconate), this is simply not the case (even if this author himself earlier made use of similar expressions). Catholic Action as a lay institution needs no special crowning of its members via ordination. The most one can say is that for some specific individuals the diaconate would represent the crowning of their work in Catholic Action. Winninger has not the slightest fear of an increase in clericalization because of the diaconate. On the contrary, he believes that the diaconate will be an effective antidote to "paternalism." He also has no fear that the diaconate will have a detrimental effect on recruitment for the priesthood. On the contrary, the priest will be able to give himself completely over to his priestly tasks once he is freed by the deacon from tasks proper to deacons. The ideal of the priest completely dedicated to the things of the spirit will shine brightly, it will regain its former attraction and awaken many priestly vocations of high quality. Finally, Winninger wants to find out if the institution of unmarried deacons has any possibilities, but not at the expense of the married diaconate. He affirms this possibility. Since the secular institutes (which do live the evangelical counsels) are clearly experiencing a period of great success, a sufficient number of celibate deacons will be found. However, it may be said that Winninger has clearly spoken out in favor of married deacons in an article co-written with the author in the *Nouvelle Revue Theologique* (April 1961).

In the spring of 1959, a little book appeared, published by Herder-Wien (Seelssorger-Verlag) and entitled *Kommt der Diakon der fruehen Kirche wieder?* [*Will the Deacon of the Early Church Return?*]. In this book, Hornef summarizes in a systematic way those thoughts that he had set forth in numerous articles. Since then, the publication has also appeared in French, Italian, and Brazilian Portugese. The English and Spanish translations are ready for publication. What is said in it in terms of a theological foundation is mainly a repetition of the thoughts of Karl Rahner (see above). The diaconate is seen as essentially a priestly office, as an office unto itself. The practical pastoral points of view stand in the forefront (the author is of course a layman). The diaconate is dealt with according to various characteristics and possibilities: the parish community, pastoral care in the deacon's own *milieu,* the missions and diaconal ministry in institutions. The liturgical aspect (Mass with a deacon) as well as charitable works have retained their respective importance. The economic aspect is also dealt with. The pros and cons of the discussion as things stand at that point in time are thoroughly reviewed and directions for new development are indicated. On the whole there has been no basic change from the outline of the first 1949 article, even though some change in details has taken place.

The acceptance of the works of Schamoni, Winninger, and Hornef in the professional literature was—*with ever decreasing exceptions*—thoroughly positive. The fact that, after the appearance of the writings of Winninger and Hornef (March 1959), over eighty articles and monographs about the topic appeared in seven different languages, indicates just how strong and world wide the interest in the rebirth of the diaconate is. It is just not possible here to touch upon all of the topics covered in these writings. We will mention only a few.

A new view is offered in the essay "The Role of the Deacon in Today's Church" [*"Du role des diacres dans l'Eglise d'aujourd'hui"*] by M.D. Epagneul in *Nouvelle Revue Theologique* (February 1959), which has since then published several articles dealing with the topic. In his article, Epagneul, the founder and first prior general of the *"Freres Missionnaires des Campagnes,"* makes clear the great value ordination to the diaconate has for the lay brothers of this society and the lay members of *"Auxiliaires du clerge"* (a secular institute). Both communities are dedicated to pastoral care. The possibility would also have great significance even for missionary societies. Life lived according to the counsels would therefore make room for a celibate deacon also.

Etudes of Paris (R. Rouquette, SJ, May 1959; H. Holstein, SJ, September 1960) offered some ideas that were partly worked out in reference to specifically French circumstances. The doubts expressed about married deacons do not serve as the primary reason for this article being mentioned here. However, the notion that only celibacy attracts high-minded men and only such vocations are authentic must be challenged. The life of the married deacon is not a "sacrifice of lesser value" than that of unmarried deacons or priests. The sacrifices may differ partly in their nature, but it cannot be stated as a general principle that they are of lesser value. Recruitment should not be based on the possibility of marriage; God calls a person to the celibate priesthood or to the diaconate. More serious doubts arise with respect to the lay apostolate, especially Catholic Action. No thought, as Rouquette assumes, is being given to ordaining the leaders of Catholic Action to the diaconate. They must remain laymen if the true purpose of Catholic Action is to be fulfilled—or they should resign! However, there is also no danger that the place of the laity in the Church will be adversely affected because of the diaconate. By the same token, there is certainly no intent to transfer all of the diaconal functions to the laity. Here reference must be made to the comments of Winninger and Hornef in *Nouvelle Revue Theologique* (April 1961). See also *Caritas,* Lucerne, 2/1960.

Mention should be made also of the article by F. Lepargneur, OP, in *Nouvelle Revue Theologique* (March 1960); it deals in detail with the circumstances in Latin America. Lepargneur gives his whole-hearted support to the rebirth of the diaconate, stresses the need for part-time deacons for the inconceivably large parishes of Latin America, for the numerous chapels and small shrines without a pastor. Nevertheless, he does not believe that Latin America is ready at this time for the rebirth of the diaconate. What is urgently needed is for the people to be more deeply grounded in basic Christian truths. Consequently, first must come reform of the seminary, reform of preaching and catechesis. Only then can the deacon be effectively introduced. But should not the deacon be able to assist in the much needed renewal? When P. Lepargneur recently wrote to this author, he expressed the opinion that the difficulties in Latin America are surmountable:

> I am more and more convinced that this campaign promoting the renewal of the diaconate is useful, necessary and that it will bear fruit at the council. . . . I believe and I hope, more than I have ever said, that the decision for the diaconate will be positive; this matter seems to be to have reached maturity lately. All in all I believe that the inevitable difficulties are small in the face of the positive support for it that one can and ought to expect.

Leopold Denis, SJ, in the *Revue du clerge Africain* [*African Clergy Review*] (Mayidi, Congo) has called attention to a difficulty with a specifically African character: the married deacon (the only kind suitable in Africa) would lack the necessary freedom to live out his vocation because of his dependence on his extended family (the clan). Just how much a change from one's homeland would help in this case, only the missionaries can say.

In 1960, a larger historical and theological study by Jean Colson (Paris) *La fonction diaconale aux origines de l'Eglise* [*The Diaconal Functions in the Early Church*] (Desclee de Brouwer, Paris) followed the writings of Winninger and Hornef. The magazine *L'ami du clerge*, Langres 7/1961, says in its review of this book, that the friends of the restoration of the diaconate are able to find completely suitable arguments for their proposal. The Evangelical Publishing House of Stuttgart published *Quellen zur Geschichte des Diakonates* [*Sources for a History of the Diaconate*] (Part I, "Antiquity and Middle Ages"), edited by Pastor Herbert Krimm, professor at the Institute for the Scientific Study of the Diaconate at the University of Heidelberg. Further, *Paroisse et Liturgie* [*Parish and Liturgy*] has published a monograph by A. Kerkvoorde, OSB, *Ou en est le problem du diaconat?* [*Where Does the Diaconate Stand?*] (Bruges, 1961). Kerkvoorde deals primarily with the pastoral and liturgical side of the diaconate. He is of the opinion that the definitive new shape of the diaconate, whose rebirth he frankly welcomes, can only succeed within the framework of a comprehensive reform. But he wants to see the restoration get underway now, via indults and on an experimental basis—consistent with what Y. Congar has said: One must begin, since only actual praxis will uncover where the real difficulties lie (and show us the ways to overcome them—the author). In Portugal, a small book by J. Paulo Nunes (Publisher Logos, Lisbon 1961) has appeared, entitled *A Hora Do Diacono.*

In France, Prelate J. Rodhain of Paris, the general secretary of *"Secours catholique,"* has provided the initial impetus for the proposal and because of this, it has received significant support and assistance from *"Caritas Internationalis"* (See also Rodhain's "A Letter to a Superior of a Major Seminary concerning the Diaconate and Its Re-establishment . . ."). The Program Commission of *"Caritas Internationalis"* met under his chairmanship from the 14th to the 16th of March 1959 in Royaumont near Paris. During this conference, four lectures were given concerning questions about the diaconate. One of them—"The Diaconate as an Ecclesiastical Office in the Light of Today's Pastoral Situation"—was given by Hannes Kramer, the leader of the Freiburg Diaconate Circle. The conference report says about it: "Kramer's lecture is all the more significant because it gives a report about a lived experiment, about a real effort to return to the diaconate." In accordance with the decision made by the executive committee of *"Caritas Internationalis"* at a meeting in Geneva (September 1959), a request was sent to the Council to allow the office of deacon to be restored.

At the invitation of the president of the German *Caritas* Society, an informative talk on the rebirth of the diaconate was given in Munich on the occasion of the Eucharistic Congress on August 3, 1960 in the *Caritas* House. About sixty persons—priests, religious, and lay—from twelve countries were present. Prof. Fleckenstein (Wuerzburg); Director Kolbe (editor of the *Liturgical Yearbook*); Msgr. Rodhain (Paris); Prof. Hofinger (Manila); Fr. Schamoni, and this writer gave short lectures from the viewpoint of the pastoral situation, the liturgy, charitable service, the missions, concerning the assignment of deacons to mission churches and concerning the current status of the proposal. Unfortunately, because of other congress events, the discussions were too brief. *Diaconate Circle Working Paper,* 5/1960 contains a detailed report.

The International Study Week for Mission Catechesis took place directly prior to the Eucharistic Congress in Eichstaett. Even though no talks expressly related to the restoration of the diaconate were given, unlike what happened in Nijmegen, nevertheless the proposal was mentioned directly or indirectly in some individual talks (Pierre Jacquemart, MEP, Bangalore, and Bishop W. J. Duschak, SVD, Calapan, Philippines). In any case, it can be said that everything that was said here about the intellectual and spiritual development of catechists runs parallel to our proposal. The sooner the catechist receives a truly fundamental education and spiritual formation, the sooner he will be qualified to be ordained as lector, acolyte, and deacon (cf. no. 7 of the resolutions of Eichstaett "The Catechists"). A narrower circle of experts and interested parties met under the direction of Prof. Rahner in September 1961 in Freiburg im Breisgau for talks concerning the question of the diaconate (lectures by Prof. Rahner, Prof. Colson, H. Kramer, and Director Wollasch). In October 1961, the "Austrian Theology Conference" in Vienna (under the leadership of Prelate Rudolf) dedicated its two days of proceedings entirely to the question of the diaconate (lectures by Schamoni and Hornef).

Now a further word concerning the development of the diaconate circles. Professional obligations took H. Kramer from Freiburg to Munich (today, he is employed at the *Caritas* Center in Freiburg). In Munich, it was not long before a group of young people from among the *Caritas* workers with the same common goal was formed. Recently, a group was also formed in and around Cologne following a weekend conference of the Catholic Academies from Cologne-Bensberg and Aachen. This weekend conference was devoted to the rebirth of the diaconate; Hornef and Kramer gave several lectures. The

Cologne group (under the leadership of Josef Volker, Bergisch-Gladbach) is composed of people from every profession, unlike the groups in Freiburg and Munich. Another circle is in the process of formation in Aachen. The Trier circle was formed in March 1962. The spirit of the diaconate—community spirit—is fostered in the monthly work and family meetings of the groups and in the monthly communal celebration of the Holy Sacrifice of the Mass. A community prayer also promotes the cause. The circles have their own "leading ideas," conceived as the result of ten years of communal reflection. In the spring of 1961, retreat days were held for the circle in Freiburg under the leadership of P. Dr. Robert Svoboda, OSC. Circle membership has increased to sixty persons in all. There will be certainly sufficient young men if the Church opens the doors to the diaconate.

The responsible preparatory commissions of the approaching council are already busy with the question. In almost every publication at the council the diaconate proposal is mentioned and affirmed. May the spirit of God lead the council to open the way to the diaconate. Not in such a way that the diaconate will be reestablished throughout the whole Church overnight, but rather in a manner that will allow bishops who consider the situation ripe in their own dioceses to revive the office of deacon on the basis of a legal framework, which will guarantee coherent development.

Notes

1. See the author's articles in the January/February 1956 issue of *Die Besinnung* (*Reflections*) and in issues no. 13/14 (1958) and no. 41 (1960) of the *Allgemeine Sonntagzeitung.*

2. For example, in 1926 P. Aupiais of the *Missions Africaines* and even Pastor L. Quesbes of Vourles (Diocese of Lyon) in 1829 made their case for the restoration of the minor orders. See also the reference to Cardinal C. Constantini made by (Father) Schamoni in his *Concentration Camp Notes.*

3. In my private possession.

4. We thank Fr. Pies from the bottom of our hearts for the fact that shortly before his death he nonetheless gave us one more extensive article on this topic ("Theology and Faith," vol. 3 [1960]).

5. It appears to be providential that the Mass with a deacon has been revived at just the right time. As soon as the new regulations for Holy Week Liturgy with only one deacon were announced, the Decennial Faculties of the Propaganda Congregation authorized bishops to allow solemn celebrations and other solemn liturgical functions to be held with the assistance of just one deacon.

Born in 1929 after the end of the war, Hannes entered into the forest ranger service in the Black Forest area in southwest Germany. It was there, while still very young that Hannes believed he first receive a call from the Lord to serve the Church as a deacon. Convinced of this, he began to prepare himself by entering the Institute for Social Service in Freiburg in Breisgau. In 1951, Hannes with six other social workers founded the first Diakonatskreis, *or "Deacon Circle." A Franciscan spirituality helped to mold the members of this Circle and their emerging notion of a servant Church. In 1954, Hannes had moved on to Munich where he founded a second Circle, assisted by two others from the Freiburg group. Other Circles followed in centers of Catholic life in Germany: Cologne, Aachen, and Rottenburg.*

In 1955, Hannes was working in a center or shelter for displaced homeless foreigners who were refugees from the East. This was the focus of his diaconal ministry at that time and served to help to develop further Hannes' concept of a restored and renewed diaconate. The practice of his profession at the Bavarian State Office for Foreign and Homeless Refugees and diaconal ministry converged. Service at the eucharistic table and service at the table of his brothers and sisters, in Hannes, became integrated.

From the beginning, wives and fiancees of the members of the Deacon Circle joined in monthly meetings. Their presence contributed significantly to the ongoing development of the diaconate in which the dynamics of marriage, family, and profession were being fused. The concepts of the role of the wife of the deacon and his children began to take shape. These were seedlings that were to bear much good fruit.

It is important to understand that in the late-1940s and 1950s this emergence of the diaconate came about through "private" initiative (we believe at the prompting of the Holy Spirit) and without any "official" church sponsorship or encouragement.

The council fathers in their decree Ad Gentes *(no. 16) declared: It is "beneficial that those who perform a truly diaconal ministry be strengthened by the imposition of hands, a tradition going back to the apostles, and be more closely joined to the altar so that they may more effectively carry out their ministry through the sacramental grace of the diaconate."*

Surely, we must include Hannes Kramer and those associated with him more than forty years ago among those who performed a truly diaconal ministry and who pioneered in bringing forth the restored and renewed diaconate of our day.

The following article was written circa 1961. Deacon Hannes Kramer was among the first permanent deacons ordained following the restoration of the Permanent Diaconate shortly after the close of the Second Vatican Council.

Samuel M. Taub

The Spiritual Life of the Deacon

by Hannes Kramer

According to canon 135 of the *Code of Canon Law,* all those in major orders (i.e., deacons) also are obliged to pray the daily office. It would appear, therefore, that the central question for the topic at hand is whether or not this obligation would be enjoined upon the permanent deacon, who will be carrying out diaconal duties upon the restoration of the diaconate as a distinct office unto itself. Several preliminary remarks would seem to be both necessary and helpful in clarifying this question.

a) The Obligation of the Deacon to Pray the Office

At the time the obligation to pray the entire office of canonical hours was introduced into the Latin Rite Roman Catholic Church, the diaconate as a distinct office unto itself no longer existed. It was, at that time, already oriented toward the priesthood and was tied to celibacy.

In the early Church, the prayer-life of all Christians was primarily the prayer of the Church. In addition to the new cult of eucharistic celebration, the old cult of the liturgy of the word was also celebrated. The earliest as well as later independent forms of the liturgy of the word (as the prayer-life of the community) were also associated with the celebration of the Mass. Furthermore, the bishop with his clergy, and subsequently the presbyter in the church for which he was ordained, prayed morning and evening prayer. On certain days, this was also done with the people, who for their part took pains to pray part of the office freely and unconstrained according to the Roman day (at the 3rd, 6th, and 9th hours). The regular obligation to pray the office evolved as part of the monastic life.

These monks, in turn, subsequently had their own influence on the cathedral and episcopal church, where they introduced the Liturgy of the Hours and displaced the old cathedral payer. It was in this way that the Roman Office undoubtedly received its decidedly monastic character, which has been retained down to our very day.[1]

It is therefore understandable that the history of the early Church reveals nothing extraordinary about the prayer-life of the (also married) deacons of that period. The obligation of prayer which has up to now been enjoined upon deacons, whose goal is to become celibate priests, cannot simply be assumed, accepted, or required of a restored diaconate as a separate office, which differs from the transitional step to the priesthood on the basis of its separate vocation and distinctive calling, its special function and corresponding formation, its specific task, and its own mission. The obligations of the cleric with respect to prayer is, generally speaking, to be viewed and to be determined on the basis of his service in and to the Church, as well as in the basis of the sum total of all of his obligations.

b) The Extent and Content of the Deacon's Obligatory Prayer-Life

We have assumed that the restored diaconate will include the possibility of being married. For that reason alone, the extent of the prayer-life to be enjoined upon a deacon cannot be determined on the basis of the monastic form of prayer-life.

In those instances where additional rules or obligations stemming from membership in a religious community, a secular institute, or an order would be enjoined upon deacons, the rules and obligations of such a life-style would have to be kept basically separate from the prayer-life required universally of all deacons. Nonetheless, it would be inappropriate right from the start to follow the line of thought, which would only require the deacon to pray the office in an abbreviated form. Abbreviated prayer time based on an obligatory recitation of a "Little Office" from the standpoint of content does not conform with the essential spirituality needs of a married deacon. The men who belong to the Diaconate Circle have as married men over a long period of time prayed both the Roman Office as well as the *Little Divine Office,*[2] by Fr. Hildebrand

Fleischmann, OSB, in German and find that this is not compatible with the rhythm of family life. Even the latter [*Little Divine Office*] is basically geared to the cloistered life-style. It is expected and requisite for the interior truthfulness of the prayer that he at least attempt to pray the breviary according to the rhythm of the hours. Right from the start this is an impossibility for the married man. Even if he were to ignore this rhythm—which would certainly be excusable—the married man would be isolating himself too much from the family. Praying the breviary alone does not give him, his wife, and the children that which they need most. This could represent a possible danger for the active deacon bound up in day-to-day affairs; for we should not, when we pray, just quickly rattle something off like the heathens, "who believe that their prayer will be heard on the strength of the sheer volume of their words!"

Even an abbreviated office would still be problematical, since it would not be tailored to the life-style and would have to be recited quickly, should one wish to find time for other appropriate forms of prayer. It would certainly be consistent with the formational wisdom of the Church to not only require but to ensure that the married deacon find time for prayer, including personal prayer. Prayer is necessary for his service.

In the service of love and care for the salvation of our neighbor, there are just many—too many—things that can only be prayed *for*. Love in action should draw its strength from conversation with the God of love. The prayer of the deacon, however, must necessarily differ in content and scope from that of monks or of a priest. When wise and experienced priests warn that priestly spirituality requires additional spiritual nourishment over and above the "formal" reading/praying of a breviary divided into fictitious hours,[3] then vis-à-vis the deacon, one should begin with a prayer-life that corresponds to his spirituality. The cultivation of his interior prayer-life, his personal relationship with God, and—for the married person—prayer in and with the family is crucial here. Given the little time he can spend with his family, he should be able to pray *with* the family as much as possible and as befits his own personal situation. Seen in this light, a family breviary similar to that written by Dr. H. Kunkel[4] can only be used as a prayer guide for a specific period of time when the children are of a certain age, just as a breviary for the laity[5] can only be used from time to time and then only specific sections thereof. That it would appear to be an error to prescribe the obligatory use of this or that breviary for the deacons of the world will be made clear in what follows. It should also be pointed out here that a decision simply to require the deacon to pray an abbreviated part of the office would be neither practical nor expedient.

Now genuine difficulties arise. Within the Catholic Church of the Latin Rite of our day, there exist no possible precedents for comparison with respect to the spiritual life of a married cleric as there are in the Eastern Churches. In the non-Catholic East, there has never, ever been "prayer obligations" in the sense we would understand; deacons, however, are required to be actively present during Mass, and to this very day, priests and deacons still celebrate Matins and Vespers in their church. We are striving here, however, to raise questions concerning the order of prayer of the Roman Catholic Church within the framework of her offices, official structure, devotional endeavors, and prayer-life.

This discussion, therefore, is based on the (in some cases) more than ten-year-long practical experiences of young married men, who as friends of the restoration of the diaconate, banded together in Diaconate Circles and—to the extent this is possible today—have striven to lead an appropriate spiritual life.

It is intended to indicate a *basic direction* for the religious and spiritual life formation of a married deacon. Much of what is contained herein can and should grow and mature over time and out of practical experience.

c) The Perfection of the Diaconal State in Relationship to the other States in Life

The point here is to enable the deacon to lead a spiritual life that is consistent with his vocation, his mission, and duties, as well as with his life-style. His personal life, job responsibilities, family, and everyday life all also need to be folded into his prayer-life, wherein they can be sanctified and enhanced. However, before this can be discussed, several comments concerning the piety appropriate to the state of married deacon vis-à-vis the other states in life are appropriate.

The single ideal of perfection for all states, which found its inimitable expression in the Sermon on the Mount, that song of love that was lived out by Christ, can be lived in various ways. The means by which this objective can be pursued are for the most part almost always the same. The observance of the evangelical counsels is, however, not the same thing as the pursuit of perfection. It makes no difference that all life-styles are structured consistent with the counsels and that living the counsels according to the Gospel is the most direct way. In order to find greater clarity with respect to the piety of the three states of life of priests, monks, and lay people, we can differentiate more accurately between clergy and laity in how they differ with respect to *office*—and between monks and laity in how they differ with respect to the manner and mode in which they strive for *holiness*.

Holiness can be realized along the path of God's commandments or according to the word and example of Christ, the counsels. Both compliment each other spiritually and have their objective in the perfection of love and their unity in following Christ in his cross, death, resurrection, and glory. Therefore, this singular characteristic, this accent on pursuit of holiness according to one's state in life is also always effective in any other state of life being rightly lived. Holiness can be attained in both ways by both laity and *clergy* and, therefore, also by the diaconate.

Office is both the starting point and the wellspring of specific devout attitudes, since inherent in it is an abundance of formational motives for prayer and action. It is precisely that which fits into the concrete life situation and mission in the life of a deacon in service and vocation that should be the content of his ascetical formation.

Clergy and laity are baptized and confirmed and, therefore, share in those offices and tasks that are appropriate to the universal priesthood. Baptism and confirmation are also interiorly proximate to the sacrament of orders. What is common to all offices based on sacramental ordination is that they are carried out [by office-bearers] as representatives of Christ and in fulfillment of his mission.

The sacramental ordination of the distinctive presbyterate and the sacrament of marriage (with their abundant graces of office and state of life), therefore, always also have in common a close proximity to the mission of Christ, to his high-priesthood, to the Lord as the head of the Body. However, they are not oriented toward the *individual* discipleship of Christ, but rather toward the "official character" of Christ as the Redeemer, that is to say directed to the *community,* to humankind and not primarily to personal perfection. Sacramental ordination and marriage are "ordered to the perfection of the community" (Thomas of Aquinas, *S. T. Supplement* q. 34, a2 and ad2). This means that marriage and ordination have a personal and institutional relationship: he who holds office must minister to others; by virtue of office all the forms of charity have a special mission (personal relationship). Community is a structured order, not just a collection of individuals, and as such it requires appropriate institutions, which are not to be sought in the "hereafter" but, rather, in the order of salvation here on earth. The concern here is the redemption of the world and its natural institutions.[6]

By way of the common aspects, we can conclude the following about the pursuit of perfection by the deacon according to the nature of his state in life: his pursuit of perfection can follow either the road of the evangelical counsels or the commandments of God. Common to both roads is the goal of the perfection of love, and both are one in the discipleship of Christ. In the pursuit of perfection according to one's state in life, the diaconal office does not exclude the marital relationship. Sacramental ordination and sacramental marriage both have in common a very close relationship to the mission of Christ, to the Lord as head of the Body. This also holds true for their office as it relates to both human concern for others as well as for the building up of the community of the Body of Christ. It is critical that we constantly examine the common aspects of Christian piety and formation in light of the distinctive aspects of the individual state in life with respect to its current life-style.

I.

The obligatory nature of the spiritual life of the deacon is greater than that of an individual not bound to Christ by ordination, and it is not some kind of private pious activity. The core of his spiritual life is a piety that is appropriate to his personal call, his office, and his life-style. Christian asceticism, if it is to be genuine, robust, and healthy, must be rooted and anchored in liturgy and in the sacraments, in the primordial sacrament of the Church, and remain so. Only in that way will it be possible to discover spiritual attitude toward prayer, sacrifice, sickness, and need; toward austerity and joy and sorrow. Spiritual life should become a reality by means of a "yes" to the will of God, for the life of the world, for the glorification of God in the fulfillment of the mission of Christ to collaborate in the preparation of the new heaven and new earth in our creation and in the economy of our salvation.

1. The Personal Behavior of the Deacon

Should one now address the question of a specific personal behavior, of a single typology and personal life realization on the part of the deacon, or should one not simply right from the outset leave everything up to an original, individual, and differentiated realization according to the character of each person?

Every personal life should be formed or shaped according to the commission: "Become who you are"—a completely personal and unalterable commission from God. The goal of asceticism is for the human being newly reborn in Christ to gain the ability to reflect the perfection of his heavenly Father in his personal life, not only with respect to the special duties of the individual as a member of the mystical Body of Christ, but also with respect to his individuality. Based on that prior understanding, even in its practical significance, we are not free to answer the question that has been asked in any way we want: *Sacred Scripture* explicitly addresses the personal behavior and attributes of the deacon. These words are still today the yardstick to be used for personal evaluation prior to ordination and by which the married deacon should order his life. In Paul's first letter to Timothy (3:8-13), he requires that deacons *hold fast to the mystery of faith*. In our day, faith has become weak. It has become weak over against rationalism, materialism; over against the excessive demands for affluence, and so forth. It has become weak because it has itself become lazy about the positive content of the deposit of faith. Faith, however, is power—it is "conviction about things we do not see" (Heb 11:1). The rejection of materialism, pleasure-seeking, and self-aggrandizement is not the only thing it demands. It calls for belief in the power of grace in the sacraments; it means being put to the test and being faithful in everyday life. It is animated by credal confession and the power of personal witness. Faith without works is dead.

Therefore, since Christian faith and Christian life are inextricably bound together, according to Paul, deacons must preserve the truth of the Gospel with blameless consciences. For he who does not give witness to the Christian truth of the Gospel by means of his life will also soon, at least theoretically, betray it or, at the very least, be guilty of only wearing the mask of faith. Just as the deacon can only hold fast to the faith if he truly believes it, loves it, and lives it, so too can he only preserve the Gospel with a blameless conscience if he knows it and conforms his life to it.

If the deacon wishes to be "full of the Spirit and of wisdom" (Acts 6:3), then this divine life within him is an inner strength, which is not intended to remain hidden but, rather, to be visible/seen. He who is open to the Spirit of holiness bears fruit. "The fruit of the Spirit is love, joy, peace, patient endurance, kindness, generosity, faith, mildness, and chastity" (Gal 5:22). To strive for these basic behavioral attributes and to put them increasingly into practice in one's life is, according to Paul, the specific task of the deacon, as it is the task of every Christian, albeit not perhaps in the same special way. This conduct should be augmented by the cardinal virtues, which actually should be the mark of every Christian: prudence, justice, fortitude, and temperance. Paul really does not explicitly cite these virtues but, rather, uses concrete examples to say that deacons should be "truthful, straightforward, may not overindulge in drink or give in to greed" (Tm 3:8-13).

Today, we know more than ever, that the spiritual fulfillment of concrete human and Christian existence is piety, the worship of God. By the same token, this fulfillment is only really possible if the individual constantly works at being a disciple of Christ. The service of the deacon obligates him to an ascetical life, so that he himself does not become immersed in the immanence of the world and so that his service, without the personal witness of love, does not become shallow make-work. The realization of a well-ordered diaconal life by someone, who does not choose the direct path of the evangelical counsels, is characterized by balance and stability through the exercise of that moderation appropriate for his service. Experience teaches that under certain circumstances it can be easier to forego "everything" than to observe moderation in conjunction "with everything"—let us say as a married deacon.

Our industrialized and automated age is confronted with the pressures of constant growth and relentless expansion; this is also manifested in the dynamics of the ever-increasing growth of human needs. Above all, we in the Western world are confronted with the acute danger of being lost to the immoderation of a practical materialism. The entire world of material goods must, however, serve the physical and spiritual development of all humanity. "We should use things as if they were all held in common." And yet we see that there are great spiritual crises in certain areas of the world with apparently high standards of living and that, on the other hand, throughout today's world there exists an unbelievable degree of bodily suffering, hunger, and sickness.

The deacon is the servant of the Church in the manifold forms of its service of love. The mentality of serving humbly is the genuine attitude of service. Openness to simple service should be the mark of the deacon. The witness of love should correspond to the service of love. Love of God and of neighbor can only be achieved with a certain measure of detachment from the inner world of life. This includes claims to dependencies in the area of one's body, one's environment, and one's contemporaries, as well as to "absolute" freedom. This is in no way contradictory to the affirmation of the world, to the free (interiorly and exteriorly) development of one's personality, to a "yes" to the will of God, to married love, or to one's personal vocation. However, our vocation, our mission, the fulfillment of the will of God are all carried out in the shadow of the cross. In the realization of the divine plan of love, on the path to perfection, we find ourselves in a constant struggle with a world beset by the disorder of sin. The deacon is in Sacred Scripture expressly called to not only reject the negative immoderation of sin, sexual immorality, greed, and thirst for power, but also to a positive moderation, which corresponds to his mission.

a) For our times, in addition to the celibate deacon or the deacon living according to the evangelical counsels, it is again valid to call for the existence of the married deacon not obligated to total conti-

nence, but rather solidly anchored in the chastity appropriate to his state in life, a chastity that can only be fulfilled in love and in self-denial.

His witness on behalf of the beleaguered or destitute individual is empty, if he himself is not living with a clear conscience. Only in this way can he help another free himself from love of self and self-centered possessiveness, thereby becoming free in his own right for many others. In a special way, the deacon is called upon to provide relief from bodily distress; his service frequently provides him deeper insight into the intimate union between body and soul than it might to a pastor. Only if he lives this unity convincingly and also glorifies God in his own body (as a gift from God) through his service will he appear credible before God and the world.

b) The deacon of today should not only be allowed to fulfill his office in a life of total poverty. As an individual with possessions, he should also be free to love selflessly, to not only call for "spiritual poverty" but also to advocate giving up any claims to excessive wealth and to do so himself.

The proper and equitable use of possessions has hardly any previous time been so seriously and universally demanded of us as it is today. How can a deacon ask his fellow human beings for the gift of love for the poor, the suffering, the sick, and the hungry if he himself does not share? All gifts, even spiritual gifts, which God has "granted" (i.e., loaned) to us, have only been entrusted to our temporary stewardship. We must also share them with others; not in such a way, however, that we suffer privation, but rather so there is equity. Again here, moderation is appropriate. The deacon does not fight for but rather against poverty and privation; he shares the gifts of corporal and spiritual mercy. How can he try to dissuade people from becoming consumed by materialism and enslaved by temporal worldliness, if he has not freed himself from selfish attachments to possessions and a disquieting pursuit of them?

If a deacon unnecessarily overburdens himself and his family financially, he may unduly restrict his mission. Inordinate demands on him could very quickly lead to the loss of his freedom. A family requires, to be sure, certain necessities for its growth and for a happy, free, and fruitful life; by the same token, to become caught up in possessions and a striving for wealth often leads to worldly perdition.

c) It is not only the ecclesiastical obedience required of individuals bound by the evangelical counsels that is required of the deacon today; the designation of his vocation as service would surely be untrue, if the deacon cannot constantly function and obey in humility.

A spirit of humble service should characterize the service of all ecclesiastical office-holders in the exercise of their official authority. The deacon, however, is called in a special way to service in the Church. In so doing, he serves God first, the Church of Christ, and his bishop. The servant has a lord master over him. Even if this Lord is always God, we are still expected to serve God in other human beings. Even at a time when hierarchical and patriarchal authority is being subjected to a severe diminution of its prestige, genuine obedience, based on free, inner respect for and trust in the bearer of the full apostolic office of bishop, must be strengthened. It is of significance that the deacon be able to carry out those tasks appropriate to him in direct association with the episcopate in relative independence and responsibility. The appropriate integration and incorporation of the deacon into the entirety of the Church, to include according him a due and proper place in the life of the Church as an unmistakable number thereof, should foster a healthy self-confidence and the courage to serve. It should free him from pride and a thirst for power and enable him to be a better listener, more alert and more prepared for the call of love. He who is hobbled by pride and arrogance, vanity and self-importance, highhandedness and inflexibility should not become a deacon. The diaconate is service and not power.

Moderation and temperance, therefore, for the married deacon means: self-control, mastery over oneself, not allowing oneself to become inordinately attached to the things of the world, to be free for God by the proper use of the things of this world. It also means to serve humbly and obediently, to be a faithful steward of the gifts of love, to take seriously the duty of fraternal correction, to be prepared for sacrifice and doing without, and to live a chastity appropriate for one's state in life. Moderation is not an unbearable hardship. Those who have learned the simple life to be found in the Good News of Christ are the people who are genuinely happy, not those who worry and fret about looking out for themselves.

2. Living the Vocation of Deacon—An Expression of His Spiritual–Ascetical Outlook

The diaconate is a lifelong call to service. This service can only be understood as a permanent office, which substantially includes a habitual participation in orders consistent with his state and his calling.

Living the vocation of deacon should be fulfilled as an ideal as the ultimate reason for his action. It should, therefore, be directed toward love of God and of neighbor, which finds its appropriate expression in *life* (a life of love!). The vocation of deacon has to do with the devout life (not merely with devout prayer).

The service of the deacon with respect to liturgy, acts of charity, and catechesis will be especially characterized by his attitude: Participation in liturgical life is sharing in life, sharing in suffering, and sharing in the crucifixion. The focal point and starting point, the wellspring of his daily diaconal activity is the altar, the eucharistic liturgy.

"I have greatly desired to eat this [Passover] meal with you. . . ." The deacon should daily desire to eat this meal of the New Covenant, which is "the primary expression of Christian life, the fundamental act of his redeemed existence" (H. Spaemann) in memory of Christ and his mission ("Do this in memory of me"), as well as in thanksgiving. The communal celebration of the Eucharist opens one's eyes for conforming one's life to Christ, permits one to live in a covenant relationship with God, and shows us the way to surrender and salvation.

How can he bring the life-giving bread to the sick and the suffering with true conviction, if his own life is not being constantly renewed, preserved, and enriched by the celebration and reception of the holy Eucharist? How can he, furthermore, dare to advise another—frequently, a stranger—or to guide the lost and the rejected onto new paths without constant reading and reflection on the Sacred Scripture, in order to know, to recognize, and to follow him, who is the Way, the Truth, and the Life? This service to others and for others cannot be performed unless one listens to the will of God in prayer and supplication, with a willingness to be used increasingly as an instrument of divine will (i.e., to empty oneself and to become free, ready, and capable of carrying out the divine mission).

This requires a solidarity with God, hard work, and an openness to God's grace. For these reasons alone the deacon requires special grace for his office. He can only bring others in contact with God if he himself knows the true value of this contact and does not allow his own relationship [with God] to be broken. Furthermore, if he also makes the effort to maintain a correct relationship through regular sacramental confession and an openness to fraternal correction, there will be an extremely intimate interaction between his liturgical activity and his interior prayer-life/attitude of sacrifice, as well as between his service to God and his service to fellow human beings.

The spirituality of the deacon has, therefore, its liturgical aspects; he has lifelong vocation ties to the place of worship and to the sacred; he is both a "bestower of blessings" and a "bestower of [sacramental] gifts." Proclamation of the word requires that the proclaimer be thoroughly imbued with the Good

News. It is an act of devoutness. Who will believe the words, if they are not witnessed by deeds? Between the proclamation of the life-giving word of the life of the Gospel there exists, above all, close communication not only for him who hears the Good News but also for him who proclaims it. The service of the deacon on behalf of his neighbor is not social action based on belief in progress but, rather, genuine pastoral care and, therefore, loving sacrifice for an individual and for the community. He believes, proclaims, and exemplifies the fact that which we have done for the least of our brothers, we have done for Christ. His mission must, therefore, be felt over and above his functions, not through affected piety or a "pastoral tone" but, rather, stemming from the essence and core of a priestly person and a life consecrated to God.

The witness of his office requires a constant pursuit of those virtues mentioned earlier and of a spirit of love. Virtue as "perfectly transformed strength" (cf. Augustine) gives the individual the strength to complete the task and, at the same time, makes the selfless work possible. Finally and definitely, the deacon will only be able to do justice to his office to the extent that he bears witness to it by his own life.

Ministerial and official activity is no proving-ground for unusual personal opinions, devoid of personal sacrifice or the charisma of the office-bearers. Mind and heart, body and soul, reason and will—all of the powers of a human being—must first be made ready to carry out the mission by means of a genuine and sound asceticism. Formation appropriate to the mission of the diaconate is not only a question of credibility, but also of the possibility of carrying out diaconal service. When the disciples unsuccessfully attempted to cure the boy possessed by the devil, they asked the Master, after he had successfully healed the sick boy, why they were unable to do so. After he had first scolded them about their lack of faith, Jesus answered clearly and succinctly: "This kind you can only drive out by fasting and prayer" (Mk 9:20). Prayer, fasting, vigils, spiritual reading, examinations of conscience, and spiritual direction—these are means made available by the Holy Spirit to lead oneself and others to salvation, to union with God.

3. The Married Life and Family Life of the Deacon

In a very definite sense, the bond between family life and vocation in life is primordial: personal life, vocation in life, marriage, and family are mutually dependent and all mold the entire spiritual and moral formation of the married deacon.

Emphasis is once again being placed on marriage as the vocation of starting a family. The meaning and task of marital love, wherein the lovers become witnesses of the love of God for each other and for those entrusted to care, is moving back into a place of prominence—along side of the purpose of marriage, which is seen as the procreation and preservation of human life.

> The mutual interior formation of the married couple, the constant effort to lead each other to perfection can even be, as is stated in the *Roman Catechism* (cf. II, ch. VIII, q. 3), quite correctly and truthfully designated as the main purpose and actual meaning of marriage. Therefore, one should not understand marriage in the narrow sense of an institution for the procreation and raising of children but, rather, in its broadest sense as complete community of life (*Casti Connubii*, no. 24).[7]

It is clear today, that everything that makes up a marriage belongs to the sphere of redemption and should be understood as an object of Christian piety. The total reality appropriate to marriage in its dignity as an institution right from the outset is taken up in the sacrament itself: the loving relationship of the married couple, the strongest expression of which is the child; the Christian home environment of the family; the work that goes into maintaining the stability of the family (which cannot be separated from the home environment); everything that belongs to the many-sided reality of marriage and family. Married life and family life will, therefore, no longer be seen as a concession to human weakness but, rather, that it has experienced a positive reevaluation, which points up the fact that in marriage "the saving action of Christ pours forth directly into the world in need of salvation." Married couples should, therefore, not contribute to each other's salvation in spite of marriage but, rather, in and through marriage. Christian marriage is not condemned to mediocrity. By the same token, the struggle for perfection in any state in life is equally valid for married life: "He who wants to be my disciple must deny himself, take up his cross daily, and follow me."[8]

For the married deacon, the mission conferred upon him in the sacrament of marriage is conjoined with and expanded by the mission conferred upon him through ordination. The witness of married love, in which natural human love toward spouse and children is permeated with the love of God, is united in a singular way with his service of love (liturgy, charity, and catechesis) in the official Church. The proper use of natural values is united with his renunciation of [material] abundance in favor of the poor.

The common struggle for perfection and chastity according to their state in life, which is obligatory in a very unique way for diaconal married couples, becomes a living testimony and a special incentive for the [faith] community.

The married couples follow the path of sanctification within the Church in a most intimate mutuality and unanimity. The married deacon, over and above his service to his family, has an additional special sacred mission to those human beings entrusted to his care by virtue of his diaconal responsibilities. All of this also requires ascetical discipline in the family. It is to be found in proper holistic education, a healthy family pedogogy, the religious education of the children, in an assiduous self-education, and in the credible behavior of the spouses. This has an effect on the structure of family life (cf. Lebensordnung). A special sign of the spirituality of a Christian family is the togetherness of will and struggle, of prayer and sacrifice, of moderation and renunciation, of joy and of sorrow. For the deacon, the conscious inclusion of the requests of the faith community (i.e., of his mission in a discrete form) in the spiritual life of the family would be part of this struggle. The goal of a deacon's family life and married life remains the same: to shape a community of love, the center of which is Christ himself. The family, which is included in the community of the economy of salvation, is in an existential and direct sense a little church, a church that is open to the world around it and in which it lives, open to the parish and to the universal Church, above all in works of love for God and neighbor, of hospitality and personal contact with fellow human beings. Such a family cannot be an obstacle for the mission of a deacon. It is in the closest possible harmony with his ordination, disposed to the perfection of the community, open to his service and his support, his steadiness and his mission all at the same time. In spite of all the possible human weaknesses (which are also present in celibacy), marriage in the diaconate should also be viewed as a mystery with respect to Christ and the Church. For St. Paul (cf. 1 Tm 3:8-13) also recognizes the special mission of the married deacon for his family and the significance of the family for the deacon. He justifiably requires as a precondition for those who would become deacons, that they must have proven themselves to be capable fathers, to manage their families well, and to raise their children correctly. For the "private life" of a man will have an effect on his public (i.e., ecclesial) activity.

The apostle Paul does not overlook the wives of deacons as a further significant factor for a well-ordered family life. He therefore requires that the wives "be honorable, not gossips, but serious and faithful in all things. . . ." In accordance with the spirit of early Christianity and the essence of marriage, which is based on unanimity, total dedication, and finality with respect to Christ and the Church, it is understandable that Paul would wish the following: He who wants to become a deacon should as a rule only have been married once and that his marriage should have been successful (an exception to this rule would be the situation, for example, where a mother of young children passes away and the husband would feel compelled to remarry out of love and concern for the children).

After mature reflection on all points of view, the Diaconate Circles agreed upon the following recommendation in this most serious matter:

> On the one hand, the recommendation to marry an appropriate length of time *before* ordination represents a relatively safe guarantee for marital stability and for individual and conjugal growth within the marriage. On the other hand, because of the uniqueness and total dedication of the call to the sacrament of marriage, it is very difficult to give the gift of self *only before* the sacrament of ordination. That could lead to overreactions in both directions (a hasty "renunciation" of marriage in favor of a "timely" ordination; or, a rash marriage without the benefit of a sufficiently long verification of mutual compatibility, so as not to have to remain single or put off ordination for a lengthy period of time). For precisely this reason, it was decided at the Council of Ancyra (314) that deacons could declare before their ordination that they expressly reserved the right to consider the possibility of marriage at a later time. Therefore, we propose that the deacon *as a rule* should be married before ordination; a marriage after ordination should, however, be permitted unless there is a clear theological argument to the effect that he can no longer marry after ordination.[9]

Properly viewed, in all of the above, what is required of the deacon and his family is not excessive: they are to give witness to love. The deacon should give a good account of himself as husband and father. Even though it may be unclear in Sacred Scripture as to whether the text refers to his wife or to a deaconess, it is, however, certain that the wife also should give evidence of qualities that ensure a well-ordered Christian family life. But since in the same text of the Letter to Timothy the cardinal virtues are also stated as requisites for the deacon, similar conclusions may be drawn about his family life: inwardly and outwardly neither greed nor inordinate pleasure-seeking, neither discord nor disarray should hold sway. From this, we also see that the *family life* of the deacon of today should be a simple Christian life by an attitude of loving service appropriate to his office, loving service in its many forms. Each family will then be able to have its own appropriate life-style.

Summing up Section I, parts 1-3, it can be stated that the spiritual life of the deacon with respect to its rhythm, form, extent, and content should be determined by and lived out within the areas of his personal and professional life, of his marriage and family life. Generally speaking, how the proper balance is to be found among these various areas of a deacon's life would also be worked out in the spiritual realm and especially in his prayer-life, which will be dealt with in depth in the section that follows.

II.
Prayer-Life

"Without prayer a human being will not persevere for long in his spiritual life, so we must seek refuge daily in this powerful resource" (St. Philip Neri). If this holds true for every human being, how much more so than for him, who in his service to others has surrendered to the will of God with respect to salvation and love? Only constant contact with God, attention to and acceptance of his will and word prepare one for this service. Prayer then as a (geformate?) formal "lovingly responsive acceptance of the loving will of God" (Rahner-Vorgrimler, *Little Dictionary of Theology*) is a basic function of the Church and therefore of its members; it is, therefore, also a basic function of diaconal service. As every Christian is called to do, so too is the deacon called in a special way to sanctify both his life—in his prayer-life and in his daily routine—and work by incessantly earnest prayer. Insofar as *prayer-life* is both generally speaking and in particular for the deacon as well more than obligatory prayer, it encompasses official prayer, liturgical-public prayer, and so-called private prayer as a prayer form. With respect to content, the Church of Christ prefers right at the outset for itself and its members a prayer-life of prayers of praise and thanksgiving as well as the prayer of worship, which is centered in the eucharistic prayers. Conversation with God presupposes that we understand how to listen to the word of God. He has spoken to us and proclaimed his word in the Gospel.

He speaks to us in life. The Gospel is nourishment for daily life. Genuine conversation between a human being and his God will, however, always make known to God his supplications and concerns and those of his brothers, his family, and the world, in the knowledge that he hears, elevates, and lastly, in the final sense of redemption, promotes the good of all those requests we make to him in prayer of supplication. To personal and interior prayer belongs above all contemplation, meditation on the truths of the faith and the demands thereof in order to realize that which is known in life. Meditation will also lead individuals in our time to acknowledgment of their mistakes, more frequent confession, penitential prayer, and perhaps even lead married couples to go to confession together to a common confessor.

The individual who seriously meditates before God will perceive that this prayer is a permanent call to devote oneself to one's fellow human beings. Meditation becomes the bridge of prayer into one's everyday life. The prayer of the Church, beginning with the Old Testament psalms as songs of praise, thanksgiving, supplication, lamentation, instruction, and repentance on through the Good News of the New Testament and the eucharistic prayer of thanksgiving as the central source and epicenter of our prayers, to the structured prayer of the great prayers of ancient and modern times, right up to the personal dialogue of every single human being—is life with God. Every mode of genuine Christian prayer is, however, always also the prayer of the Church—it is prayer "in Christ and the Church " (Eph 3:21).

1. These basic elements of the prayer-life of the Church must be also included in the special prayer-life of the deacon so that he prays with the Church and as Church. The prayer-life of a married deacon includes liturgical public prayer; personal prayer; prayer with his spouse, his children, and his entire family. On the one hand, it will have fixed forms, which come from the existing treasures of the Church, and be solid enough to structure the day; on the other hand, it will be sufficiently flexible to fit into the daily schedule of the deacon, suitable for the ages of the children, and appropriate for the current occupation and family-life situation. The decisive importance of a prayer-life appropriate for the various areas of a deacon's life is to be found in the foregoing Section I.

Family prayer and family liturgies are by no means private events; they are rather preparations, in a form suitable for the Church in miniature [which is the family], for the official prayer and liturgies of the Church. They are extensions thereof and are the prayer of the Church. This is still true, even if they do not always make use of the official customs of the Church. It remains to be seen, however, how well united family prayer-life is to the formal prayer of the Church from an ecclesial standpoint.[10]

Above all, we need to mention here communal celebration of Holy Eucharist. Its importance for the deacon's personal life and *especially* for his vocational life has already been sufficiently emphasized. Holy Mass should actually be the center of family life. Family attendance together at Sunday Mass should be the norm. Just as guests invited to a banquet would not normally refuse any of the dishes served to them on such an occasion, so too life in and with Christ should normally include and not exclude participation in his banquet (i.e., reception of the gifts offered there). Every Mass is for a husband and wife, regardless of whether or not they can participate together, a genuine renewal of their marriage covenant, by which "they are absorbed into the spousal mystery which exists between Christ and the Church," because "the Eucharist is that sacrament wherein the Lord continuously renews his spousal covenant with the Church."

In fact, Dillersberger[11] maintains that the fifth chapter of the Letter to Ephesians, concerning marriage, presupposes "the entire Christian practice of worship" as the substratum and foundation of the Pauline model [of Church]. Just as the Mass understood as sacrament of the covenant represents a community of life and love, so too is it for married couples an advanced school for their communities of life and love *in* and *by* their families. The eucharistic celebration should continue on to make its spirit felt in all areas of family life. Daily scripture reading—whether alone or when possible with one's wife or if their children are old enough also with them—will lead an individual and his family safely and imperceptibly in everything to a life lived according to the word of God. It will lead individual family members and the family as a whole to a building up of the Body of Christ in all areas of activity—if the Good News is transformed in their lives. The living proclamation of Sacred Scripture on the part of a father is an important presupposition for the transformation of lives through Scripture. The vocational and spiritual life of a deacon would be impoverished and stunted without the reading of Scripture; it would be unthinkable. Let us just mention here for a moment the catechetical tasks, which the married deacon is supposed to assume.

Family prayer-life will be adapted to the ecclesial year, special feast days and weekdays; the Church does not cease to exist at the door of the parish church, but is rather continued, made actual, and established in a cell-like way in the family. Certain parts of the official liturgy and the Liturgy of the Hours could be adapted for the family in a scaled-down form (e.g., sections of the church prayers before and after meals, morning or evening prayer). However, it is extremely important that the official liturgy of the Church be prepared and carried on in the family. This corresponds in the final analysis to the essence of both the Church and the family, and in a special way, it also holds true for important family events, the preparations for them, and their commemoration (baptism, first penance, first communion, confirmation, marriage, and death). There is evidence that it is quite possible for a family to conduct days of recollection and retreats as well as devotions right at home.

It should be at least mentioned here that parents also need to deem it important that the home be properly arranged for such activity. At the very least, there should be a suitable place where the family can gather for prayer ("God's corner"). The treasure of Christian hymns suitable for the seasons of the church year as the living psalms of the human beings of our time will bring the children of all age groups together with their parents in a joyous and thankful community of life and love. Such special occasions of family life and family teaching moments should also include free-form prayer, especially on the part of the father—prayers that not only include the cares of his own family, but prayers of praise, thanksgiving, repentance, and supplication in loving solidarity with the needs of others, of the world, and of all creation, which longs for salvation. To this would belong family rosary devotion by way of special response to the world-wide request for "the consecration of the world [*consecratio mundi*]." Every family has the obligation to fulfill its own God-given calling in accordance with its abilities, its structure, the ages of the children, and so forth. In this regard, fathers as the heads of families have a special task. The "father's blessing" would be an example of this. This blessing is not reserved to only those times when children leave home. A father should give this blessing to his wife and children daily. He should not only bless the family bread every now and again; he should lead grace before and after meals, and at least bless the gifts, especially since the Lord has in a special way "given each Christian group seated at table this sense: that of a mystical communal meal with the Lord of Glory."[12]

In addition to public liturgical, official, and common prayer, there will always be personal individual prayer, from which children, spouse, and parents would be excluded. The personal identity of a spouse or child is not subsumed by the family. It will only be allowed to complete its own proper development and to live up to its own very personal calling for itself and for others by means of a deeply interior, vocal conversation between the individual and God—a conversation that should not be interrupted.

As husband and father, the ordained deacon carries an important and serious responsibility with respect to the fact that the liturgy of the Church, including the "little church" (i.e., the family), is "the preparation for and pledge of the heavenly liturgy."[13] His family in this regard can be a humble, missionary sign in an era of an incredibly high number of family and marriage crises; liturgy is clearly the central focus of Christian spirituality. Furthermore, the close connection and "relationship" of both of the Church's social sacraments—marriage and the priesthood—is visible in the prayer-life of the deacon. It follows therefore that in the concrete official prayer-life of the married deacon both spheres are closely related and are complemented by his personal prayer. It has been shown that assisting at the holy sacrifice of the Mass, the reading of Sacred Scripture, personal prayer, and family prayer—all consistent with the liturgy of the Church—are important and essential for the personal, professional, and family life of a deacon. Ostensibly, this attenuates the significance of praying of the official breviary (Liturgy of the Hours) as it is practiced in priestly and monastic life. Is not this also a consequence of Acts 6:1-6, wherein the overburdened apostles determined that they should call "deacons" to service at tables, so that they could devote themselves to prayer and preaching? The resolution of this question as it pertains to the restoration of the diaconate rests with the highest authority of the Church.

For all of the above-mentioned reasons, the Diaconate Circle community urgently advises and recommends the approval of a prayer-life schema focused on the sacrificial celebration of the holy Eucharist, daily scripture reading, family prayer, and personal prayer. The compilation of a special diaconal prayer book, which takes into account the educational background of a deacon, is also recommended. Such a prayer book should be in the vernacular, if for no other reason that to encourage diaconal families to pray together, and should be attuned to the mission, the profession, the responsibilities, and also to the family life of a deacon. Furthermore, in this way, his praying will be consistent with the official prayer of the Church.

2. Concretely, the following prayer-life of the deacon with the Church and as the prayer of the Church could be his official and permanent responsibility:[14]

> a) attendance and assisting at holy Mass daily if possible; depending on the situation, also functioning liturgically as deacon (*missa cum diacono,* liturgy of the word, and distribution of holy communion);

> b) daily scripture reading, if possible together with his wife;

> c) daily contemplation, spiritual reading, and/or adoration of the holy Eucharist.

> A proper prayer book for the deacons of the world in the vernacular could include the most esteemed prayers from the Old and New Testaments, from all the psalms, selected texts by ancient and modern theologians, great saints, prayers from the *Imitation of Christ,* the prayers of the Church for the chief petitions of the day, for the various times of the day and of the church year, and so forth—so that they could all be prayed in a living rhythm.

> d) For the *married deacon,* very special significance should be attached *to the communal, intimate, and blessed prayer of the family* (with wife, with children, and with both wife and children) at certain times of the day, on the various church feast days

throughout the year, for special family occasions, and so forth. Obligatory prayer time or an obligatory prayer schedule should not be mandated and should not be divided into strict categories of scripture reading, contemplation, adoration or family prayer, so that the deacon will be able to truly realize an interior and personal prayer-life; to be able to lift up the petitions of the day in prayer, contemplation, and worship; and to be able to foster family prayer in the appropriate manner.

A vital prayer-life loosely configured to the normal rhythm of the day, which would include holy Mass, scripture reading, contemplation, or spiritual reading, adoration and family prayer would consume approximately an hour each day and could still be construed both as prayer with the Church and the prayer of the Church.

3. *In addition, the deacon should:*

a) pray the Rosary and practice forms of eucharistic devotion;

b) frequent the sacrament of confession approximately once a month;

c) make an annual retreat, with his wife, if at all possible.

If asked the question as to what is more obligatory for any deacon throughout the world—prayer or service to his neighbor—he should respond along with St. Vincent de Paul in his exhortation to his nuns:

Do not worry or feel guilty if you cannot find time for it (prayer or spiritual reading); since if what you are doing is being done for the right reason, your prayer is not being neglected. And if there were ever a good reason to do so, that reason is most certainly service to your neighbor. For if you neglect God for God's sake—one work for another urgent and meritorious work—then you do not neglect God. If you interrupt your prayer time or your spiritual reading or even your silence to minister to a person in need, please be assured that by doing so you are also serving God.

The spiritual life is one of loving devotion to God and to one's brother in imitation of Christ.

Notes

1. Cf. S. Baeumer, *History of the Breviary* (Freiburg, 1895) and J. Pascher, *The Liturgy of the Hours of the Roman Church* (Munich, 1954).

2. Herder Verlag, Freiburg, 1962.

3. R. Grosche in *Word and Truth*, Special Edition: "Council Survey" (Freiburg, 1961), p. 595.

4. Published privately by the author (Wuerzburg, 1953).

5. Cf. also H. Bacht, the article "Lay Breviary" in *Lexicon of Catholic Theology*, VI:743.

6. Cf. F. Wulf, "Christian Witness in the Secular and Religious State" in *Society and Life* 27 (1954): 379-383; F. Wulf, "Priestly Piety, Religious Piety, Lay Piety" in *Society and Life* 29 (1956): 427-439; as well as H. Seiler, "The Spirituality of the Christian in the World" in *Society and Life* 27 (1954): 358-368.

7. Pius XI, Encyclical *On Christian Marriage* (December 31, 1930), quotes in the German-Latin Herder edition of 1931.

8. Cf. B. Haering, *Marriage in Our Day* (Salzburg, 1961); A. Auer, *The Christian Open to the World—Fundamental and Historical Aspects of Lay Piety* (Duesseldorf, 1960); Y. Congar, *The Layman* (Stuttgart, n.d.).

9. *The Working Papers of the Diaconate Circle* 3/July (Freiburg, 1961): 30.

10. Cf. H. Oster, "That They May Remain in Your Praise . . ." (Mainz, 1958); K. Becker, *Liturgy and Lay Piety* (Hirschberg), nos. 1-6 and 12 (1959), as well as no. 1/2 (1960); L. Winterswyl, *Lay Liturgy* (Wuerzburg and Colmar, n.d.).

11. J. Dillersberger, *The New God—A Biblical-Theological Essay on the Letters to the Ephesians* (Salzburg-Leipzig, 1935), pp. 179ff.

12. J. Dillersberger, *Luke*, vol. VI (Salzburg, 1949), p. 187.

13. Pius XII, Encyclical *On the Sacred Liturgy* (November 20, 1947) *Mediator Dei*, no. 25.

14. Cf. earlier in this volume, H. Kramer, "The Liturgical Ministry of the Deacon," pp. 362-379. (Reference here is to an earlier article in *Diaconia in Christo* by the same author.)

At the time this essay was written (circa 1961), there was a certain confusion and misinformation circulating in ecclesiastical circles and in the then-current literature, concerning the precise canonical status of the deacon. Since the diaconate had not yet been restored, most information being circulated—whether oral or written—was exploratory and tentative. Prof. Winninger (Strasbourg, France) was concerned that this misinformation and other forms of misunderstanding be cleared up, especially in academic and theological circles. We should also bear in mind that the order of subdeacon and the minor orders had not yet been canonically suppressed. It should be mentioned this article was written for a primarily european readership. In his desire to bring clarity out of confusion, Prof. Winninger contributes important insights about the nature of the role of the deacon vis-à-vis both priests and lay persons. Of special importance for the contemporary permanent diaconate is the strong position taken by Prof. Winninger, concerning the fact that the diaconate does not diminish the lay apostolate (lay ministry).

Samuel M. Taub

The Deacon and the Lay Person

by Paul Winninger

It is the objective of this article to sketch out briefly the differences and the relationships between deacon and lay person with respect to the reinstitution of the diaconate as a permanent office.

The results of the exposition can be summarized in three statements:

1. The deacon is not a layman but, rather, a cleric.

2. The deacon can, however, assume the role/task of mediator between priest and people.

3. Diaconal office and the apostolate of the laity do differ but do not compete with one another.

I. The Deacon Is a Member of the Hierarchy

Some authors, particularly at the outset of the movement to restore the diaconate, unfortunately used designations such as "lay deacons" or "diaconate of the laity." These expressions are inaccurate, even contradictory, and therefore nonsensical. Thus, they should be avoided.

Deacons are, of course, drawn from the laity, just as priests are. They are certainly ordained, instituted into the initial degree of the sacrament of orders and are marked with the indelible character thereof. As members of the clergy, deacons enter the hierarchy.

"In the Church, holy orders, established by Christ, differentiate clerics from laity for leadership of the faithful and for the ministry of [public] divine worship" (*Code of Canon Law*, c. 948).

The Council of Trent states the following concerning the ranks of holy orders: "In the Catholic Church, there exists a divinely instituted hierarchy, which is comprised of bishops, priests and ministers." At the very least, deacons are understood to be included under "ministers," since holy Scripture explicitly mentions not only priests, but deacons also." One can dispute the sacramental character of the lower orders, even that of the subdeacon; there is no doubt, however, that the diaconate belongs to the sacrament of holy orders.

From a juridical point of view, the *Code* [of Canon Law] classifies those who have received tonsure and the lower orders, and especially deacons, as clergy (cf. c. 108). Even though Pius XII, at the October 1957 Congress for the Lay Apostolate held in Rome, stimulated the idea of a possible restoration of the diaconate, he took no position about the plan. He considered the idea "not yet mature enough." But he did take pains to correct the error of those who spoke of a "lay diaconate" by explaining that: "The diaconate would find its place *together with the presbyterate,* in the distinct ordering which we have set forth" (what is meant is the differentiation between clergy and laity, between the hierarchial apostolate and simple cooperation in the work of this apostolate).

The deacon is, therefore, no longer a layman, but rather a cleric; he is ordained.

II. The Deacon as Mediator between Priest and People

Although the deacon clearly belongs to the hierarchy, we may still say, that he—especially in certain circumstances—stands as a mediator between priest and people. Since he is on the first or lowest level of the three degrees of holy order, he stands nearer to the lay person than does the priest. The reality of this proximity manifests itself in two ways:

1. *By his functions.* The deacon is consecrated, but does not consecrate; his service in the areas of charity, catechesis, administration, and liturgy can be performed by lay persons, and to some extent this is already a reality.

2. *By his life-style.* He can, under certain circumstances, hold a civilian position, and he can be married.

The appropriateness of the institution of this mediating order by the apostles has generally been confirmed by modern sociology. Its benefit is all the greater, the more complex the social organism is. The civil and ecclesial communities of our day are in actuality such organisms.

Elsewhere in this book, significant light will be shed on the "mediator role" of the deacon and diaconal service in a detailed description of diaconal duties. A brief enumeration of these will suffice here:

1. Deacons by virtue of their appointments are, to a significant extent, mediators (see Acts 6); the apostles appoint them to carry out certain tasks of a material and administrative nature between themselves and the faithful.

2. Liturgically, the deacon is a mediator, still retained to this day in the Greek rite and considered essential. It is a major shortcoming that he is missing from the simple Latin rite; this is the reason for the abnormal, solo action of the priest at the altar and for attempts at more or less confused and inappropriate substitutions (e.g., using child altar servers, male and female lectors and sacristans).

3. In *Diaspora* and mission countries, the deacon, as leader of the local [ecclesial] community, is the unifying bond, who is the link between it and priest and bishop.

4. In a more general way, the deacon—particularly in today's society, which is more and more becoming a conglomeration of lukewarm or unchurched Christians and atheists—can carry out this task of mediation successfully in many different ways by means of his service and his personal behavior. He has access to those social circles to which

53

access would be very difficult for a priest. He can approach people who would refuse to have any direct contact with a priest and lead these people to the priest. Deacons can move about more freely in those fringe areas where the interests of Church and state intersect than can priests, since they would be less likely to be suspected of clericalism by an affable partner. Deacons are especially well-suited for the position of negotiator.

5. In the special case of the de-Christianized workplace, the hierarchy has no presence in the workplace because of the prohibition against priests working in factories—an active laity not withstanding. Cardinal Pizzardo's letter of prohibition sets the record straight by calling attention to the fact that "the apostles instituted the diaconate to free themselves from secular tasks so as to be able to devote themselves to prayer and preaching." Is this not a discreet allusion to the fact that the Church might not have any serious objections to deacons being allowed once again to attempt to resume this role? By so doing, the ordained hierarchy would again have a presence in the workplace, and contact with the workers would be reestablished.

6. On the other hand, a certain number of deacons, in a specific way, will render "the world of technology itself with its own values intelligible to the hierarchy in an up-to-date and effective way. This 'up-to-date-ness' and effectiveness, which appears to be of great value to the work of the holy Church in modern society, can only be handled by priests in exceptional cases."

Briefly stated, in reality, some of the problems that accrue today to the role of the laity in the Church and relationships between clergy and laity are problems of the diaconate. A genuine, institutionally effective, juridically correct, and theologically well-grounded solution to these problems can be found only through the diaconate.

III. The Diaconate Does Not Diminish Lay Apostolate

The restoration of the diaconate has been unsettling for some. After all, isn't one running the risk of dividing the apostolate of the laity, of suppressing its recent blossoming by siphoning off the active laymen from Catholic Action and thereby robbing this apostolate of its "best and brightest?" Won't those activities presently being performed by laymen now become "clericalized?" Won't such a thing work against the recent, successful increase in participation in the life of the Church on the part of the laity? These objections are based on the idea that the various aspects of diaconal service could also be carried out by lay persons, by virtue of their sacramental baptism and confirmation, which bestows "a royal priesthood" on all Christians. The reestablishment of the diaconate would therefore seem to be of no use. This argument continually reappears, especially according to H. Holstein: "It is not *necessary* to be ordained in order to engage in works of charity, to preside at Sunday scripture service, to teach catechism, etc." Such talk only misrepresents the problem and creates confusion. The lay apostolate and the diaconate differ from each other, complement each other, and do not compete against each other—the laity does not compete against the priesthood, and the baptized state does not compete against the ordained state. This is easily understood in the relationship between the active layman and the priest, who consecrates and therefore must be consecrated. It is less readily seen at first glance as far as the deacon is concerned, above all because of the historical decline of this order, but especially because the duties of the deacon are numerically uncertain, change according to the conditions of the time, and to some extent are already being carried out by laymen; to the extent that these duties are not consecrational, they do not necessarily require ordination—particularly, if one examines them in isolation. If one follows, however, that "uselessness of ordination to carry out this or that service" line of thought to its endpoint, one would immediately arrive at the conclusion that the order of deacon is unnecessary and should be dropped from the repository of Catholic faith. One can see how erroneous such a conclusion is since it proceeds from an erroneous premise: the principle that ordination for ecclesiastical office-holders, who themselves do not consecrate, is of no use. In order to draw correct conclusions in this area, we must proceed from the solid truth of actual relationships from sacramental theology and ecclesiology, and attempt to build a unified construct. The task at hand is not to first isolate individual activities and inquire as to whether or not ordination is necessary to carry them out; it is rather to *build up the Body of the Church*. To do so, active lay persons and deacons are necessary.

We will develop this thesis in five brief steps.

1. The Sacraments are there and mutually compliment one another.

The sacraments must be viewed as they were intended by virtue of their divine institution—to compliment each other, not to compete with one another. On the one hand, it is essential to set forth in all their importance the responsibilities that accrue to all Christians by virtue of baptism and confirmation (e.g., missionary work). But it is just as essential that the entire richness of the sacrament of orders, in particular the diaconate, which up to now has been repressed, be unfolded.

True progress in theological thought always manifests itself in a synthetic synopsis of the whole, which does not tolerate any unbalanced accents. In this twentieth century, we are experiencing a time of grace in which everything in the Church is coming together in a harmonious rearrangement: the rethinking of the total meaning of baptism, confirmation, marriage, and also of orders and, specifically, the rediscovery of the diaconate. To neglect the sacrament of ordination in favor of the other sacraments or Catholic Action would be to fall into a kind of laicism; it would mean an unfortunate degradation of ordained office, which would ultimately be harmful to the laity, the hierarchy and the entire Church.

In the early Church, which to be sure need not be slavishly copied as a model in every age, but nonetheless should be consulted as the ideal image, the faith was spread largely by the laity, who became missionaries directly by virtue of their baptism. And yet there were deacons in those days! The one did not render the other superfluous, but rather they both complimented one another in a vibrant unity within the organically structured Church. In the ages that followed, the dying out of the diaconate did not result in a rebirth of lay missionaries but, rather, just the opposite. In view of the priesthood, which was universal and all-powerful, both [the laity and the diaconate] became inactive; this glut of priests in the Church, which has hardly withdrawn from the sphere of secular power, has fortunately begun to lessen. The restoration of the diaconate is logically and directly bound up with the renewed consciousness of the laity themselves [about their role] in the Church, which itself is rediscovering the organic diversity of tasks (i.e., of the members of the unified Body of Christ) in accordance with Paul's writings.

2. Nonconsecrational hierarchical tasks also require ordination.

In the Church, a *societas perfecta,* there is a large number of tasks—which by the way may change depending on time and place—that are carried out jointly in mutual assistance and complimentarity by both clergy and laity. The hierarchy has been primarily instituted to consecrate, to proclaim, and to lead. Ordination does not only confer the power to consecrate and should not be requisite for that reason alone; it also confers upon the higher degrees of the clergy the authority to preach/proclaim and to lead. Orders or hierarchy are simply identical with this threefold authority. Of course, it is not easy, especially on the level of the diaconate, to distribute or demarcate in precise manner the lesser or auxiliary forms of proclamation and administration between clergy and laity. Two reliable basic principles may be cited here, however: First of all, the apostles instituted the diaconate for a specific and rather well-defined ministry; and second, it has been church tradition to ordain those who hold permanent, if lesser, office. At present, a list of some of the major and more important diaconal ministerial duties would include: administration, preaching, leadership in priest-less communities, certain liturgical functions (solemn baptism, distribution of the Eucharist, presiding at a Sunday worship service when a priest is not available, burial services, and officiating at weddings). Yes, lay persons could also function in this capacity, but they could only do so as a surrogate and, incidentally, under extraordinary circumstances. Under normal circumstances, these actions are hierarchical in nature; their regular and permanent exercise properly belongs to the sphere of activities of the ordained state. Scripture, tradition, and hierarchial structure are all tied to ordination and, in this particular situation, to the diaconate, so it would be a mistake to want to dispute this fact in partiality to the lay state. Charity assumes a special place among these ministerial duties. It is the responsibility of clergy and laity alike. However, it is very significant that it also be officially carried out by the hierarchy, wherever possible by the diaconate.

3. Catholic Action is not diaconal in nature.

Within the framework of a theology of the diaconate, which is clear and secure in its principles (if not necessarily in all its applications), it is also advisable to describe clearly the role of the lay person, which is twofold.

With the shortage of priests, lay persons can be delegated to carry out a wide range of auxiliary services that are normally reserved to the hierarchy (e.g., religious education [catechism] classes and some liturgical functions). In those instances, however, they are not acting on the strength of their special vocation as Christian lay persons, but rather in a surrogate manner on the strength of their having been delegated to do so. If at some future time deacons were to appropriate a portion of these services into their official duties, this should not be a cause for complaint on the part of the laity. On the contrary, this would simply represent a restoration of the normal situation, consistent with tradition and the intent of the Council of Trent, which recommended ordination for the holders of such offices. In any event, there are countless needs—the harvest is great and the workers are few. Lay persons of good will always have opportunities to engage themselves actively in the multiplicity of helping services, particularly in the area of their most special vocation: Christian witness.

By the same token, lay persons are truly called to the "*consecratio mundi* [consecration of the world]." This is their fundamental mission; they are irreplaceable here. This is the actual missionary task of Catholic Action, at least as it is understood in France: to bring the Good News by word and deed into their de-Christianized environment. It is then the duty of every baptized person; it is the vocation of every confirmed person to give witness to Christ and to his Church in the home, in the neighborhood, and in the factory. This is not a special, ordained office; it means to be leaven, the light of the world and the salt of the earth. Each person should serve in accordance with his [or her] state, both the lay person and the cleric. This mission does not imply ordination. On the contrary, the active Christian in the final analysis ceases to be a lay person or even a witness *per se* in those situations, where the witness of a lay person carries more weight than that of a cleric.

4. Over against Catholic Action, the diaconate serves as a necessary framework for the establishment of the hierarchial structure of the Church.

It is, therefore, easily seen how the state and work of the lay person differ from that of the deacon in both the parish and the diocese.

The active lay person is, by his life, a witness for Christ in his environment; he is actually to be found everywhere and in innumerable locations. His action can neither be exactly defined nor delineated. This action cannot be strictly enjoined on anyone, either for a certain period of time or in a limited field of endeavor. It is devoid of prescribed forms and canonical jurisdiction.

By the same token, deacons as "office bearers" belong to the hierarchy. They are limited in numbers by the functions they can perform; the Church calls as candidates only those she needs. Let us assume that there would be an equal number of priests and deacons or the ratio is as it was in Jerusalem, seven to twelve—basically, one deacon per location or per parish. And yet as far as Catholic Action is concerned, there is no limitation [of members]. The deacon has a permanent function; he is ordained for a hierarchial office. Once he receives an official assignment, he possesses a canonical jurisdiction.

The hierarchial character of a deacon in a priest-less community in *diaspora* and missionary countries needs to be especially emphasized. These people are basically without an actual hierarchial presence that can represent the Church at the local level—and this is indispensable. The deacon can ensure this presence by catechizing, preaching for the community on Sundays, organizing charitable works, and serving the community as its leader. This office is both ontological by virtue of its divine institution and hierarchial. It could never be filled by a lay person except in accidental circumstances. This is confirmed by psychological considerations, as well as by Sacred Scripture and history. We know of no example of a Christian Church that, upon the loss of the hierarchy, continued to exist as a Catholic Church. Christ describes the Church, universal as well as local, using the image of a flock, which is under the leadership of a shepherd.

The lay person by definition is *not* a shepherd. Although he can and must be a missionary, he cannot call the faithful together for church; he can never set himself in the place of the hierarchy. A priest can take a deacon's place; the higher rank of Holy Orders can assume the duties of those of lesser rank, and the bishop possesses the fullness of hierarchial authority. But it does not work the other way around; a lay person can never take the place of a deacon, except *per modum actus*.

The theology of the parish community as local church clearly reveals two truths. On the one hand, the Church is visible for Christians in a local community, where it is concretely lived and experienced. When this does not happen, there is a danger, that the concept of Church is no longer valid. On the other hand, a group of baptized persons is only rendered real and permanent by the presence of a shepherd, of at least a deacon. If in a situation where a community is threatened by dissolution, a lay person takes over the reins, then he is in truth already no longer a lay person; he becomes a shepherd by virtue of the functions he has assumed. In accordance with his authority and by his choice—even without the requisite ordination—he is a deacon or a priest, an *episkopos* (overseer, guardian).

5. The deacon and the lay person stand in the same relationship to one another as the priest and the lay person.

Having stated the above, it is sufficient to clarify in a word the relationship between the deacon and Catholic Action: it is basically identical to the relationship between the priest and Catholic Action. By virtue of his status and in accordance with his charisms and jurisdiction, the deacon can support a group of active lay persons by encouragement and with advice. A particularly important task for a deacon in a priest-less community is his effort to awaken a missionary spirit, as well as to organize an elite group capable of radiating the truth of the Gospel into various walks of life.

The diaconate and Catholic Action are specifically different. It is unfortunate that some have occasionally referred to the diaconate as the "crowning of Catholic Action" in the sense that the latter organization should aspire to ordination as the consummation of its activity.

This would only be appropriate in an individual situation of an apostolic vocation, which has its roots in Catholic Action and is subsequently translated into the desire to consecrate one's life to the Church (as also happens when an active layman may later enter the seminary and become a priest). Catholic Action is the officially designated service of the laity to the Church; it should therefore be sufficient unto itself. If there are those who see in the diaconate a threat to the lay apostolate, it should be noted that this fear does not emanate from theologians or the leadership of Catholic Action, at least not in France. Clearly, their silence right up to the present moment appears to indicate that they have understood the planned diaconate to be what it is—a clerical office, specifically distinct from the cooperation of the laity, a relief and a refinement for the priesthood, an office that promises to restore the entire sacrament of holy orders to its fullness.

In this rather comprehensive overview essay of the history of the diaconate from the first millennium, Fr. Croce (Innsbruck) synthesizes for us some key lessons, which those who are concerned with the restored permanent diaconate should study and internalize. These lessons should come as no surprise to anyone even vaguely familiar with the recent history of the restored diaconate, for they have to do with the human condition. Furthermore, Fr. Croce's research confirms those who have shaped the structure and the formation of the restored diaconate in so many dioceses in the United States. It is evident that those responsible for preparing the documentation for Vatican II and the documents issued by Rome in those years immediately following Vatican II were more than a little conversant with the history of the diaconate during the first millennium. At the very least, Fr. Croce seems convinced that the original reasons why the apostles of the infant Church perceived the need for deacons are still valid as the second millennium comes to a close. In any case, to paraphrase Santayana, perhaps the most important lesson to be learned is that those who do not study the mistakes of the past are condemned to repeat them.

In the interest of greater readability, the 243 footnotes in Fr. Croce's original German essay have not been included in the translation that follows. Those who have an interest in this deeper level of scholarship are referred to the original German text.

Samuel M. Taub

From the History of the Diaconate

by Walter Croce, SJ

The current efforts to restore anew the diaconate may be justified only to the extent that they serve genuine pastoral concerns. Nevertheless, they must also find their justification in the light of history; for the modern reconstruction of an institution that is almost as old as the Church itself must, in the final analysis, come about in harmony with tradition.

The practice of recent centuries indeed points to a development which, it would appear, opens up only slight possibilities for a greater use of deacons. According to the law currently in effect, the deacon is only assigned some liturgical functions and the right to exercise the office of preaching. In practice, not even these possibilities are fully utilized, so one is left with no alternative but to ask why this reticence? Is it completely unjustifiable, or is it in the final analysis an expression of a deeper or possibly even ancient ecclesial conviction?

Church law in citing its source for canon 1342 makes reference to the *Roman Pontifical,* which contains the following well-know statement: "It is proper for deacons to minister at the altar, to baptize and to preach." These words were inserted by Durandus (1230-1296) into the declaration *Provehendi filii,* in which the responsibilities of the deacon were described as just cited. However, Durandus does not understand [the original Latin verb] *praedicare* in the sense of "to preach," but rather he means solely the proclamation of the Gospel. Correspondingly, he states in his explanatory section: "they (i.e., deacons) are authorized to proclaim (*praedicare*), that is, to publicly read the Gospel." [Translator's note: Over time, the original primary meaning of the Latin verb *praedicare* shifted from "to proclaim publicly" to "to preach." In the Middle Ages, its technical meaning became "to preach"]. Therefore, it appears that this editor (Durandus) of the *Pontifical* implies something more than was its intended sense. Durandus even views the normal functions of the deacon as merely assisting functions, and he was by no means inclined to see the deacon as one of the ordinary ministers of the sacrament of baptism. He therefore recognized only a twofold office for the deacon (in contrast to the threefold of the *Pontifical*): "to proclaim publicly to the people and to assist the priest." For further clarification, he states:

> . . . they are authorized to assist priests and to minister in all things which are carried out in the Sacraments of Christ, in baptism, anointing, the paten, the chalice . . . and to proclaim, i.e., to read publicly the Gospel. [Finally, he emphatically pronounces]: nevertheless they [deacons] are not permitted to baptize or to distribute the Lord's body except in an emergency in the absence of and by delegation from a bishop or priest.

We see then that the situation at the end of the thirteenth century is hardly any different than that of today. At that time, the deacon was not called upon to preach or to baptize (other than in exceptional circumstances). Now, it is indeed correct that Durandus adopted from older sources that statement in the *Pontifical* in which the functions of the deacon were enumerated, and so it is possible for us to interpret this statement, at least for an earlier period, differently than Durandus would permit us to do at the end of the thirteenth century. Our source could only be the *Roman Curial Pontifical*, which also dates from the thirteenth century and is therefore not very distant from the time of Durandus. Generally speaking, this source does not provide us with any point of departure for an interpretation, which would differ from that of Durandus. On the other hand, it does reveal that texts older than the *Roman Curial Pontifical* do not go beyond Durandus in the definition of diaconal responsibilities. The twelfth-century *Roman Pontifical* does not contain *any* reference to any diaconal functions, and in both the *Salzburg Pontifical* (eleventh century) as well as the *Roman-German Pontifical* (tenth/eleventh centuries), there are only references to service at the altar and to the conferral of baptism in some form; there is no mention of preaching. The *Pontifical of Egbert of York,* which belongs roughly to the same time period, outlines the deacon's sphere of activity as follows:

> Deacons are authorized to minister at the altar, to proclaim the Gospel in the church, to baptize and to distribute communion in place of priests, to wash the feet of pilgrims and to bury the dead.

These words, which are free of any punctiliousness and therefore, most deserving of our trust, grant to the deacon only the right to administer baptism and distribute communion in place of a priest.

Any preaching activity does not even come into question. Only the public reading of the Gospel during Mass is included in his responsibilities. That this must have been the case in earlier centuries is demonstrated for us, among others, by the Synod of Vaison (529), which determined that a deacon may read to the people excerpts from patristic homilies, in the event that the priest-pastor is prevented by illness from being present. It was inconceivable that a deacon would preach in place of the priest in such a situation. The sphere of competence of the deacon is even more clearly delineated in the *Apostolic Constitutions.* Therein, one finds that the right to baptize is reserved exclusively to bishops and priests, with deacons only assisting them; even the right to teach is reserved to the priest. Whereas, it is said of the deacon: "he does not bless, he does not baptize, he does not offer [the Holy Sacrifice of the Mass] . . .," he is still permitted to distribute holy Eucharist not as a priest but, rather, as a minister to priests.

And finally, the public proclamation of the Gospel belongs to both deacon and priest. One must, therefore, admit that today's practice, whereby deacons are only permitted with serious reservations to preach and to baptize, is consistent with tradition; even if today's practice is in apparent contradiction to the declarations of the *Pontifical,* these two functions have never belonged to their sphere of office.

On the other hand, it is a fact that the diaconate not only existed in ancient Christianity but was of great significance. Already in Pauline communities, deacons were working side-by-side with their bishop; Clement of Rome attributes their existence to divine intervention and sees them prefigured in Old Testament prophecy. For Ignatius of Antioch, they are an essential component of the hierarchy; therefore, everyone should also "respect the deacons as Christ," not just bishops and priests. According to Ignatius, "there can be no Church" without this three-tiered hierarchy.

The *Didaskalia* requires that a sufficient number of deacons be available in every city, and as we may conclude from the letters of Cyprian, there must have actually been a rather large number of deacons available in all of the larger cities. The Synod of Neocaesarea (314-325) does indeed limit their number [in each city?] to seven by citing the Acts of the Apostles, but that does not diminish the importance of their office. So we cannot assume that the early Christian diaconate was an empty degree of Holy Orders as it is today. There were certainly important responsibilities associated with the diaconate, but we will have to look for them in areas other than teaching and expressly sacramental functions.

Diaconate as Service

In the *Church Order of Hippolytus* (of Rome) one finds the statement that during diaconal ordination, only the bishop is to lay hands on the candidate and not the entire presbyterate. The reason given is: "They are not ordained to the priesthood but for service to the bishop." With these words, the responsibility of deacon is designated as service and this, in turn, is contrasted with priesthood. There is, therefore, a significant difference between service and priesthood, and the two should not be confused. The rite of laying on of hands is, of course, the same for both the ordination of the priest and of the deacon, but it does not have in both cases the same sense nor the same effect. The *Canons of Hippolytus* expressly highlight and emphasize this difference, after they have set forth the rite of laying on of hands for diaconal ordination: "and therefore he does not belong to the order of priesthood, but to that of deacon as befits a servant of God."

The ordinance from the *Church Order of Hippolytus* reappeared in a slightly revised version in the *Testament of Our Lord* and became normative in the West, having been incorporated into the *Ancient Statutes of the Church.* In addition to these, it found its way into the *Gelasian Sacramentary,* the *Frankish Missal,* the *Gallicanized Orders* of the eighth century and into the *Carolingian Pontificals.* Even Durandus included it in his *Pontifical* as a rubric, and so it is that we find it again in the current *Roman Pontifical.* In the *Ancient Statutes of the Church,* the canon from the *Church Order of Hippolytus* was somewhat abbreviated. One no longer finds the expression "service to the bishop," but rather: "is consecrated not for the priesthood but for service." In this garbled form, the canon also made its way into later liturgical texts that relied on the *Statutes.* Furthermore, it is still widely held with conviction down to our day that the specific responsibility of the deacon consists in service and that he has no share in [ministerial] priesthood.

From time to time, the Church has pointedly emphasized this difference. The Synod of Nicaea (325) notified deacons that they are only "servants of the bishop and lesser than priests." The Fourth Council of Toledo (633) forbids them from wearing two orarions, pointing out that not even bishops or priests are permitted to do so, much less "their servants." Even the author of the *Apostolic Constitutions* feels compelled to remind deacons that they have been called for "service." Even their name, he says, points to that fact. Since the differentiation in titles of office are not without meaning, very real differences are expressed therein. If this were not the case, it would have sufficed to designate all ecclesial office-holders with the same name. However, bishops are called to the episcopacy, priests to priesthood, and deacons to service. This is an argument that can hardly be disputed.

It is a fact, that ecclesial titles of office, which were not fixed right from the very beginning and owe their existence to the spontaneous linguistic creativity of the community, have each retained the specifically typical characteristic of the office-holder. If then a group of clerics received the name "deacon" as a permanent title of office, one can conclude that only relatively modest services were associated with the affairs of their office.

What these services were comprised of is seldom indicated in any precise or exhaustive way. Frequently, what is to be found is stated negatively—what the deacon is not permitted to do. Usually, however, it is quite generally stated: he is there for service to the Church, to priests, and above all for service to the bishop.

The *Church Order of Hippolytus* grounds the rite of diaconal ordination (i.e., the laying on of hands by the bishop alone) precisely in the fact that the deacon is ordained for the service of the bishop:

. . . for service to the bishop, to do those things, which are delegated to him. He has not been called to become a teacher for all clerics, but rather to ascertain what is necessary and to tell the bishop about it. He is likewise not called to attain to the elevated nature which priests share, but rather he should pay careful attention to that which is fitting, so that the bishop will trust him and instruct him in that which is desirable.

According to the *Didaskalia,* the deacon should be ready to carry out the orders of the bishop and always be at his disposal. *The Testament of Our Lord* also sees the task of the deacon primarily as being ready to receive and carry out assignments from the bishop. So, in a special way, the deacon was to be found at the bishop's side, and it depended upon the bishop as to which assignments he would carry out on a situation-by-situation basis. This connection between deacon and bishop was so close that occasionally it was compared to the relationship between Christ and his Father:

> Just as Christ does nothing without his Father, so also the deacon does nothing without the bishop, and just as the Son is herald and prophet of the Father, so too is the deacon the emissary and voice of the bishop.

The *Didaskalia* sees this connectedness as the ideal, and many things important for the Church are dependent upon its realization. She therefore cautions bishops and deacons:

> [B]e of one mind . . . and diligently nourish the people together, because according to the mind of the Lord you are of one mind. . . . The deacon should be the ear, heart and soul of the bishop, since if you both are of one mind, peace will be found in the Church through your harmony.

Certainly, this concord would not always be realized. In a larger college of deacons, it was probably not even possible for all of them to work in such close proximity to the bishop or to enjoy his trust. Usually, it was a single individual, who had an especially close relationship with the bishop. The bishop spoke of him as "his deacon" and thus gave an impetus to the development of the archdiaconate. In any case, the deacon according to his original call was the servant of the bishop and secondarily, of course, an assistant to priests and therefore to the entire Church.

This association *with* and subordination *to* priest-pastors, as well as the basic willingness to undertake any service assigned to them, comprised the essential core of the scope of the diaconal office. *Diakonia* thus became a permanent concept that was clearly fenced off from the *leitourgia* of the high priest and which could be placed in a direct parallel with the *didaskein* of teachers and the *episkopein* of bishops. The fact that the exercise of this office demanded of the office-holder high moral qualities and, above all, great unselfishness was already also well-known in those days. For that reason, the *Didaskalia* placed special emphasis of these words of our Lord:

> He who among you wish to be great, let him become your servant, and he who among you wishes to be first, let him become your slave; just as the Son of Man did not come to be served but rather to serve and to give his life as a ransom for the many.

To which it adds this admonition:

> Thus, O deacons, should you also conduct yourselves. If the Lord of heaven and earth has served us, suffered and endured everything he did for our sake, how much more then must we treat our brothers in the same way, since we have become imitators of Christ and have sought after his place!

For Ignatius of Antioch, deacons have been "entrusted with the service of Jesus Christ," and it was precisely for this reason that "he loved them so much."

Forms of Service

Since the deacon is called for the service of the bishop, "to do that which they have been delegated to do," it can generally be expected that his scope of service cannot accurately be determined in advance. It is the bishop's prerogative to use his deacons as he sees fit. Thus, Ignatius of Antioch asked the deacon Burrus solely to be his companion as he undertook his journey of imprisonment [to Rome] along the route of the Christian communities in Asia Minor. He dictated to him his Letters to the Philadelphians and to the community of Smyrna and found in him "assistance and solicitude in every respect," because he was a genuine role model of service to God. In the same manner as Burrus, the deacons Rheus and Agathopus as well as the deacon Philip of Cilicia also attached themselves to Ignatius and accompanied him to Troas. When Ignatius learned there that the storm of persecution had in the meanwhile subsided in his episcopal see of Antioch, he suggested to the community of Philadelphia that a deacon be designated to travel to Antioch in order to congratulate the believers there on their newly achieved peace. Naturally, such journeys were only possible as long as the deacons in the community were not engaged in more important tasks. Cyprian, for example, no longer took the risk of releasing any of the clerics in Carthage to serve as mere emissaries. Therefore, he appointed Saturus to lector and the Confessor

Optatus to subdeacon and sent the two of them to Rome with letters. In spite of this plentiful availability, which perfectly suited the nature of the diaconate, it was not long before certain functions crystallized into tasks that can be described as specifically diaconal. For the most part, they fall into the areas of charity, liturgy, and pastoral care.

1. Charitable Activity

The *Church Order of Hippolytus* already mentions that the deacon is called "to take care of the sick and to make reports to the bishops concerning them." The instruction in the *Didaskalia* reads similarly: "Deacons, you should therefore visit all who are living in poverty and report back to the bishop about those who are suffering!" The *Apostolic Constitutions,* the *Canons of Hippolytus,* the *Testament of Our Lord* all also place emphasis on this activity. The personal attributes expected of a deacon always include benevolence, mercy, and concern for widows, orphans, and the poor. In the Ordination Prayer, which has been preserved for us in the *Testament of Our Lord,* the bishop prays that the deacons will show love for widows and orphans, whereas the *Shepherd of Hermas* complains with deep bitterness about deacons, who are derelict in their service, because they have deprived widows and orphans of sustenance, which they consume for themselves. All these texts clearly show that very early on deacons were entrusted with charitable tasks.

That should not surprise us. The exercise of charity is, after all, a basic duty of ecclesial life, and we know how seriously concerned the Church in the early centuries of Christianity was with respect to the fulfillment of the law of love. It was not only the author of the Acts of the Apostles but also Justin the Martyr, who in his time could say:

> We come to the aid of all in need. Each of the rich gives willingly according to his own free judgement. What has been collected is handed over to a supervisor, who supports widows and orphans and all who are in need because of sickness or any other reason. He also helps prisoners and newly arrived strangers. For anyone who is in need of anything, there is a helper.

As these words already demonstrate, the charitable activity of the Church was not only carried out with great enthusiasm, it was also organized. Donations were turned over to the bishop, and he had the task of distributing them among the poor. For the bishop knows best:

> . . . who is in need, and he distributes the gifts to all in such a way that one individual does not receive an allotment several times in one day or in one week while another received nothing. If he hears from someone, that he is in direst need, then the bishop deals with him as an administrator of God, as is fitting.

The leadership of caring for the poor, then, was in the hands of the bishop. We also have numerous examples that serve as proof for us of the concern and circumspection with which bishops of early Christianity ministered to the poor. The letters of Cyprian of Carthage contain more than once this instruction:

> . . . to the extent possible, concern for the poor must be shown in all possible ways. In order to protect them from want, we must provide them with the means necessary to prevent poverty from accomplishing among the oppressed that which the storm of persecution was unable to accomplish among the believers.

Understandably, it was impossible for the bishop himself to carry out the myriad charitable tasks, which were especially difficult to administer during the periods of persecution. The words from the Acts of the Apostles were still true: "it is not right that we neglect the Word of God to wait on tables." Therefore, it was necessary for the bishop to turn over the responsibility for the care of the poor for the most part to others, and for this purpose now he not only had priests but also deacons at his disposal. In Acts 5:6-10, young men are mentioned, who assist the apostles in administering the alms that have been received. It is not out of place to view these young people as the precursors of later deacons or even possibly as the first nonordained deacons. In later times, deacons were also engaged in providing ancillary services in charitable work. They were to begin to visit the believers in their homes to determine if someone were sick or in need and to report this to the bishop. According to the *Testament of Our Lord,* this task was also obligatory for priests, who were to look after the sick in their homes along with deacons. In so doing, they were also supposed to determine the needs of the sick and to ensure that the Church came to the aid of these people. They could even visit boarding houses to inquire there about any individuals who might be sick or in need of assistance. Where a seaport city might be concerned, a deacon might be expected to make a search along the beach to look for any deceased ship-wrecked individuals, who he could at least properly then clothe and bury. Providing the bishop with information about the needy and distressed in his community was naturally only part of the charitable work carried out by a deacon. He also assisted the bishop in the receipt and distribution of contributions. The *Didaskalia* called therefore, above all, for a sufficient number of deacons so that assistance could be rendered to individual believers as quickly as possible. In this connection, the *Didaskalia* not only mentions deacons but also women (usually referred to as "widows" in other places), since only women could provide to other women the help they needed. Deacons, therefore, working on behalf of the bishops, had to limit their activities to visits to men only.

In a special way, the bishop was dependent upon the effectiveness of priests and deacons, if he himself for any reason was personally prevented from carrying out his ministry to the poor. This was the case with Cyprian, who during the Decian persecution was forced to relinquish almost entirely to his clerics the care of the needy. From his freely chosen exile location, he could only exhort by letters his priests and deacons not to allow either those imprisoned for the faith or the rest of the poor to go without food, clothing, or money. Incidentally, he had distributed all of the collection monies among his clerics, so that a greater number of both priests and deacons would have the necessary means to provide support to those seeking help. In Rome, at approximately the same time, Pope Fabian (235-250) divided the city into seven districts and assigned a deacon to each one of them. This measure also contributed to the improved organization of welfare work. We know that at the very least there were in Rome at that time approximately 1,500 poor who were being supported on a regular basis, and since this could hardly have been carried out without strict organization, it is as least probable that the division of the city into districts was associated with carrying out the charitable assistance. From all of these reports, we can also learn how deacons were used to do the charitable work. They did not work independently but were rather closely tied to official directives from the bishop. If they had to act quickly to come to the aid of a needy person, then they were at least to report back to the bishop about the situation, lest a rumor get started and an attempt be made to play the bishop and deacon off against each other. Neither were they independent from priests but, rather, were supposed to cooperate with them. Therefore, deacons actually functioned only as assistants of the bishop and priests. They were also expected to perform many extremely menial services (e.g., the *Testament of Our Lord* expected of deacons that they would wash the sick and the lame; anoint, dress, and bury the dead; Cyprian asked them to claim the bodies of those who died for the faith and to record the dates of their death). That deacons did in fact discharge these duties faithfully is proven to us in a letter, in which Bishop Dionysius of Alexandria praises not only the laity and the priests but also singles out the deacons in a special way because, during the plague that struck the city following the Decian persecution, "they showed no concern for themselves but, rather, fearlessly looked after the sick, nursed them with care and ministered to them in Christ." In so doing, many caught the plague themselves and, as a result "the most able—priests, deacons, and laity—lost their lives." So, if several centuries later, we read in the *Pontifical of Egbert of York* these words: "deacons are authorized . . . to wash to feet of pilgrims and to bury the dead," then at least this corresponds completely to the facts from the first four centuries. Further, it is simply not pious allegory when the *Irish Collection of Canons* in the chapter entitled: "Concerning the Degrees [of Orders] in which Christ was Present" states: "the deacon (was Christ), when he washed the feet of the disciples."

2. Liturgy

In Ignatius of Antioch we read this statement, the meaning of which is not easy to discern despite its simple construction: "It is necessary that deacons, who here are (servants) of the mysteries of Jesus Christ, also be suitable to all in every respect. For they are not servants of food and drink, but rather helpers of God's Church." What is Ignatius trying to say with these words? Does he wish to reject the service of waiting on tables as an activity that is totally out of the question for deacons? We have no reason to assume that. Ignatius would thereby not only be turning against a reliable ecclesial practice, he would also be renouncing the origin of the diaconate! Then, perhaps, the statement should be only understood in the sense that Ignatius would have it understood that the service of food and drink is not a profane service, but rather service to God's Church. Deacons, even when they are serving (waiting on) tables, stand in the precincts of "the mysteries of Jesus Christ." The practice of charity has its origin right there. It was not without reason that, in the early centuries, the Agape meal and the celebration of the Eucharist were bound up together. This also holds true for the contributions that the bishop distributed to the poor through his deacons, since these contributions were not presented as oblations during the sacrifice [of the Mass] at the altar. In other words, worship and charitable activity are intimately intertwined, and it can be further concluded that deacons, who have been called in a special way to minister to the poor, also have their position "in the precincts of sacrifice."

It was probably in this way that early on deacons were also assigned certain liturgical functions. Such functions were intended primarily to be those that, in some way, gave expression to the mutual relationship between worship and charity.

Taking this into consideration, it is easy to understand that deacons were initially required to take part in *Agape* meals. *Agape* meals, on one hand, symbolized palpable assistance for the poor and, on the other hand, in the form of the private *Agape* meals, which had been detached from the celebration of the Eucharist beginning in the second century, they embodied ritual-like, and therefore, liturgical characteristics. It was the task of the deacon to recommend needy persons who would participate in the love meal; at the meal itself at dusk, he would ritually carry light into the room, and in the absence of a bishop or priest, he would preside and give the blessing. Further, during Sunday eucharistic celebrations, he would participate liturgically. Here are the words of Bishop Ignatius of Antioch:

> Strive to celebrate only a *single* Eucharist, since as "there is only one flesh of Our Lord Jesus Christ, one cup in which his blood is united and one altar, so too is there also only" one bishop together with his priests and deacons.

The *Didaskalia* and the *Apostolic Constitutions* give us a rather clear picture of the functions of a deacon during the celebration of the Eucharist. This picture requires only slight enhancements from other sources. Before the liturgy begins, deacons (or at least one of them) took a place at the doors of the church. They were to observe those coming in and ensure that they went to the places assigned to them. As soon as the liturgy began, the deacons closed the doors; those arriving late were not allowed in. During the liturgy, the deacons shared their duties. Some remained among the believers to ensure quiet and order. At least one, however, stood at the altar to assist during the eucharistic sacrifice. He was also designated to proclaim the Gospel, unless he was preempted in this task by a priest.

Prayer and participation in the celebration on the part of the believers was also led by deacons. Their own participation in the liturgy was given greater expression in the preparation of the gifts of bread and wine and, above all, in the distribution of holy communion. The bringing up of the gifts was given special mention by Justin in his description of the eucharistic celebration and was therefore significant in its importance. The *Church Order of Hippolytus* and the *Apostolic Constitutions* expressly assign this act to deacons. Just as they initially brought the gifts of the community to the altar, so too was it appropriate for them at the end to return a portion of the gifts, transformed and consecrated, to the believers. The first clear evidence of this is found in the words of Justin the Martyr. Later testimony is found in the *Church Order of Hippolytus*, the writings of Cyprian, the *Apostolic Constitutions*, and in the

Testament of Our Lord. As opposed to Justin, all of the other authors only mention the presentation of the chalice as a right to which the deacon was entitled, and according to the *Church Order of Hippolytus,* they only had this right if there were not enough priests present to distribute holy communion. These limitations notwithstanding, they still had the uncontested right to offer the chalice containing the Precious Blood to the believers. Even the Synod of Nicaea only speaks out against the abuses of deacons giving the Eucharist to priests and of receiving communion themselves before the bishop does; the right itself does not come up for discussion. That which was left over from the eucharistic gifts was again entrusted to deacons; they brought it into the *pastophorium* for safe-keeping and used it as needed to bring holy communion to the sick in their homes.

Outside of the Sunday eucharistic celebration, deacons assisted priests when they offered the holy sacrifice for those imprisoned for their faith. They also assisted the bishop in the conferring of sacraments, and here we would be referring of course to relatively insignificant services. They guided the person to be baptized to the baptismal font, climbed into the water with him, anointed him, and handed him milk and honey following the baptism. For confirmation, they carried the container with the holy oils, vested the confirmed with the confirmation garment, and during the consecration by the bishop, held the Book of the Gospels above the head of the elect. Other than such assisting services, they did not perform any other functions, since the conferral of sacraments as such basically remained reserved to priests. The deacon could only confer baptism with the permission of the bishop, but after all, this is a right granted even to lay persons in an emergency. Cyprian of Carthage tells us that in an emergency a deacon could also undertake the reconciliation of a penitent; this practice is confirmed for us by the Synod of Elvira. It should be mentioned, however, that at that time the sacramental nature of this act was hardly acknowledged. In the penitential discipline of the third and fourth centuries, "peace with the Church" was given greater prominence and attention than reconciliation with God. So one could hold the opinion that under certain circumstances even a deacon could administer reconciliation, since why should he not be capable of granting "peace with the Church" to the penitent? Naturally, in the final analysis it was a case of error.

In any event, in view of his office, the deacon found himself in direct proximity to the most sacred mysteries. This close contact with them was understood very early on as the highest honor, in fact no less than the deepest core of the diaconal office. The oldest ordination prayer handed down to us points out that the goal of the election, which occurs during the act of

73

ordination, is that the deacon in the Church "may distribute the Most Sacred gift that can be offered to God." *The Apostolic Traditions* use this to substantiate the particular uniqueness of the rite of ordination, which consists of the laying on of hands. Ordination to the clerical state is intended for liturgy.

With respect to the widow it is written:

> . . . she is instituted and united with the others by word and not by the laying on of hands, since she neither offers [the Holy Sacrifice of the Mass] nor conducts liturgy.

So it is once again clear that what has repeatedly been reiterated since Ignatius of Antioch, namely, that the deacon together with priest and bishop comprise the hierarchy of the Church. These three are a single unity and are likewise set apart from both the laity and the lesser clerics. Their distinctiveness, however, lies in their privilege to approach sacred liturgy.

This concept of the diaconate eventually brought with itself an expectation that its incumbents would have a life-style that corresponded to this direct proximity to the mysteries. In his time, Ignatius of Antioch, who acknowledged that deacons are "servants of the mysteries of Jesus Christ," immediately drew the conclusion that "they must strive to be acceptable to all" and must "guard against accusations as they would guard against fire." Cyprian also states that the motive for the blamelessness of their conduct is that they are destined for the altar and the sacrifice [of the Mass]. Accordingly, he also requires a more thorough examination before admission to the diaconate so that no unworthy individual gains access to service at the altar. In particular, it was believed that the requirement of celibacy should derive from a designation for service at the altar. In this regard, bishop, priest, and deacon were always viewed together, although here a differentiation between "priesthood" and "service" would have certainly been possible—and probably, even appropriate. However, it is striking that this differentiation is never made here. In his day, Paul required of both a deacon as well as of a bishop that he be married only once. The Synod of Elvira bound both of them to continence because they both perform service at the altar. The Second Council of Carthage (390) places this same requirement on all three degrees, because all "by virtue of their consecrations are joined together by the bond of chastity." Bishop, priest, and levite "serve the Divine Mysteries," and it is fitting that all "who come in contact with these Mysteries [and] serve at the altar" should observe chastity. At least for the western Church, since its earliest times, the exercise of liturgical powers and celibacy were bound together, and since the deacon found himself together with the bishop and the priests "within the place of sacrifice," he too had to share this life-style with them.

3. Pastoral Care

The care provided by priests and deacons in the homes of believers was, above all, one of charity. They wanted to help with sundry kinds of material needs. However, there was also a pastoral mission associated with this work. The bishop needed to know the status of religious and moral life in his community. The priests and deacons, who came in contact with all levels of the population during their home visitations and who were privy to the problems confronting the people, were in the best position to advise the bishop about conditions in the community. Some of the difficulties they could solve themselves. For example, when confessors, who paid the price of imprisonment for the courage of their faith, frequently did not know how they should react to those who had asked them for the letter of recommendation they needed to regain communion with the Church, it was the deacons who could and should have given them the correct advice. They knew who were worthy and who were not. Generally speaking, they also were better acquainted with the demands of the Gospel than were the confessors and were in a position to prevent many ill-considered reacceptances back into the Church. Other cases needed to be referred to the bishop for his decision. The basic principle understood for the faithful was that a request was first made to the deacons and through them to the bishop. The *Didaskalia* even added that the reason for this was that one could not come to God except through Christ. This process was a great relief for the bishop. In this way, he was no longer burdened by petty, insignificant matters, especially since he, as is set forth in the *Testament of Our Lord,* insisted that deacons should only bring the various matters requiring his attention before him once a week, namely, on Sundays. This way, he could make his decisions in peace and have his answers delivered by the deacons. It is, therefore, with some justification that the *Didaskalia* calls deacons "the eye and the ear of the bishop."

Within the community, catechumens were commended in a special way to the care of deacons. According to the *Apostolic Constitutions,* the process of coming forward for the catechumenate was to be handled by deacons. The *Testament of Our Lord* mentions that deacons visit the homes of catechumens to give encouragement to the undecided and to instruct the unknowledgeable. It cannot be determined from this source, however, as to what this instruction consisted of. Can it be concluded from this that the instruction of the catechumens was in general assigned to deacons? Sometimes, this conclusion is drawn without proper reflection. In actuality, however, we are aware of only one case in which we know with certainty that people were continually referred to a deacon "so that he would instruct them in the rudimentary fundamentals of the Christian faith." This individual was the deacon Deogratias of Carthage. This example, however, shows that we are dealing here with a special set of circumstances. Deogratias was asked to provide the introductory catechesis because he had a pleasant lecture style and a thorough knowledge of Christian teachings. Therefore, he was not assigned catechetical responsibility because he was a deacon but, rather, because of his distinct personal attributes. It appears therefore that this is an exception, and we simply cannot assume that regular catechetical activity was a normal part of the diaconal sphere of action. This is also suggested by the fact that Deogratias was initially rather confused as to how he should structure his catechesis and had to ask St. Augustine for guidance. If deacons had been instructing catechumens regularly over a long period of time, such guidance would have certainly been unnecessary. Besides we know that, in general, special instructors (*doctores*) were used to instruct the catechumens. They are mentioned in the *Church Order of Hippolytus* as well as in the eighth book of the *Apostolic Constitutions*. What was expected of them was nothing more than appropriate teaching skills and competent theological formation. With priests, it could be assumed that this was the case; as evidenced in the letters of Cyprian, it is understood that in many instances priests functioned as "*doctores audientium,*" that is, as catechists. However, lay persons were also considered suitable for this work. For this reason, the *Church Order of Hippolytus* leaves both options open: "whether ecclesiastical doctor or lay [doctor]." We also understand it to be the case, when Eusebius reports to us that Origen, as a lay person, instructed catechumens and even directed the catechetical school in Alexandria. Given such provisions, it would naturally also have been possible to use deacons, who possessed the appropriate skills as teachers of catechumens. In spite of this, however, this was not done, except in special circumstances. We cannot, therefore, state that catechetical activity belonged to the normal tasks of deacons.

As with catechumens, deacons were also expected to take penitents into their care. The *Testament of Our Lord* cites a case involving a serious moral transgression and assigns to the deacon the responsibility to investigate the case and make a report about it to the bishop. After that he is to "instruct" the penitents, and this "instruction" is to be understood in the same sense intended by Cyprian, when he made it obligatory for ecclesiastical leaders to notify those who had fallen about the conditions that they must fulfill if they wish to be accepted back into the church community.

Whether or to what extent the faithful were provided with any kind of pastoral leadership on the part of deacons is not clear from our sources. In the

Pseudo-Clementines, the faithful are clearly exhorted to accept the "doctrine of faith" from the bishop, the "admonitions of life" from priests, and the "order of discipline" from deacons. However, these and similar positions have been sufficiently interpreted if we refer to the various disciplinary instructions that deacons are to give during the liturgy.

Greater influence and greater responsibility were thrust on deacons, however, as soon as they became the only relatively independent pastoral ministers in a community. These situations arose occasionally as, in the third and fourth centuries, rural Christian communities began to multiply and could no longer always be provided with pastoral care from the bishop's see city. The bishops also generally endeavored to assign priests or pastors in the villages, but when there were insufficient number of them available to the bishops, the parish was turned over to the leadership of a deacon. The first clear testimony to that effect is found in canon 77 of the Synod of Elvira (306), where we read: "If a deacon, ruling a people without a bishop or presbyter, has baptized some of them, the bishop must bring them to the perfection of it through his blessing." What is being said here is not only that a deacon could lead a community, but also that he unquestionably had the right to confer baptism. It was pointed out, however, that in such a case the baptism must be enhanced by the bishop's blessing (which we should readily understand as confirmation). When we consider how firmly the ancient Church ordinarily reserved the right to baptize to the bishop and priests, we can judge the magnanimity contained in this canon. It is hardly possible today to assess how often or how seldom these deacon-pastors made their appearance. The sources do not provide much help in this regard. Other than the Synod of Elvira, only Gregory of Tours mentions a certain Cantinus, who "in his diaconate ruled the church of that distant village of Iciodor." The decree of the Synod of Antioch (341), which forbade deacons from leaving their parishes, does not permit us to conclude that there were independent deacon-pastors. Based on all of these observations, we can nevertheless state that deacons were frequently employed as pastoral helpers and displayed an effectiveness that should not be underestimated.

The Crisis of the Diaconate

The first four centuries, to which we have given our attention thus far, depicted an upward movement in the history of the diaconate. Were they also the peak of its development?

This question can only be answered if we also look at the development of the diaconate in the period that immediately follows. Toward the end of the fourth century, the unknown author of a tract takes a sharp jab [at the diaconate]. For a long time, the tract was attributed to St. Augustine, and now it is included in the works of Ambrosiaster. It carries the strange title, *Concerning the Boasting of Roman Levites*. The author takes issue here with the opinion, commonly held at that time, that deacons in no way stand beneath priests but, rather, can claim for themselves the same rank. St. Jerome must also have had knowledge of this same trend, since in a letter to Evangelus, he takes a position similar to that of Ambrosiaster and attempts to turn this thesis upside down with all of his characteristic vehemence. The argumentation of the two authors is of far less interest to us than is the situation that forms the basis for the dispute, at least as it is indirectly outlined in both documents. We learn from them that Roman deacons over time have become accustomed to distancing themselves from the more menial service tasks and leaving them to be carried out by lesser clerics. Now, they no longer carry either the altar or the sacred vessels; furthermore, they no longer hand water to the priest so that he can wash his hands. They do, however, indeed arrogate to themselves rights that only belong to priests. At banquets (understood here are private *Agape* meals), in the absence of the bishop, they not only usurp the place of priests but they also share the blessing with them. They make themselves conspicuous by their endless home visitations and all kinds of gossip, and because of their status, their tale-bearing is not without its effect. For this reason, they are feared by some; others flatter and bribe them to wangle recommendations for themselves. In this way, the diaconal office admittedly becomes very lucrative, and if it were only a question of money, the priest would have had to be envious of every deacon. We will have to take into account that this description in and of itself is only intended to apply to conditions in Rome, and that, furthermore, it could be one-sided—or probably, even prejudiced. Nevertheless, it makes us aware of problems that deserve our attention and, at the very least, need to be examined.

The first criticism that Ambrosiaster allows himself is based on the fact that, over time, other lesser ecclesial offices developed along side the diaconate. This is an indisputable fact. "The growing Church gave birth to ecclesiastical offices." Based on this assumption, it is more than understandable that deacons would endeavor to unload some of their workload to others. It is laughable that Ambroisiaster would interpret it as a sign of dangerous arrogance that deacons no longer handed water to the priests but, rather, that this was now done by subdeacons. This development was necessary. In this way, deacons would be freed up for other, more important duties. Admittedly, if we wish to enumerate which activities the deacons from the fourth century on were to keep themselves free for, we immediately run into trouble. While we observe that they withdraw from areas of activity, we cannot enumerate which new activities replaced the former ones. For example, from the fourth and fifth centuries on, deacons hardly play any role whatsoever in the area of works of charity. It was indeed taken for granted until just recently that deacons had been extensively involved in welfare activities as leaders of the *Diakonia* houses—those social welfare institutions that had created a Christian sense of responsibility in the distress-filled days of the declining Roman empire. This opinion can no longer be supported in light of the results of the latest research. These *Diakonia* houses [*Diaconiae*], which had been established in the East beginning in the fourth century and in the West since the seventh century, were actually directed by either a monk (if they were monastic institutions) or a lay person, and not by a deacon. Even the personnel assigned to assist at these institutions were either monks or lay persons, not deacons.

It was a similar story with the "hospitality houses" [*Xenodochien*], which had been established in most larger cities after the end of the persecutions to provide shelter for pilgrims, the sick, foundlings, and elderly in need of care. Some of these houses were erected and maintained by lay persons, in which cases they were directed by lay persons. But even bishops and popes hardly ever looked to deacons for cooperation in their own efforts to establish "hospitality houses." St. Augustine, for example, turned to the priest Leporius when he wanted to establish a guest home for pilgrims in Hippo. Pope St. Gregory the Great exhorted the Archpriest Epiphanius to renovate the "hospitality houses" in Sardinia, which had fallen into serious disrepair due to the neglect of the senile Bishop Januarius.

The Church did strive to turn over the administration of its established institutions to clerics, but the research sources always mention only priests or lesser clerics in this regard—deacons are never mentioned. In general, deacons do not even appear in subordinate positions. Seldom do we discover an inscription, wherein a deacon is identified as a medical attendant. That should come as no surprise, since hospital nursing personnel in the East were from the so-called *parabolani,* who were possibly lesser clerics, but more likely members of a kind of brotherhood. In the West, they were lay volunteer auxiliaries. It is difficult to determine just what the situation was during this period with respect to the charitable activity of the district deacons of Rome. The sources say nothing about it at all. It is likely that by this time this organizational structure had been overhauled and replaced by other arrangements. Perhaps, the previous involvement of the district deacons with charitable work was now by this time reduced to nothing more than the extended house visitations to affluent persons mentioned by Ambrosiaster. Therefore, apparently deacons had gradually withdrawn more and more from charitable work. It would, however, still have been the desire of the Church that deacons care for the poor. The Roman Synod of A.D. 595 denounced the sad fact that deacons only seemed to be active as singers [of psalms] instead of being guardians of the poor, but it would appear that little attention was paid to the admonition. Deacons moved into other areas of activity and no longer showed any serious interest in charitable activity. Therefore, their assistance was no longer sought, and when the administration of charitable works was reorganized during the Carolingian reform, no one gave any thought to reinstating deacons in it. Once again, the care of the poor would be primarily the task of the bishop, just as it was in the beginning; he would be responsible for the establishment of hospitals and for appointing a worthy canon to be director of same.

Another important area of responsibility, which one could suppose might have fallen to deacons after they had been relieved of less important tasks, would be the area of treasury administration. Even in the earliest centuries, deacons were exposed to a certain extent to this area in conjunction with their charitable activities. When toward the end of the fourth century, the bishop was compelled to turn over the administration of the treasury to a qualified manager, what could be more appropriate than to appoint deacons as managers? In actuality, however, only a limited number of them were recruited for this position. For example, we are told that Pope St. Gregory the Great appointed the deacon Anatholius as *"vicedominus"* [roughly translated, "vicar general"] and entrusted the administration of the diocese [*episcopium*] to him. The deacon Cyprian was appointed "rector of the patrimony" in Sicily by him. The Synod of Toledo (655) deals with the case, where a deacon under certain circumstances could even give away Church goods. Deacons were hardly ever appointed as managers (of the treasury). This office was usually assigned to a priest, and even occasionally to an archdeacon. Even for the administration of patrimonies, Pope St. Gregory the Great as a rule chose subdeacons, not deacons. The reason for this is not immediately clear. Were deacons, generally speaking, too young and not reliable enough to assign them to such a responsible office as that of manager (of the treasury)? Did they lack the knowledge or other special skills that would be necessary prerequisites for such an assignment? It is a fact that the educational level of deacons was not always all that high. The *ostraca,* dating from circa A.D. 600, discussed by Deissman indicate that deacons could certainly read, since before they could be ordained, they had to memorize one gospel and twenty-five psalms. However, a priest would have to write their application to the bishop for them.

In any case, the bishop was free to select whomever he wanted to administer the treasury. The Council of Chalcedon only stipulated the basic guideline that it should be assigned to a cleric from the bishop's own diocese. The individual's hierarchical rank was completely irrelevant. Pope St. Gregory the Great apparently followed a practice of recruiting "rectors of the patrimony," whereby he would first seek out men who were qualified for the task and then admit them to the clerical state. In doing so, he only needed to appoint them subdeacons; deacons could fulfill other missions.

Following these negative comments, it becomes even more urgent for us to determine what tasks deacons actually devoted their time to in the second period of their history. In this regard, the letters of Pope St. Gregory the Great can again give some clues. A document written to the deacon Honoratus contains an order that Honoratus should admonish the commanding officer Theodorus not to move mercilessly against the population during the capture of the Duchy of Sardinia. In another letter, Honoratus is asked to take Bishop Anastasius, who had been banished by the emperor, under his care. Another deacon, Savinian, was sent by the pope to Constantinople with a letter for Bishop John, in which Gregory tells the bishop that Savinian will verbally explain the entire situation to him in private and that the bishop should try to settle the situation with him. On another occasion, Savinian is sent to Patricus of the East to congratulate him about the fact that he was back in the good graces of the emperor. It was not only the pope, however, who used deacons this way; other bishops also sent their deacons with letters to Rome or to the imperial court or even to other bishops. We see, therefore, some deacons appearing in high positions as emissaries of bishops and as papal *nuncios*.

Some deacons also had the opportunity to be promoted to the honor of archdeacon, and in this position they held an extremely influential office. Honoratus, the archdeacon of Bishop Natalis of Salona, administered all of the church goods [in that diocese] and enjoyed such independence that if he had to, he could prevail against the bishop himself. Thus, Honoratus could not be persuaded to hand over to the bishop a portion of the church treasury so that the bishop could bestow gifts upon his relatives. When that resulted in his being replaced as archdeacon by the bishop, following which he was to have been ordained a priest, he found a powerful protector in Pope St. Gregory the Great, who compelled Bishop Natalis to rescind this move. In this case, we can also see how sought after the office of archdeacon must have been. In a certain sense, it was more highly esteemed than the priesthood. Even Pope St. Gregory the Great accused Bishop Natalis of seemingly calling deacon Honoratus to "higher honors," while in fact wanting to demote him.

The reason why the archdiaconate was so highly esteemed did lay primarily in the fact that the archdeacon was frequently the first claimant to the bishop's chair. The archdeacon Savinian even followed Pope St. Gregory the Great on the papal throne. Given these prescriptions, it is no wonder that the office of archdeacon was time and time again the goal of ambitions aspirants. On more than one occasion, Pope St. Gregory the Great was compelled to intervene and put a stop to this ambitious pursuit of the office of archdeacon. Thus, he gives Archbishop Januarius a direct order to move deacon Liberatus to the bottom place among his brother office-holders, because this individual was unbelievably pride-filled and only concerned about moving higher and higher up the ecclesiastical ladder. The pope even had to replace his own archdeacon Lawrence because of arrogance and other shortcomings, about which Gregory preferred to remain silent. There is also evidence that the competence of a deacon and especially the relationships of trust a deacon could have with his bishop could also provoke jealousy on the part of his colleagues, as can be seen in another of Gregory's letters. In this letter, Gregory explains that he has inquired into the character of the deacon Peter and concluded that he is above reproach: He is completely loyal to his bishop and of value to the Church. Therefore, neither he nor his Bishop Gregory have anything to fear. I would pay no further attention to the slanderers. Naturally, only one deacon among the deacons of a city could be promoted to archdeacon. Also not all of them could be used as *nuncios* or emissaries. Most remained in the position of an ordinary deacon. What about these deacons? What functions did they perform?

At the Synod of Trullo (692), one of the topics of discussion must have been the number of deacons in the various [particular] Churches. Canon 16 makes reference to the corresponding canon of the Synod of Neocaesarea and simultaneously takes issue with it. It is noted that the situation in those earlier days was completely different. The seven deacons of the Acts of the Apostles were not called to the service of the Mysteries, but rather to service at tables. Apparently, this argument was intended to justify the large number of deacons at that time in Constantinople (there must have been around 150 of them). At the same time, we perceive that "service of the Mysteries" (that is, in the celebration of [divine] liturgy) was viewed as the most important diaconal task. In the same manner, Justinian had also justified the increasingly larger number of clerics: "it is permissible to appoint twice as many ministers as there originally were for the service of the sacred cult." He saw himself compelled, however, to limit the number of clerics; he set the overall total at 425 and the number of deacons at 100. However, he only did this in order to spare the

Church from an intolerable financial burden. The fact that where this question is concerned, not only money and the solemnity of the divine liturgy but also, under certain circumstances, even other factors needed to be taken into account, apparently was neither recognized nor given any consideration. All other concerns, whether of a charitable or pastoral nature, were obviously completely eclipsed by cultic requirements. The preoccupation of deacons with liturgical functions certainly was particularly typical of the eastern Church. However, in the West following the end of the persecutions, more and more importance began to be placed on the ceremonial development of the divine liturgy. It was thus that deacons came to view the celebration of liturgy as their primary area of activity. The protest of the Synod of Rome in A.D. 595 had already given us evidence that deacons preferred the singing of psalms to caring for the poor. In this regard, Gregory mentions that this practice had been spreading for some time; probably, even he could do nothing to change it. This appears to be confirmed by several inscriptions that can be found on the graves of deacons from this period, in which the deceased are memorialized as cantors of Davidic poetry. The melodies of the Easter "Exultet" have preserved for us right down to this very day an example of that vocal art, which was cherished with such love and joy by the deacons of those earlier days. The deacon, therefore, felt himself to be a minister of the altar. That is what we read on many inscriptions, and we sense something about the accomplishments of life, when we learn that the deacon Rogatian, for example, lived seventy-eight years as a most respected minister of the altar for God. Furthermore, occasionally it is even called to our attention, that deacon X also ministered to the poor; from the example we just cited about the cantor of Davidic poetry, it is also mentioned at the end that he was Dives to the poor, even though poor himself—but this attribute was cited secondarily.

At the beginning of the ninth century, Amalar Von Metz reads in the writings of St. Jerome that according to the testimony of the Acts of the Apostles, deacons are called to service at tables. He comes to the conclusion that it is therefore logical that "It belongs to the service of deacons, that they bring to the altar of God that which is necessary for the Heavenly Banquet." Thus, he has completely forgotten that the work of charity belongs to the service of deacons. He can no longer understand the word *tables* in its originally intended sense; he understands it to mean the table of the Lord and applies it to cultic worship. In one sense, which could hardly be outdone, this new understanding of the diaconate is set forth in the document, *Concerning the Seven Orders of the Church*. Its author is anonymous, and even determining it original date is problematical. It certainly dates from the sixth or seventh century and, fittingly, enhances the picture of the diaconate we have from that time period. It says of the deacons:

> God has become their portion; they no longer depart from the Temple of the Lord, whether by day or by night. They are the altar of Christ, upon which the Mysteries are consummated and the sacrifice is offered. What could be more worthy than the altar in the Temple of God?

They are then compared to Levi, to his priestly tribe, who has become the head of all priests:

> Without him priests would have no name, no origin and no office . . . just as the priest is given the power to consecrate, so is the servant given the power to dispense the sacrament. Unless they wish to be arrogant, priests are also not allowed to take the chalice from the Lord's table, unless it is handed to them by the deacon. In this way the servant of the sanctuary is elevated to preeminence, while the priest, after he has consecrated (the gifts), is slightly humbled. He honors the servant and thereby recognizes that he owes him respect. Our God, the Almighty, has so established it that "he who wants to be greater becomes lesser, and he who appears lesser, emerges as the greater" . . . the priest needs the deacon as much as the deacon needs the priest.

Here, we see the diaconate and the priesthood allied with one another and the diaconate viewed as the indispensable compliment of the priesthood. This accentuation of the diaconate is decidedly overstated. We recall the words of Ambrosiaster: "he is trying to place Levites on the same footing with (high) priests and deacons with presbyters . . .," but it appears that at this time no one takes offense with this anymore. Isidore of Seville quotes several places from this document, compares the deacons to the seven chubby-cheeked angels from the Apocalypse as well as with the seven candlesticks, and goes so far as to state: "Without them (i.e., deacons) a priest has a name, but does not have an office." The deacon has thereby become almost exclusively a liturgical functionary. He appears to no longer recognize any other mission.

It may be that deacons assigned to individual parishes as part-time clergy felt somewhat differently. This was often the case in the larger and more remote locations, especially when there was a shortage of priests. Pope St. Gregory the Great ordered Bishop Balbinus to ordain a priest [*presbyter cardinalis*] and two deacons for a church in his diocese, "which was so bereft of priests that not even the dying could be confessed nor the children baptized." The Synod of Toledo (633) mentions cases where deacons were assigned to parishes as assistants. For the eighth century, this practice was confirmed by the synodal statutes of St. Boniface and the Synod of Frankfurt. Even in the eleventh century, the Synod of Coyaca requires that every church have a sufficient number of priests, deacons, and ecclesiastical books. Synods also give us a glimpse at the activity of these deacons. The Synod of Tarragon (516) decrees that priests and deacons assigned to a rural church are to rotate liturgical responsibility. One week the priest should recite matins and vespers, the next week the deacon. On Saturday, all the other clerics must be present at vespers, so that on Sunday a full staff is on hand. Service at the Sunday Mass was naturally one of the deacon's tasks, as well as the care of the lighting. Prior to the Feast of Easter, he had to go to the cathedral church for the chrism. Other duties of an exceptional nature were never mentioned. There is no mention of either any kind of conferring of sacraments or of any pastoral functions in the documents. Occasionally, it also happened that deacons were the only clergy serving in smaller oratories. In times past, there was even a regulation that only priests could be assigned as ecclesiastical leaders at baptismal churches. This ordinance would make no sense if elsewhere instead of priests only deacons or lesser clerics had not taken care of liturgy. We certainly cannot attribute it to the initiative of the bishop that in some places only deacons took care of a church, especially if pious and wealthy lords of the manor set great store in having at least a deacon or some other cleric at their side. The bishops tolerated this customer and simply notified owners of private churches that they could only arrange for the services of deacons and lesser clerics with the permission of the bishop. In general, bishops strove, to the extent it was possible, to assign a priest to every church according to canon 11 of the Synod of Aachen in A.D. 817, "every church should have its own priest," and some time later, this requirement is repeated:

> . . . whenever possible the bishop should assign to each church its own priest, so that he can administer it independently or under the supervision of a priest prior (senior pastor). In many towns there are no priests; they can certainly celebrate Mass in all of the churches assigned to them, but they cannot see to all of the other services, because there are too many churches. As a result, where baptism of the sick, the confessions of penitents or bringing communion to those in danger of death are all concerned, there are many who lose out.

For us, the reasons cited are first of all very illuminating. It did not occur to the Synod, in these emergency situations where too few priests were available, to entrust to deacons at least those pastoral functions that did not absolutely require the priestly office. Deacons were, in this respect, viewed as very lowly assistants to the priest. Deacons were not permitted to provide actual pastoral care at the rural oratories. Given this precondition, it naturally did not make a great deal of sense to leave deacons as solitary clergymen at rural churches. Therefore, again and again one perceived the tendency to recall deacons from these "outstations" and to assign them to the cathedral. The Synod of Emerita (666) guaranteed the bishop the right to recall deacons from rural parishes and to transfer them to the cathedral. In and of itself, this is understandable—the deacon is ordained for the service of the bishop. In the early Middle Ages, there were also other reasons for this. It was disadvantageous for reasons of both the formation and the discipline of clerics to have them spend their lives at a rural oratory far removed from the bishop's see. On the other hand, the bishop was duty bound to see to the education of his clerics. The Synod of Rome (826) gives the bishop the right to exclude his clerics from holy service for as long as it takes them to acquire the appropriate learning. This educational responsibility that the bishop had could only be carried out in the episcopal city. Therefore, we can recognize in all of the capitular legislation the tendency to gather the clerics at the cathedral and to bind them in duty to communal life. "Let no one who has received the tonsure be without a canonical or regular way of life, and let no priest or deacon or abbot be free of episcopal supervision."

Clerics lived in the cathedral according to the rule of the canons, and even deacons were not exempted. Chrodegang actually mentions deacons several times in his *Rule*. Their activity consisted primarily of participation in choir prayer within the framework of canonical life. They also performed a certain amount of manual labor and accompanied the priests on Sundays and holy days whenever they traveled to convents to celebrate High Mass. They assisted the priests in the liturgy and were also witnesses to their behavior. Generally speaking, the deacons were a group of clerics, who were distinguishable from the other clerics by nothing other than their degree of orders. In the nonliturgical sphere, they engaged in no special activity that could be considered theirs alone.

Summary

The diaconate—about which, Ignatius of Antioch had said, "was instituted according to the will of Jesus Christ"—had lost its significance before the completion of the first millennium. Nonetheless, even in the period of its decline, we see deacons who were outstanding personalities. Alcuin, who was the successor of Aelbert in the York School and court theologian to Charlemagne, wanted to be nothing else his entire life long than a deacon. Paul the Deacon, biographer of Pope St. Gregory the Great, and John the Deacon will forever be known by the hierarchical title of their degree of orders. Yet neither their fame nor their scholarship had anything to do with their position as deacon. They were not summoned to the Frankish court nor drawn into the circle of the papal Curia as deacons because of their personal attributes. Precisely because the diaconal office no longer occupied their time, they were able to quietly devote their lives to science and literary work. Thus, their names alone give evidence of how far along the demise of the diaconate was during their lifetime. We ask ourselves how this came about. To some extent, one can point to the fact that the growing decentralization of ecclesial life, the development of the parish system, and also the "unpropitiousness of temporal conditions" took their job away from deacons task by task. These reasons may explain some things, but certainly not everything. For example, it is by no means clear why the diaconate would suffer a loss in importance because of the decentralization of ecclesial administration. Just when it was becoming necessary for the bishop to turn over to others some of the tasks that he himself had performed up to that time, the hour of the deacons should have come. Since developments actually turned out differently, then other reasons must have been decisive. Maybe we might succeed in identifying them.

When Hippolytus of Rome formulated the statement: "[the deacon] is not ordained to the priesthood, but for the service of the bishop, to do those things which are delegated to him . . .," a simple and clear formula seemed to have been found, which could give proper direction for the effectiveness of deacons. Service and priesthood were clearly differentiated and also separated, since service—and not priesthood—devolved upon the deacon.

On the other hand, this service encompasses a broad area of activity. Everything the bishop assigns to deacons (i.e., tasks that are not exclusively priestly functions) belongs to their scope of activity. After all, the deacon is ordained for service (i.e., he is officially called and duty bound to serve). That is how the diaconate became an office. Therein lie the meaning and essence of the office—the intent was to create with it an institution that would ensure forever the execution of important tasks, which should never be missing from the Church. In this way, one would have thought at least the necessary preconditions would be in place to permit the diaconate to develop into a permanent and valuable institution in the Church. In spite of this—as history has shown—things were not as clear in concrete reality as they were expressed in the words of Hippolytus. For example, What are simple "services"? What is included in specifically priestly functions that needs to be excluded from the scope of the diaconate? and Where is the dividing line between them? As we have seen, in the second century deacons were already permitted to administer the communion chalice. Later on, they could also baptize, at least now and then under certain circumstances. According to the *Church Order of Hippolytus,* they could (it would appear, in cases of emergency) anoint the sick. Were these functions that truly corresponded to the meaning of the diaconate? Or were these just tasks only permitted to priests that were usurped by deacons? In any case, it is fair to ask whether the carrying out of such tasks represents that service for which deacons are called. Was the origin of the diaconate not to be found in the wish of the apostles to be relieved of having to wait on tables, so as to be able to proclaim readily the word of God?

There is also a fringe area of pastoral care, about which the priest cannot worry without neglecting his service in the sanctuary. Should not the diaconal sphere of activity be sought in exactly this fringe area? These questions are not easily clarified, and they actually were clarified in the early period of the diaconate. It is certain that deacons were employed in both areas—first and above all in the "fringe area" but, then, also in that area that touches upon that which is clearly priestly service. It is, likewise, certain that the development of the diaconate took a strange turn later on. It was not long before the diaconal ranks evidenced a tendency to abandon their work in the fringe area and to push their way into the sanctuary. Even if church regulations spelled out time and time again, "the deacon does not bless, does not baptize, does not offer [the holy sacrifice of the Mass]," we can recognize the effort to counteract the above-mentioned tendency. Such statements are also an indication of just how vigorously deacons were striving to move closer to the priestly office. The Synod of Arles (314), which had to suppress the attempt of some deacons to offer the holy sacrifice of the Mass, provides us with even more striking evidence of this. Such encroachments were naturally doomed to failure; they were also limited to exceptional cases. However, the tendency itself did not change.

Ultimately, it led to the situation where deacons confined themselves primarily to the celebration of liturgy and, in the bargain, took upon themselves the obligation of celibacy, so as to be able "to touch the sacred Mysteries." The relationship between deacon and priest was finally reduced to the formula: "without the deacons, the priest has no name, he has no office." In the meanwhile, the lesser clerics and quite frequently also the laity took over those tasks that had comprised the original and most germinal sphere of activity of deacons. Basically, there was nothing to stand in the way of this. The lesser ecclesiastical offices, which were called "diaconal streams" (*rivuli diaconatus*), represented a legitimate and possibly even a necessary expansion of the diaconate. If, however, this expansion is so aggressively pushed forward that of itself it creates a vacuum in the diaconate, then this development can hardly be positive.

The same thing can be said about the use of the laity. In and of itself, there is certainly nothing wrong with the laity taking over some of the services normally provided by deacons by virtue of their office. But if these tasks, in the final analysis, are only carried out by lay volunteers while those who are obliged by their office to carry them out steer clear of them, then such a development is no longer healthy. Unfortunately, this is what happened to the development of the diaconate. It should, therefore, come as no surprise to us that a certain counter-reaction asserted itself very early on.

Initially, this was to be seen in the fact that certain functions were strictly limited to emergencies. The deacon should only baptize, anoint the sick, or distribute holy communion in an emergency. It was further seen in the constantly problematical relationship between deacons and priests. In a way that strikes us today as remarkable (because it sounds so thoroughly petty and yet as a symptom is important), it was necessary to emphasize over and over again that deacons were of a lesser rank than priests, that they should not sit down in the presence of priests before they were invited to do so, nor were they permitted to speak unless they were asked to do so. Pope Gelasius also declared that the deacon was not permitted to have a seat in the presbytery (i.e., on the presbyterial bench in the sanctuary area). These indirect and frequently overt competitive struggles were certainly not very pleasant, but they actually happened. They were also a consequence of those developments that took the diaconate in a direction that was no longer consistent with its original purpose. The greatest tragedy was possibly in that dichotomy that continually encumbered the diaconate, whereby the holders of this office were, on the one hand, bound by the obligation of celibacy to a life-style that is proper to the priest, although on the other hand, they were clearly not priests. In the synodal documents, we read with deep regret about the constantly recurring charges that incontinence persists among the clergy. Just like priests, deacons therefore also had to take an oath of chastity before their ordination; yet, in the final analysis, the only alternative, should they not keep their oath, was to threaten them with the loss of their income.

Ultimately, the decisive reason as to why the diaconate as an office experienced its downfall will probably never be determined with complete unambiguousness. It was very problematical; perhaps, what was most lacking was its own self-understanding. However, the concern remained. Hinckmar of Rheims, in the ninth century, asked every pastor in his diocese if he had a cleric who can teach school or is capable of either reading or chanting the epistle, as he sees fit. It is explicitly the Church that needs the diaconate if the priesthood is to remain free to carry out its own mission.

Dom Augustinus Kerkvoorde, OSB, was born at Wetteren, Belgium on January 9, 1913. He was professed in the St. Andrew's Abbey (Brugge) on February 2, 1934, and ordained a priest on July 23, 1939. In 1936, he was a Doctoral Candidate in Arts and Sciences, with a focus on German philology. He was granted a Licentiate in Sacred Theology in 1939 by the University of Louvain and a Doctorate in Sacred Theology in 1943. From 1945 to 1962, Dom Augustinus wrote extensively in the areas of sacramental theology and eucharistic spirituality. Dom Augustinus became interested in the possibility of the renewal of the diaconate as a lifetime ministry and opened to married men as part of the renewal of the Church and her ministry, which followed in the wake of World War II. In the 1950s, discussions that inspired writings on this possibility had reached the Low Countries from Germany. When invited by Prof. Karl Rahner, SJ, to contribute to the compilation that became Diakonia in Christo, *Dom Augustinus was ready with this theology of the diaconate, which he had formulated in the preceding years.*

Samuel M. Taub

The Theology of the Diaconate

by Dom Augustinus Kerkvoorde, OSB

I. The Problem

1. The Council of Trent has defined that the diaconate, or more precisely, the minor office of the Church, belongs to the divinely instituted hierarchy. In October 1957, at the International Congress on the Apostolate of the Laity, Pope Pius XII called to mind the fact that a layman who is ordained a deacon ceases to be a "layman" and is received into the hierarchy. Where does the diaconate or, better yet, the minor office or, still better yet, the offices—for the problem must be looked at in its relationships and its historical development—fit in with respect to the "hierarchy" of the Church, "the sacrament of orders," and the "visible and external priesthood" established by Christ?

2. It is not our intent to question the literature about this subject, nor tradition understood in its broadest sense (i.e., not only as the handing on of the teachings but also the transmission of institutions, liturgy, legal norms, and customs), nor even the ordinary and extraordinary Magisterium of the Church (e.g., popes, bishops, councils, definitive statements, encyclicals, promulgations, regulations, interpretations, catechisms, and so forth). Others collaborating on this volume have taken on this assignment. Our primary concern here is to examine theology (i.e., the theologians). These individuals, of course, use the "sources" or "*loci theologici*" they cite as the basis of their thought. However, the weight of their commentaries and inferences rests just as much on the presentation and explication of Christian teaching as on the frame-work itself. Therefore, our question is: Does the scholarship of the theologians make possible a complete, unambiguous, and well-grounded theory about this subject? What conclusions can be drawn from their scholarship?

3. Furthermore, there is no intent here to outline a "theology of the diaconate" but, rather, to examine whether and to what extent such a theology already exists. To anticipate directly the answer to this question right up front: Up until very recent time there had been no need for such a theology, since the office of deacon in the Church had practically ceased to exist. Although the deacon in the Eastern Church still exercises a certain liturgical role, this role is very restricted in comparison to that of the deacon in the early Church. In the western Church, it really only exists theoretically as a function of service in some solemn ceremonies—and even then this service of a "deacon" is usually exercised by a priest. The law of the western Church accords to the diaconate a general measure of significance with respect to its ordination rite as preparatory to priesthood, but the short span of time an individual spends in this wholly "theoretical" function could never arouse a demand for a thoroughly elaborated dogma about the diaconate.

There are numerous theologies and apologetical works about the papacy, the office of bishop, the priesthood, the lay state, the religious state, Catholic Action, apostolates, missions, and so forth. Even though these "theologies" are not totally clear or from one mold—and especially since the boundaries between the various "offices" and "ranks" have not yet been clearly delineated and continue to give rise to endless discussions—at least none of these "ranks" can complain about the lack of theoreticians for those subjects. On the contrary, all of them can easily complain that there are all too many theoreticians who are sources of confusion and inaccuracies.

On the other hand, there is, as far as we know, no independent theology of the diaconate. The number of authors and works we cite should not delude us. None of them deals with the diaconate exclusively, say, to help deacons correctly understand and exercise their functions in the Church. What we will present here will only be individual fragments (*membra disjecta*) scattered throughout the various writings on orders in general, the priesthood, the sacraments or the Church. At the time these treatises were being developed— the high middle ages where the sacraments are concerned and the modern age as far as ecclesiology is concerned—the diaconate remained nothing more than an archeological relic that had lost its practical significance. In the East, the situation is a little different, and yet even there we do not find any notable reflections about the theological significance of the diaconate.

4. Nonetheless, it is still worthwhile to collect the fragments and to look at the findings that can be derived from them for any outline of the theology of the diaconate. Once it becomes apparent that this rank may be revived in the near term, such theologies will undoubtedly spring up like mushrooms. The number of articles that have already appeared in periodicals can give us a foretaste of the nature of the literature dealing with this topic. There will be plenty of routine authors and publishers who will pounce on this unexpected inheritance. If by that time theology has not succeeded in setting up some clear and simple principles for the restoration of the diaconate, and if its deepest meaning has not been made visible for both the learned and for the simple faithful, then this ancient and divinely established institution will easily soon be in danger of going down the same path as many other ecclesiastical institutions. The diaconate, which should take its normal place in the Church as an institution that will bring both balance and vitality, runs the risk of becoming a superfluous organ, smothered and frustrated—that is, if it is not first choked to death in the literature and in controversy before it can even be reborn.

Such a danger is in no way illusory. The abundance of literature dealing with the other "ranks" in the Church contains both good treatises, which always deal with the essentials and with evangelical simplicity, as well as those that are always the same—filled with may digressions, rhetorical skirmishes, and completely useless, flippant controversies. This fact should steer defenders of the diaconate to follow a course of great common sense. Theology—and here, we mean true theology, which can precisely state a problem and earnestly seeks to probe deeply into it and strives to perceive its consequences and enlighten public opinion so that it does not drown in murky academic scholarship—must be on its guard, not only to be able to rebut objections and sort out bad articles, but also to be able to eradicate relentlessly stylistic cleverness, dogmatic obstinacy, particularism or sensitivity, tasteless construction, exaggeration, oratorical drivel, or senseless extravagance.

5. And now our modest investigation arrives at the essential question: *What is the diaconate as seen through the eyes of theology?* Viewed theologically, what is the essential nature of this sacramental office and what is its place in the hierarchy of the Church? We will omit here discussions about the institution, the matter, the form, the minister, the recipient, and the effects of the sacrament; we will only mention them occasionally to the extent that they have a relational bearing on our essential question. By the same token, we will simultaneously expand the subject both upwards and downwards in order to shed light on its relationships to the other levels of the hierarchy. It is impossible to determine precisely the position of a given theologian with respect to the diaconate, without evaluating his position to the episcopacy, presbyterate, or hierarchical priesthood, as well as to the laity or the royal priesthood of the faithful. While it would seem to be appropriate to broaden the scope of our discussion to the priesthood of Christ, it would unfortunately take us too far here.

6. We believe we must pull into this discussion, above all, the "nearest relatives" of the diaconate: the subdiaconate and the minor orders. Undoubtedly, contemporary theology is inclined to group the diaconate together with the presbyerate and episcopate as "sacramental orders," whereas the subdiaconate and the minor orders are assigned to the lay state as "sacramentals." Canon law, however, sees in these orders, higher and lower, rather different steps of the sacrament of orders and an entry way to the priesthood, and this is consistent with high scholasticism and the Councils of Florence and Trent. Historically and logically, the subdiaconate and minor orders probably emerged from the lay state. From the beginning, nevertheless, they have been viewed as ecclesiastical and, in a certain sense, as hierarchical functions (with the exception of exorcist) and have been grouped together with the diaconate (or more precisely with *diakonia*—the lesser service), which occupies an intermediate position between the priesthood itself and the lay state. In any event, theology is confronted here with a serious and significant problem, which in our opinion must be resolved before a general restoration of the diaconate can be envisaged. Otherwise, the confusion will only become greater—to the detriment of all the "ranks."

7. We prefer to carry out our investigation retrogressively, to follow the *ordo praeposterus,* as St. Jerome would say (i.e., to begin with the chronologically most recent theologians). We will cite them here without differentiating

their direction or school of thought, their field of specialization or their affiliation. This method might not appear to be very logical; nevertheless, in our opinion, it offers several advantages. First of all, we begin with the contemporary state of theology, the explication of which is less difficult than that of the earlier centuries: The theology of the earlier periods used a different language and faced different situations—facts that must always be taken into account when it comes to careful interpretation. Second, since theology continues to make progress (although sometimes one is tempted to be skeptical about that!) this method makes it possible to present here the most representative authors, those who speak most clearly and comprehensively about the subject matter. Third, all theologians stand on the shoulders of their predecessors (even if they do not copy them word-for-word) and study their doctrinal propositions, in that they interpret or criticize, adapt, and classify them; thus, it will be easy for us to track back through their positions to those of their predecessors and, in this way, to trace out the main lines of theological tradition. This will spare us a great deal of repetition.

8. By "theologians," we understand not only dogmatists but also moralists, canonists, liturgists, historians, and exegetes to the extent that they can shed light on our problem, which is preeminently dogmatic in nature. The solution presented here does not in any way show preference to these individuals or the theses cited. The remarks that we add and our conclusions will make our own position sufficiently clear.

Finally, as we present the chronologically most recent theologians, we will however exclude those who have already addressed themselves explicitly to the possible restoration of the diaconate. Elsewhere in this volume are to be found the views of the most significant among them, as well as a comprehensive bibliography of that which has already been written on the topic of the renewal of the diaconate. We will make an exception to this rule with respect to the article by Fr. Schillebeeckx in the (Dutch) *Theological Dictionary*. This article deals extensively with the possible renewal of the diaconate and the minor orders. We do so, first of all, because this essay rests on a noteworthy theological foundation and, second, because it is written in the Dutch language and could therefore easily escape the attention of those who are especially interested in this problem.

9. Our investigation has also proven to be disappointing and difficult from other points of view. It may not be so bad that the theologians do not agree among themselves about a certain number of dogmatic opinions. What is rather ludicrous is to have to observe how a group of serious men present

these using the words *probably, certainly,* or even *generally,* who then in turn refute other opinions in exact detail—opinions that other, no less serious, people for their part set forth using the words *probably, certainly,* or *generally*—whereby the one group presumes to oppose the other group using no less "certain" arguments. What conclusion can one draw from this? Should it be that even these terms need to be interpreted in order to be understood? It is hoped that we will be permitted to opine that simplicity and exactitude of meaning are not even close to being achieved here.

10. In the special case of the sacrament of orders, their difficulty is exacerbated by the ambiguity of terminology. It does not only apply to the earliest centuries of Christianity, where the terminology for the priesthood and orders is so difficult to determine; the confusion appears to be just as great today. What do the authors understand precisely by the terms *apostolic office, hierarchy, ordination, religious state, cleric, priesthood, orders, jurisdiction, sacramental character, office, authority of office, charism,* and so forth. This is not always easy to determine. The terminology is no less unambiguous than is the theory. It differs according to the dogmatic, historical, canonical, or exegetical position for the authors in question. At times, these authors appear to contradict themselves from one sentence to the next. It becomes even more difficult due to the fact that terms such as *orders, ordination, consecration, priest, servant* [*deacon/minister*], and *solemn ceremony* do not have an exact equivalent in the various languages, and that they are all based on different situations and connotations. We cannot be expected to make detailed allowances for all of this. Rather, we wish to pursue the major lines of thought and the conclusions that can be drawn from them.

11. One final remark. It addresses theology, in general, but also appears to have special significance for the object of our interest. Theology is a "science," whether one views it as a science of "God," of "faith," of "revelation," of the "Christian supernatural," or of "the relationships between God and the individual human being or all of humankind mediated by Jesus Christ." The object and method of theology have been sufficiently discussed. The objective of theology—and of every other science as well—can only be that which spurs on human knowledge and puts it at the service of life. However, how does such science proceed? It does so by means of hypotheses (i.e., with the help of assumptions, experiments, and mistakes). An established science plunges forward into unexplored territory on the basis of a previously known or preconceived idea (or hypothesis), in order to abandon this idea and replace it with another one, as soon as the results learned contradict it or confirm or make possible another idea. In other words, theology differs considerably

from dogma, which teaches us divinely revealed truth, which in and of itself, although not always in its expression, is indisputable.

Theology, as does every other science, therefore has *the right to err*. The (Magisterium) does not have this right. Both tasks differ essentially from each other. It is the task of the Magisterium to hand on in an unbroken line the faith and to lead people along the path of salvation established by Jesus Christ (living Tradition). Theology has greater freedom; it can and must illumine the faith and advance its propagation on the basis of knowledge. It can propose free "opinions," which the Magisterium can allow on the basis of its varying methods of review without assuming the responsibility to accept or reject them, but only to the extent that they belong to the received teachings of the Magisterium (as expressly confirmed by it). This circumstance appears to have several consequences concerning the behavior of theology toward the Magisterium, the faithful, and itself, consequences that, on closer inspection, appear obvious but are frequently overlooked! If one wants to grapple with the problem of the diaconate, these consequences should not be overlooked.

12. As far as the Magisterium is concerned, theology is not supposed to replace the Magisterium. It may not set something forth as an article of faith, as heretical, certain, or only probable, something that it is not, something that has not been expressly introduced by the Magisterium, when it is basically only a "theological opinion." Theology may strive to clarify the Magisterium; it may not, however, prejudge its decisions, either in area of teaching or practice. It may not attempt to exert pressure on the Magisterium, directly or indirectly, nor—as Dollinger would have liked to do—attempt to create a body of public opinion, "before which finally everyone would bow, including the heads of the Church and the bearers of power." It is precisely public opinion that must conform to the Magisterium as Mohler explained to Abbé Bantain. Theology can interpret the decisions of the Magisterium, but it may not publish its own interpretations and conclusions—and yet, how many of these divergent opinions have we read recently, for example, concerning the encyclicals *Mystici Corporis* or *Humani Generis*!—as the teaching of the Magisterium itself. Only the "ordinary" and "extraordinary" Magisterium has the authority and the responsibility to teach the faith and lead the Church.

13. With respect to the faithful, theology must be able to inform the faithful accurately and objectively both about the true and certain teachings of the Church as well as about the relative value of its own opinions. In so doing, it does not have the right to present its opinions or hypotheses as the official teaching of the Church. There are many examples of this to cite from

the history of theology. Have not many individuals lost their faith since the beginning of the modern age because an entire theology did not understand how to differentiate the true from the false, the certain from the doubtful, and the essential from the irrelevant in a timely manner? These people did not lose their faith in theology—one could probably easily justify that and it would have done little harm—rather, they lost their faith in the Church, whose teaching was presented in a false light, and this is much more serious. It may be gullible to believe in a certain theology, but it is never naive to believe in the Church, which possesses the guarantee of infallibility, and to dispose oneself to its practical guidance, even if one's own inner being seems to resist it. In our days, even in Christian countries, there is an almost generally accepted opinion that one is "gullible" if one "believes everything the Church says!" Are the people or is the Church at fault here? Or should a large part of the blame be attributed to theology? The current trend is for (the Church) to blame itself. The Church should neither blame herself nor doubt herself. She must untiringly carry out her role with unshakable faith in the mission with which she has been entrusted and the promises she has been given. The same cannot be said of theology, which, it appears to us, needs to examine its conscience seriously.

14. With respect to itself, theology—as any genuine science should be —is also undoubtedly proud of the fact that it knows somewhat more in its field than the average mortal, whereas it should also remain somewhat humble in the face of all that it basically does not know. It can be pleased about the fact that others can put its deeper knowledge to good use, but should not allow itself to become enmeshed in the vanity of false knowledge. Theology can be sorely tempted to do so by the substantial impetus that derives from curiosity and the admiration of the world, which can easily change a "scientist" into a man who "knows it all." Theology cannot hold up its modest discoveries as lanterns and then also present them to people as such. Fr. Bouessé concluded a paper on the post-Tridentine theology of the Eucharist, during which he mentioned names such as Lugo, Vasquez, Lessius, Franzelin, Monsabré, and Hugon, with this sentence: "*Lecon de modestie pour les théologiens que cette meprise.*" There are certainly enough other areas besides the holy sacrifice of the Mass, in which theologians have erred or will always err and where a little more modesty would do no harm whatsoever.

In other words, theology must not assume that its hypotheses are "theses" that must be proven at any price. As any honorable science, it must also base its hypothesis (which can only become a thesis after it has been thoroughly examined) on facts, and not bend the facts to conform with the hypothesis. By the way, theology shares these mistakes with other intellectual sciences, like philosophy and history ("theology's two eyes," as they were called by Dollinger), which also constantly attempt to "dogmatize" to the extent the object of their work can elude examination and judgment. The natural sciences do a much better job of differentiating between hypothesis and thesis (or "law"), since they are always required to submit their work to exacting examination. The intellectual sciences should be that much more modest, since their knowledge demands more "surety"; the damaging effects of false philosophies, historical concepts, or thelogians (ideologies) are sufficiently well-known.

15. This lengthy preface was intended to sketch out our position vis-à-vis "theological opinions," to which we will subsequently refer, including those presented as proven theses (most of which we regard only as hypotheses). In the same way, it is also intended to provide information about the value of the conclusions *we* draw: they are no more than "theological opinions." We can shine our weak light on the concept of the diaconate; it is up to the Magisterium of the Church to bring more precise focus to it, should it be deemed necessary or appropriate. We can wish for the restoration of the office of deacon under certain circumstances; it is up to the hierarchy of the Church to decide about both the restoration and the circumstances.

II. The Positions of the Theologians

1. We begin this chapter with the comments of the Flemish Dominican *E. H. Schillenbeeckx,* professor of theology at the Catholic University of Nijmegen. Here, we encounter an objective analysis of the facts and doctrines, which are associated with a clearly sketched out theological treatment in a very broad Thomistic sense. Even though he does not expressly address the diaconate, his thoughts concerning the sacrament of orders can still shed considerable light on the object of our research.

The author does a rather thorough job of developing the doctrine of sacramental character, which he sees as the key to the sacramental economy of the Church and to the mediation of salvation, which is both effected and communicated by Christ, the true Minister of the sacraments. What the Council of Trent has defined about this character is limited to a few points. However, the Thomistic view, which sees in it a participation in the priesthood of Christ, a sign of membership in the Church, and a mission of cultic worship, makes it possible to define the places of the priest and of the faithful, which, each in their own way, are consecrated through the sacraments of orders, confirmation, and baptism. Christ not only dispenses his grace in the Church via sacraments, but also through persons. The priest is a true *sacramentum-persona,* whose salvific action is linked to those visible signs established by Christ for that purpose.

According to Scholastic interpretation, the priest is *presbyter*; according to the ancient and traditional view it is the bishop. Fr. Schillebeeckx opts for the ancient interpretation and traces the essential function of priesthood back to the Eucharist. The bishop possesses the fullness of priesthood—and accordingly, the sacramental character of orders. Priesthood and the priestly character are only a sharing of those of the bishop. For its part, the diaconate would be a sharing of a lesser degree in the priesthood and the character of the priest.

The minor orders present a real problem, which is still not solved. According to Scholastic thought, they were a sharing in the diaconate; according to the modern view, they are only sacramentals. Originally, those in minor orders were lay helpers in apostolic service. Over time, minor orders developed into ritual or sacramental consecrations, simultaneously losing their significance since they were no longer exercised. With respect to a "clergy" ordained (consecrated) according to our canon law, the author differentiates between a theological point of view—sharing in a hierarchical office—and a juridical point of view, according to which those in minor orders (like religious, who do not belong to the priestly state) are assimilated to the hierarchy on the basis of the new meaning, which these (minor) orders received in the course of history as entry steps to the priesthood.

The author is inclined to the opinion that sees lay functions in the minor orders, which according to a legal fiction were compared to the clergy. These circumstances made possible a revival of these steps to ordination, which could not be allowed to become atrophied but, rather, must be adjusted to fit various needs—both as lay support for the hierarchy and as actual preparation for the hierarchical priesthood.

Observations: Is the Thomistic position—which reduces the hierarchical priesthood (according to our author the episcopacy) to an essentially eucharistic service function—correct? Is the diaconate a sacramental sharing, of a lesser degree, in the priesthood of the *presbyter* or of the bishop? If the diaconate by virtue of its sacramental character is also a *sacramentum-persona,* then what is the place of this sacrament in the hierarchical structure of the Church willed by Jesus Christ?

The original lay character of the minor orders does not appear to us to be in doubt. Later on, the Church differentiated between the *clerici* (clerics) and the *ordo sacerdotalis* (priestly order), which included bishops, priests, and deacons. This probably made it possible to solve some of the difficulties that stemmed from canon law terminology.

2. To what has just been said, let us now fold in the current position of theology vis-à-vis the diaconate, using an essay by a Dutch confrere of Fr. Schillebeeckx, *P. A. H. Maltha,* professor of theology at the Collegium Albertinum in Nymegen (Holland).

The sacramentality of the diaconate is beyond doubt, even if some theologians such as Durandus de S. Porciano, Cajetan, and Salmeron have disputed it. This is apparent from ancient tradition, from the matter and form of the ordination, from the *Decree to the Armenians* (even though its dogmatic binding force is disputed), and finally, from the Council of Trent, which clearly included the diaconate in the hierarchy.

Observations: That the diaconate is sacramental or a "sacrament" is held by all theologians today to be certain, universal—or, at the very least, more probable—teaching. They even see this teaching confirmed by the constitution of Pope Pius XII, *Sacramentum ordinis.* There is, however, an exception, namely, the opinion of Fr. Beyer, who even after the issuance of the constitution still denies the sacramentality of the diaconate on the basis of the following arguments: The deacon has no sacramental authority except to baptize, which the laity can also do; he does not have a single *potestas ordinis* (ordination empowerment); one cannot deduce either the institution of the diaconate by Christ nor its sacramentality due to its ancient origins; the liturgical laying on of hands has no sacramental effect either in diaconal or episcopal ordination, since it does not impart a single priestly power [power that Fr. Beyer recognizes solely in the consecration of the Eucharist and the forgiveness of sins]; the laying on of hands is or was a routine part of other sacraments such as confirmation, confession, or extreme unction, as well as the ordination of an abbot. This position is consistent with the author's opinion about a single sacrament of orders fulfilled completely in the *presbyter.* How all this may be responded to from Scripture, Tradition, the Magisterium, liturgy, and the practice of the Church, we will leave to the other contributors to this volume. We will only comment here that this opinion appears to be unique and stands in opposition to the entire theological tradition—Eastern and Latin, Patristic and Scholastic.

3. Let us now expand upon these findings, using the point of view of *M. Schmaus,* professor of dogmatic theology at the University of Munich and the author of the most recent and comprehensive Catholic dogmatic theology work

in the German language. Christ is the only priest in the New Testament. He fulfilled his priesthood in the total sacrifice carried out once for all. The entire Church shares in the priestly character of Christ; she is the instrument, through which the glorified Christ functions as Priest in the proclamation of the word and the conferring of the sacraments. However, not all the faithful as living members of this single edifice share in this priestly function in the same way. In the Christian Community founded by Christ, there is an order, a hierarchy, which was originally realized by the apostles and then, subsequently, by those whom the apostles installed in various offices: bishops, priests, and deacons.

These offices are passed on by means of sacramental ordination. Orders is therefore the sacrament that enables certain members of the ecclesial community to provide special services, in that they are permanently conformed to Christ in a special way that permits them to represent him in certain official acts, in service of the word or sacrament. There is but a single sacrament of ordination, although in this sacrament there are several degrees or "orders" that are intended for the various services instituted by Christ.

The sacrament of ordination, according to St. Thomas, was instituted primarily in relationship to the Eucharist. The Council of Trent also referred to priestly ordination as the heart and center of the sacrament of ordination. Episcopacy confers the fullness of priestly powers entrusted by Christ to his Church. Diaconal ordination is a preparation for priestly ordination; according to virtually universal theological teaching, it is sacramental.

In the third century, the subdiaconate and minor orders were added to these sacramental ordinations. They were introduced in the interest of liturgical dignity for cultic ceremonies; nevertheless, any baptized Christian man can exercise the corresponding offices. The ceremonies and prayers, which go along with the conferring of these offices, bear the essential characteristics of sacramentals and not sacraments. The medieval concept that held that they were sacramental still has a few proponents, but this simply does not correspond to historical reality. These orders were not instituted by Christ, but introduced by the Church. Once upon a time, they were important functions in the Church. Today, they are merely entry steps to the priesthood; the former functions are carried out partly by unordained laity, and partly by priests.

Observations: Again, we find in this conception the essential strains of Thomistic thought, which are expanded here by reference to the priesthood of Christ, the priesthood of the Church and the faithful, and the service of the word. Is it completely right to say—even according to the statement of the Council of Trent—that priestly ordination is the center point of the sacrament of orders, that the episcopacy is the completion or fullness of this order, and that diaconal ordination is the preparation for priestly ordination? Were the minor orders primarily or solely established for cultic service?

If these orders are not sacramental, how does one explain and justify the fact that, for several centuries, they were considered to be sacramental by the Latin Church?

4. Let us now turn to a canonist, Canon F. Claeys-Bouwaert, former professor of canon law at the Ghent Seminary, who not only possesses indisputable competence in the juridical and historical spheres, but also an excellent theological mind. His writings are held in high regard.

Using references from canon law and conciliar texts, he too establishes that the sacrament of orders essentially confers the power to consecrate the Body and Blood of Jesus Christ, to celebrate Mass, to distribute holy communion, and to forgive sins. Theologians debate about the nature of the character that ordination imprints upon the soul, as well as about the sacramentality of the episcopacy and the diaconate.

The sacramentality of the diaconate is not an article of faith; nonetheless, one would in all likelihood have to recognize it, and this is already happening among theologians. Tradition has discovered its institution in the Acts of the Apostles. The powers of this [degree of] orders are very limited today, whereas in earlier times they were much broader. The author cites the following: service at the altar; preaching; baptism; distribution of the Eucharist, especially under the form of wine; reading or singing the epistles and the Gospel; receiving the gifts from the faithful; maintaining order in sacred places; preparing catechumens; and mediation associated with the administration of the sacrament of penance. Most of these forms of ministry have been abandoned. The history of this retrogressive movement has apparently not yet been written, says the author.

In any case, it is appropriate to differentiate between two different aspects of the sacrament of orders: the essential aspect of priestly power in its intrinsic sense and the aspect of *assisting* in the exercise of this power. The Scholastics differentiated between ordained hierarchy and jurisdictional hierarchy. This differentiation was picked up in a pronouncement of the Magisterium and has become standard. The ordained hierarchy comprises the seven major and minor degrees except the episcopacy, which today is generally viewed as a special order. It is not the same as that of the Eastern Church, whose constitution is recognized as valid by the Latin Church. Other ecclesiastical offices, whether of more ancient or more recent origin, do not involve ordination.

Theologians do not agree as to where the Magisterium belongs in this differentiation; some would view it as a third authority within the Church. Two degrees of jurisdictional hierarchy are divinely instituted: the Supreme Pontificate and the episcopacy. The remaining degrees have been established by the Church and are therefore subject to possible changes.

Remarks: Let us fix our attention on the double aspect of orders or the hierarchical priesthood and repeat them using the original terms: the aspect of *presiding* (episcopacy and presbyterate) and that of *service* (diaconate). Let us also fix our attention on the idea expressed in the views of Fr. Schillebeeckx already discussed, namely, that the differentiation between orders and jurisdiction does not represent an adequate distribution of powers in the Church, if only because it is so difficult to situate one of the most important tasks of the hierarchy—the ministry of the word—in either of the two aspects. There are also other functions that have no proper place in them: the ministry of prayer and worship, and the ministry of Christian charity. Certain older and more recent ecclesiastical offices (including some important ones) find no corresponding sacramental expression in orders. Among these, the author includes the following: the Supreme Pontificate; those in tonsure; cantors; confessors; nurses [*parabolani*]; grave-diggers [*fossores*]; interpreters [*hermeneutae*]; and deaconesses. One could cite even more of them—old and new—and specifically cite the problems associated with the relationship between regular clergy and secular clergy, as well as the role of women in the Church.

In 1949, the author wrote that the history of the diaconate has yet to be elucidated; this gap, as of today, has been partially filled in, although in our opinion, not very satisfactorily. Above all, what is missing is a thorough overview of the specific essential status of the diaconate in the Church, the various reasons that precipitated its attenuation into a purely theoretical concern, as well as the way—when the cause is removed, the effect ceases—in which a divinely instituted diaconate could again regain its original place and appropriate significance.

5. The Christian East has done a better job of retaining the ancient concept of the hierarchical priesthood than the West. The role of the deacon in the East has remained unchanged, at least in liturgy. What could the customs and the theology of the East teach us about the diaconate? One could easily maintain that the entire theology of the hierarchy—both in the West and the East—can be traced back to a single, anonymous, probably Syrian, author of the late-fifth or early-sixth century: the famous *Pseudo-Dionysius the Are-*

opagite. According to him, there is also a celestial hierarchy of nine levels. This hierarchy—whether celestial or temporal—not only establishes social stratification, it also plays a larger role in leading its members to worship in an effort to help them assimilate God more and more through knowledge of the truth and holiness.

Divine illumination has been assigned directly to the highest level of the celestial hierarchy, with the lower levels mediated by the higher ones. It is worth noting that according to Pseudo-Dionysius, Christ himself by virtue of his nature is subject to the mediating role of the angels. This is in contrast to the classic teaching of the Greek fathers that angels are only servants or "deacons" of Christ in the salvific mission.

The nine levels in the ecclesiastical hierarchy are grouped together in three stages: the divine sacraments (Eucharist, anointing, baptism); those who are knowledgeable about these sacraments and initiate into them (bishops, priests, and deacons); and finally, those who are initiated into them by the aforementioned (monks, the baptized or *illuminati,* catechumens, demoniacs, or penitents).

Christ is the source and supporting foundation of every ecclesiastical hierarchy. We need the sacred gift of priestly powers in order to approach those beings who are superior to us. The bishop represents the fullness and completion of the structure of the human hierarchy; he is the steward of the sacraments; the bearer of the knowledge, which he passes on to his subordinates; the splendid tool of purification, illumination, and perfection. The other members of the ordained priesthood carry out their function only in union with him and in dependence upon him. Those priests selected and ordained by bishops stand by them and help them; their primary task is illumination.

The third level—that of the deacons, whom Dionysius calls "liturgists" and not by the Greek-Christian term *deacons*— exercises an office of purification. They cleanse away everyone who impedes conformity to God; guard the entrances of the church; escort out those who have not been properly initiated; read the Scriptures; sing psalms; remove the waistbands and clothing of those being baptized; assist the bishop; and exorcise catechumens.

Monks—the most thoroughly prepared of all the initiated—are instructed by the bishop and consecrated by priests, with the assistance of the deacons. They have no rightful claims to the priestly hierarchy, whom they must respect and obey; similarly, they have no mission to carry out in church, since their place is among the holy people at the gates of holiness. The holy people (*illuminati*) require the service of priests, who should gradually lead them to spiritual contemplation and union. The lowest level of the initiated, that is, the catechumens as well as penitents and demoniacs (i.e., baptized persons who have been cut off from the sacraments through sin or possession by a demon) are entrusted to the cleansing work of deacons. Holiness is essential for the hierarchy; Dionysius does not hesitate to exclude [from the sacraments] even priests living in sin.

Even though St. Thomas, consistent with the original Scholastics, concentrates his entire theory of orders on the eucharistic sacrifice, he continually makes references to the hierarchy of Dionysius and its functions. He feels the need to justify his views in relations to it:

> The purification for which the deacons of the Church are responsible is not the cleansing of sin. It is said of deacons that they cleanse to the extent that they exclude the unclean from the community of believers or properly dispose the faithful for the reception of sacraments through holy admonitions. In the same way, it can be said of priests that they illumine the holy people, not because they infuse grace into them, but because they administer the sacraments of grace to them.

> The deacon participates in a certain way in the power of the priest to illumine, when he distributes the Precious Blood. In the same way, the priest shares in the fullness of the episcopal power to administer [sacraments], when he distributes the sacrament of the Eucharist, whereby a person's conformity to Christ is rendered complete.

Gregory Barhebraeus (1225-1286), the great Syrian theologian of the thirteenth century and a contemporary of St. Thomas (whom he did not know however), mentions another hierarchy having nine levels: an upper group consisting of patriarchs, metropolitans, and bishops; a middle group to which priests, deacons, and subdeacons belong; and a lower group comprised of lectors, cantors, and exorcists. He prefers, nevertheless, to remain with the "classical" theology of the great Dionysius and only subscribe to three levels in the temporal Church, whereas there are also three in each of the celestial Churches. As far as the lower levels are concerned, he does not assign any place to them in the ecclesiastical hierarchy, since they do not involve any ordination by the laying on of hands.

Let us turn our attention now to the rather subordinated place Barhebraeus assigns to widows, deaconesses, and monks in his hierarchical theology. These "states" still occupied a position in the Church between the clergy and the faithful during the time of Pseudo-Dionysius; in Barhebraeus' day, they no longer existed or lived in communities isolated from the churches:

And one should know that at the beginning of evangelization (as the book of Clement teaches), virtuous, chaste, and God-fearing women, once they became widows, were [officially] instituted in the Church. And during the breaking of the Eucharist, they stood within the sanctuary [chancel] behind the priests on the left side.

And as with widows, deaconesses were also instituted in the Church. And as Clement stated, they stood behind the subdeacons in the sanctuary as the eucharistic gifts were brought forward. And James of Edessa says that the deaconess "had absolutely no authorized function in the sanctuary," but she does polish "the lamps and light them" [in the church] where she has been instituted. And she is not permitted to touch the altar, although in the absence of a priest or a deacon, "she removes the Mysteries from the wall tabernacle and distribute them to women or children." And when there are adult women to be baptized, she anoints them, just as she would anoint them if they are sick.

With respect to monks, Barhebraeus at times speaks of them as if they were outsiders in the Church; while they are consecrated, hands are not laid on them.

The Russian theologian A. P. Maltzev (1854-1915), speaks of the following ordination levels: episcopacy, presbyterate, diaconate, lectorate, and hypodiaconate; the last two, however, are not recognized as sacraments. He associates the psalmist and the candle-bearer with them. The Orthodox recognize only three hierarchical ranks. The lectorate and subdiaconate, which correspond to our minor orders, are for them simply functions, even though they are conferred by the bishop. From the Council of Trullo on, the subdeacon understood himself to be obligated to celibacy—a regulation that has not been observed since the sixteenth century, however. The Eastern Churches do not recognize the doctrine of sacramental character, but once orders have been conferred they cannot be conferred a second time. Also, they do not make our differentiation between ordained powers and jurisdictional powers; they simply remove an unworthy office-bearer from office. They charge that the Roman Church has added an additional office—the Papacy—at the top of the hierarchy ordained by Jesus Christ and also added the minor orders at the bottom level.

In the Greek catechism of *Gallinikos,* we read: "Clerics are not all alike." Some are deacons, others priests, and still others bishops. The functions of the deacons are very limited. They have no leadership position nor do they administer the sacraments. They may only assist at the Sacrament [Mass] and with the permission of the bishop may proclaim the word of God. Priests, who outrank deacons, also have no leadership position, even though they can administer almost all the sacraments except the sacrament of orders and the consecration of holy oils. They also proclaim the word of God. Bishops, to whom is entrusted the power to ordain priests, proclaim the word of God, administer all the sacraments without exception, and have the highest responsibility for the care of souls.

Let us augment this theology with some thoughts of the French Dominican *C. J. Dumont,* director of the Centre d'Etudes Istina in Boulogne-sur-Seine. The ordination levels recognized by the Eastern Church—presbyterate, diaconate, subdiaconate, and lectorate—are conferred for their own sake in order to be exercised, not with direct reference to promotion or ulterior advancement to the priesthood. According to the canonical-liturgical tradition of the East, it is assumed that once an individual has been invested with a higher order that individual would no longer continue to carry out the service of the lower order. A priest would never fulfill the function of a deacon; this would be equivalent to a forfeiture of rights. This is partially explained by the importance of the role of the deacon in the liturgy:

> The liturgy is as a rule always sung. The role of the deacon in this is very important, even though this office is strictly limited to liturgical celebrations. Therefore, it only requires a little time. The deacon also has a full-time job, which allows him to provide for his livelihood—at least a manual occupation that can be easily interrupted to attend to liturgical service (Mass, administering the sacraments, burials, devotions). This definitely does not require any special religious and/or spiritual formation.

Those Churches in union with Rome are attempting to abandon these customs and to harmonize their ecclesiastical discipline with the Latin Church. It has become customary for a priest to exercise the function of the deacon. One balks at the thought of making someone a deacon, who does not possess the requisite suitability for the priesthood. In the same way, the new, recently promulgated Eastern church law renders the subdiaconate an obstacle to marriage—a measure that only makes sense when thought of in conjunction with a later entrance to the diaconate and priestly office. Fr. Dumont reports that in the Orthodox Church, a large number of young people are appointed as lectors or subdeacons solely to participate in pontifical worship services, without the slightest intentions of obligating them to an ecclesiastical career.

Observations: Throughout the dissimilarity, the uncertainties, and at times—one has to admit—the singularly charming ideas of Eastern theology and customs, we find some permanent dimensions that bring us closer to ancient Christianity and the other situation in the Latin Church of the early centuries, as is still attested to, for example, in the Rule of St. Benedict. There are actually no other levels of orders other than the three major orders, which are held to have been instituted by Christ: the episcopacy, the presbyterate, and the diaconate. These orders differ significantly from minor orders, from monasticism, and from lesser offices. Deacons, lectors, and subdeacons are ordained solely on the basis of need and for the purpose of exercising their ministries, not as an honor or for meritorious distinction or with the intent that they will ultimately advance to a higher order. As Fr. Dumont points out, it is sad to have to admit that at the same point in time when there is a movement underway to restore the minor offices as orders, this structure, which has been in place for so long in the Eastern Church, is now threatened with dissolution to the same extent as happened in the Catholic Church. Let us further call attention to the important liturgical role of the deacon, who in liturgies represents the link between the priest and the faithful, and yet, on the other hand, whose social position is similar to that of our sacristans and church vocalists, who are not ordained and whose working relationships unfortunately are frequently comparable to that of a basic employee.

6. Let us turn again to our Western Church and to our scholasticism in order to listen to the French Dominican *H. Bouessé,* professor of theology at the College of Chambery-Leysse. Fundamentally an adherent of St. Thomas, he evidences great historical erudition and astounding philosophical acumen. Even so, one must also conclude that he does not possess a sense of historical reality in the same measure as his Flemish confrere, Schillebeeckx.

Following his exposition of what the priesthood of Christ means with respect to the pagan world and the Old Law, he proceeds to a study of the ministerial priesthood of the Church. Even if history does not clearly reveal in every detail how the transition from apostolic leadership to episcopal leadership occurred, it certainly does provide evidence that it did happen.

This is so because, in their lifetime, the apostles appointed men to be ambassadors and servants of Christ and his salvation—at first to assist them and later to be their successors: bishops, priests, and deacons.

> It is a certain tenet that the entire ministerial priesthood in the strict sense in the Church of Christ is the priesthood of the priest, of him whose actual function is the consecration and offering of the eucharistic sacrifice. He who does not possess this power is not a priest. He who has it is a priest. On this strictly delineated plane of the priesthood, the highest cultic function of the Church on earth, there is no difference, no nuance between

the second-level priesthood—between priest and bishop. There is also no difference in level between priest and pope.

Like St. Thomas, Fr. Bouessé is of the opinion that the episcopacy essentially has power over the Mystical Body of the Lord (not over the eucharistic Body). The episcopacy builds up the Church on earth, in that it establishes the gradual progression of the baptized and confirmed faithful and, above all, of that of bishops and priests (the diaconate is not mentioned).

Episcopacy and diaconate, as sacramental degrees of participation in the royal priesthood of Christ, have a common basis. Since neither the one nor the other is directly ordered to the Eucharist, they do not imprint any sacramental character on the soul. They impart in indelible form a consecration to ministry to the Church, to priests and to laity, and only indirectly to eucharistic ministry. The author therefore sees, over and above the participation of the faithful in the royal priesthood of Christ, a gradually and functionally different participation in this priesthood by deacon, priest, bishop, and pope.

Another indisputable tenet would be the extra-sacramental character of episcopal jurisdiction, which the author sees as being completely dependent upon that of the pope and with which he associates the authority of the magisterium in conformity with the generally held opinion [*sententia communis*]. He indeed adds here that there is no doubt that jurisdictional authority in the scheme of regular discipline goes hand in hand with the sacramental authority of the bishop.

Fr. Bouessé reserves to the presbyterate the power to sanctify the faithful through the sacraments. "In spite of all appearances, the power to ordain priests is lesser that the power to celebrate the Eucharist and is subordinate to it."

Observations: The certain tenets of Fr. Bouessé appear to us to be rather open to criticism. Can one really claim that the priesthood in the strict sense is that of the priest and of the ministry of the Eucharist? This hardly corresponds to the "priesthood" that Jesus entrusted to his apostles—and they, in turn, to bishops—whether in the Latin tradition of the first ten centuries or in the Eastern tradition, both of which normally called the bishop "*sacerdos*" or "*pontifex*," not "the priest." Can one say that the "priesthood" of the bishop or the deacon represents a sacramental sharing in the "royal" priesthood of Christ in contrast to the priesthood of the priest, who alone possesses the power over the eucharistic Body of Christ and the sanctification of the faithful by means of the sacraments? Thereby, does one not make out of the diaconate and the episcopacy simply powers of spiritual jurisdiction? And can one in this regard linearly arrange deacon, priest, bishop, and pope according to authority? Does one not also thereby do exactly that which the Orthodox accuse us of, namely, adding an order to those that were instituted by Christ? Can one so clearly define the extra-sacramental character of jurisdiction? Can this jurisdiction be understood differently from the hierarchical priesthood instituted by Christ, or would not this differentiation be viewed as all too theoretical?

Does not jurisdiction normally proceed from orders? Would not ordination that imparts no jurisdiction or a jurisdiction that would be conferred without ordination be contradictions, even if it involved the Bishop of Rome (who in this case would not yet even be a bishop)? Fr. Bouessé says nothing about the subdiaconate or the minor orders. However, can he logically abandon the Thomistic concept of the sharing in the sacramental character of the bishop by the lesser orders, in order to uphold his position of the priesthood of the priest in its essence as eucharistic ministry?

7. Let us now ask the liturgists and historians to either reinforce or refute the "certain" principles of Fr. Bouessé. We turn first to his confrere *Fr. P.-M. Gy,* professor of liturgy at Le Saulchoir Theological College (Etiolles).

The term *order* signifies the spiritual power associated with specific levels of the hierarchy, as well as with the rite in which this order is conferred. In the latter case, the author believes (along with some of the Scholastics) that we are speaking about a sacrament of ordination. The term *order* emphasizes the hierarchical and organic character of the Church, the collegial exercise of an essentially communal function. Orders comprise three unchangeable and divinely instituted levels: the episcopacy, the presbyterate, and the diaconate; these orders are sacramental. The subdiaconate and the minor orders also share in the sacrament of orders, but in an entirely external way—as sacramentals. The term *totum potestativum* (fullness of power) proposed by St. Albert and St. Thomas can be used with reference to both.

The exercise of both the episcopal and priestly priesthood essentially comprises a cultic and a *kerygmatic* function. The cultic function (Eucharist and the sacraments) presupposes empowerment by ordination, whereas the ministry of proclamation is based on jurisdiction. Only empowerment by ordination is sacramental, even though both functions are "mutually and completely connatural." One can become even more inveigled in one or the other of these two functions, but if one loses sight of the bond that unites them, one runs the risk of falling into ritualism or of no longer properly understanding the difference between priests and other Christians. Cult and proclamation must remain together.

The cultic is certainly the more important of the priestly functions, but the ministry of proclamation requires a higher degree of holiness. In this latter sense, the author cites the words of St. John Chrysostom: "The Word is the greatest, the holiest and the best of all sacrifices . . . my priestly office is to preach and to proclaim the Gospel—that is the sacrifice which I present." Bishops have generally reserved the homily to themselves as their task and only delegated it to priests by way of exception. Deacons, no less than subdeacons or the other lesser orders, do not possess priestly office; they are assistants to and collaborators with priests:

> The deacon also shares in some way in the apostolic power of proclamation, at the very least by liturgically proclaiming the Gospel; other examples of proclamation activity are seldom to be found in the history of the Church. This authority of the deacons appears to be based on the granting of equal status for both the Seven appointed by the Apostles and those deacons introduced to us by St. Paul; this equivalent status is based on Tradition.

The activity of deacons, likewise, extended into the realm of the liturgical assembly and the administration of the temporal goods of the Church. During Mass, they assisted the celebrant and led communal prayers. In the ancient Church, and still today in the East, the bishop could not confer sacraments without the participation of a deacon. This diaconal activity has been practically extinct in the Latin Church since the Middle Ages; the deacon has, to some extent, been replaced by the master of ceremonies, whereas the faithful have been left more and more on their own since that time. More recent liturgical pastoral practice has once again rediscovered the importance of the liturgical functions of the deacon. As far as the authority to administer the temporal goods of the Church is concerned, it belongs to neither priests nor to the laity, in the opinion of this author. It might possibly be one argument for the reinstitution of the real diaconate.

Those orders subordinate to the diaconate are not sacramental, although they do effect actual grace and are preparatory to the reception of sacramental orders. Their role could be compared to the prebaptismal exorcisms, but the reason for their existence is to support the deacon in his task of providing lively expression to the liturgical assembly. Despite that, these [minor] orders gradually acquired more and more of a liturgical or ritualistic sense. This is especially the case with the subdiaconate, to which the Latin Church in the twelfth century assigned the importance of a consecration to service at the altar and then with the sense of a "higher order," which carried with it the obligation of celibacy. The Council of Trent had expressed a desire to restore the minor orders, although this oft-expressed desire has in the interim never been fulfilled. The current discipline, whereby these orders have been made into steps on the way to the priesthood, and which prescribes that they all must be passed through one after another—with no practical experience in their corresponding functions—has a certain artificiality about it. These orders exist solely in seminaries and monasteries, to the great loss of liturgical pastoral practice and proclamation.

Fr. Gy, has also devoted a work to the study of the old designations for the hierarchical priesthood. In the New Testament, the Greek term *hiereus* or Latin *sacerdos,* which also appears in the pagan religions and Judaism, is reserved to Christ alone and is not quite synonymous with *presbuteros* ("presbyter").

The term *ordo* comes from ancient Rome and signifies a council (*collegium*) or a social class in contrast to the people—*populus* or *plebs.* In this sense, it was also used for the hierarchical priesthood. Since the time of Constantine, bishops, priests, and deacons seem to have taken a place in the official state hierarchy and simultaneously had the right to a title (*ordo, honor, dignitas*) as well as the official signs of office.

The term *sacerdotium,* which is used for the hierarchical functions, began to creep into ecclesiastical language around 200, at first as a designation for the bishop and then for the priest. This occurred without any clear reason as to why Christians in this case would reach back to a word, with which the New Testament had broken. "The texts, however, clearly show us that the term *sacerdotium* developed simultaneously with the term *sacrificium* [sacrifice] and in direct connection with it." This idea found its very expression in the *Apostolic Tradition* of Hippolytus: priests "sacrifice" bread and wine, whereas deacons "present the sacrificial gifts." The deacon actually may not "sacrifice"; he was not ordained to the priesthood [*non in sacerdotio ordinatur*].

How is this to be explained?

Even if there is no hard proof that *sacrificium* was expressly mentioned in the anaphora of Hippolytus and possibly did not exist since Apostolic times, Fr. Jungmann holds out the probability that in the second and third centuries, the appreciation of the Eucharist as a presentation of earthly gifts can be noted as a reaction against the exaggerated spiritualism of the Gnostics. The New Testament definitely had to stress the unique distinctiveness of the sacrifice of Christ over against the animal sacrifices of the old covenant. To combat the Gnostics, Irenaeus and his successors had again given way to the thought that creation was good and was the object of a genuine sacrifice, which God could make—in other words that the priesthood of the old covenant had a valid component, which accrued to the cult of the New Covenant.

At first, the term *sacerdos* was used only for the bishop, but gradually then also for priests, the *sacerdotes secundi ordinis* [priests of the second rank], who shared in the eucharistic priesthood of the bishop. As far as deacons are concerned, they appear to have been excluded from the priestly hierarchy. Nevertheless, Fr. Gy quotes a text by Optatus of Mileve, composed around 366/367, according to which deacons are assigned to the "priesthood of the third rank," and adds the remark: "This granting of the *sacerdotium* to the deacon is practically a singular occurrence in the Tradition."

Observations: Fr. Gy has done a much better job than Fr. Bouessé of sketching out the historical perspective of the hierarchical priesthood, which essentially and originally has been understood as that of the bishop, and in which priests share to only a lesser degree. He also points out the artificial character and dangers of too wide a gap between ordinational power and jurisdictional power. Attention is also called to the relatively late appearance of the concept of hierarchical priesthood as a function of the eucharistic sacrifice, a position that appears today to be predominant in theology.

Nevertheless, it seems to us that Fr. Gy makes too broad a division between the cultic or sacramental function of orders (Eucharist and sacraments) and the jurisdictional task of proclamation. The liturgy of the Mass encompasses, in addition to its sacramental function, the service of the word—understood in both its explicative (the form of sacraments in the broadest sense) and its *kerygmatic* components (communal prayer and the service of love [service at the altar, *Agape,* eucharistic meal]). Jurisdiction encompasses the power to administer the sacraments, as well as to proclaim the Gospel or lead the Church.

It seems to us, as well, one cannot make a clear separation between sacrament and sacramental. In its original sense, the sacramental is nothing more than an interpretation and elucidation of the sacrament. In our opinion, a sacrament cannot be restricted to that minuscule scope, which the Church has determined as juridically necessary for validity, without running the risk of creating a distorted ritualistic image of it. Fr. Gy also introduces a characteristic statement about minor orders, which obviously contains a slight contradiction: "The subdiaconate and minor orders are not sacramental, although they do effectively confer actual grace." Is a sign that effectively confers grace, strictly speaking, not already a sacrament?

The diaconate appears to us to be too widely separated from the higher degrees of orders and too closely associated with the "minor orders." St. Leo, who is quoted by the author, speaks about *sacerdotal orders,* which include bishops, priests, and deacons; the Rule of St. Benedict does also. Fr. Gy remarks that the use of the term *sacerdotium* with reference to the deacon by Optatus of Mileve is practically unique in tradition. However, there are several other examples that can be cited:

> *Jerome:* Those persons chosen to be bishops, presbyters, or deacons are either virgins or widowers; or certainly, having once received the priesthood, they remain forever chaste.

> *Leo:* No layman . . . may rise . . . to the dignity of the priesthood . . . either to the first or the second or the third degree thereof in the Church. . . . [*Translator's note:* Implied here is the understanding that progression would be up through the minor orders.]

> *Benedict:* Should an abbot desire to ordain a deacon or a presbyter, he should select one of his own men who is worthy to serve in the priesthood.

Fr. Gy speaks about the former role of the deacon in liturgy and the administration of the temporal goods of the Church. This hardly sheds any light on the essentially mediating function of the deacon in cultic service or charitable activity, on the reception of the sacrificial gifts brought forward by the faithful or the distribution of communion as well as the care of the poor, and last but not least, on the role of the deacon as the link between charitable service and the altar. This role above all, in our opinion, is that which provides the justification in tradition from its earliest beginnings right down to our own time for the firmly held sacramental ordination of the deacon and his place among "ordained" orders. The *Apostolic Tradition* does indeed exclude deacons from the priesthood, although it does include an ordination prayer, according to which it is the task of the deacon "to carry into the most sacred [sanctuary] that which will be offered up to God by the high priests." Later theology seems to have retained only the negative aspect thereof (i.e., the exclusion [of the deacon] from the *sacerdotium*). It has certainly retained the sacramental character of the diaconate, although it remains quite silent and indecisive in its determination and justification of this sacramental character.

It need not even be stated that these thoughts expressed about the diaconate in the writings of Fr. Gy in reality run counter to all of the theology cited here. The author talks about a "real restoration of the diaconate," which might possibly be justified by the task that is in actuality neither priestly nor lay by its nature. It appears to us that this would be a weak justification for a sacramental degree of orders. The most disconcerting problem related to the overall theology of the diaconate is this: How can one justify then that an "office instituted by God" must be "really restored"? Let us say it very pointedly: as a result of its own incompetent interpretation of facts and conventional customs, theology has quite simply lost sight of the significance and almost of the reality of divine institution.

We, nevertheless, would like to draw upon a concept of Fr. Gy's that we consider to be very valuable: the concept of various orders in the Church. In this connection, he remarks that Pope Pius XII returned the old designations of *order of bishops* and *order of the laity* to respectful usage. Shortly before that, he had quoted St. Leo, who speaks of an *order of Levites*. Pope Pius XII actually did repeatedly and intentionally make the clear-cut distinction between the sacramentally ordained members of the hierarchy and the laity, to include religious, who do not belong to the hierarchy, when he was speaking about the cooperation (not the participation) of the laity with the apostolate of the hierarchy. This distinction, says the pope, is divinely instituted, whereas religious orders are established by the Church. Clergy and laity, whether they belong to a religious community or not, are first and foremost members of the Church and must, each according to his [or her] place and state in life, participate in and cooperate with the apostolate of the Church.

Christ, however, entrusted to the apostles and their successors the task of proclaiming the Gospel to the entire world, when he said to them: "Do this in memory of Me!"; he charged them to watch over the flock of Christ and to establish ecclesiastical discipline. When the pope makes the contrast between clergy and laity, he does so because the clergy (priests and deacons) have been assigned as direct co-workers of the bishop in this threefold task. If a lay person has been entrusted with a spiritual task, he does not thereby in any way become a member of the hierarchy. This task does not confer on him ordinational or jurisdictional powers, "which essentially remain bound to the reception of the sacrament of orders and to its various levels."

The Apostolic Constitution *Sacramentum ordines* [*The Sacrament of Orders*] speaks exclusively of the three major traditional degrees of ordination: bishops, priests, and deacons. In his speech to participants in the Second World Congress of the Lay Apostolate [1957], which will undoubtedly be duly recorded in the annals of the restoration of the diaconate, Pope Pius XII draws a clear line of demarcation between the laity and the diaconate, which he places alongside the hierarchical priesthood. Can one conclude from that, that those in minor orders are relegated to the lay state? that the tasks that formerly belonged to these orders—tasks, as the pope also states, that had already been carried out by the laity for a long time—are really only lay functions (a factual set of circumstances that basically refers back to their historical origin)? This is not explicitly stated, but it appears to be obvious.

This idea does not in any way denigrate the lay state (whether we are concerned with religious or not)—a lay state, into which some theologians would have liked to introduce various degrees of participation in the apostolate of the hierarchy. It appears to us, however that this idea precisely establishes the true ecclesiastical significance of it. The lay state, which is ordained to the royal priesthood by means of the—in a certain sense "hierarchical"—sacraments of baptism and confirmation, is not a passive "order" in the Church. It must actively cooperate in the mission of the Church: in proclaiming the Gospel throughout the world; in the expansion of the kingdom of God; and in the building up of the Body of Christ. It is simply not necessary that all types of secondary, "nonsacramental" consecrations (there is no additional sacramental consecration in the life of the lay person other that of marriage) such as vows, missionings, promises, special consecrations—all of which undoubtedly in and of themselves are completely lawful and permitted by church law—should take precedence over the true sacraments instituted by Christ and the basic code of human personal conduct implied in these sacraments.

8. Let us now ask a patrologist, the French Jesuit *J. Danielou,* professor at the Institute Catholique in Paris, about the earlier importance of the hierarchical priesthood.

The *sacerdotium* is only one aspect of *ministerium* [ministry], and it determines ministry in its relationship to Judaic and pagan sacrifice and priesthood. The presbyterate is another aspect, and it has to do with presiding in the assembly and leadership in the community. The apostolate is a third aspect, service of the word or of spreading the faith. In reality, Christian ministry according to St. Paul is the sharing of the Mysteries of God, the economy of salvation, which is both revelation and action. The economy of salvation, which is fulfilled by Christ, is "ministerially" administered by the Church in word and sacrament. In this sense, the author cites St. Gregory of Nazianzen, St. Gregory of Nyssa, St. John Chrysostom, and Pseudo-Dionysius.

Because the priest administers the Mysteries, he himself is also a sacrament. Fr. Danielou points out the variety of designations used for him, all of which are equally appropriate. In Alexandria, they preferred to call him

"Learned One" and "Herald of Faith"; in Antioch, "Sacrificial Priest"; and in Jerusalem, "Overseer" and "Steward."

Priests are first and foremost ministers of the work—"the proclamation of the Gospel is a priestly work"—according to both Origen and St. John Chrysostom:

> When you see priests and Levites no longer concerned with the blood of goats and bulls, but rather by the grace of the Holy Spirit standing in service to the Word of God, then say that Jesus has mounted the pulpit of Moses (Origen).

The office of overseer exercised by the priest includes administration of the goods of the community; for "the Christian community is also a community of charity, when it takes care of the poor."

Observations: With such a breadth of vision, which is both farther from and nearer to the origins [of Christianity], we can much better understand how the diaconate—as service at the altar, of the word and of charity—stands alongside of the hierarchical priesthood. We can better understand how the apostles and, subsequently, their successors could "ordain" "deacons," who would assist them in their "diaconal service" (*diakonia*) or in the service of charitableness, of the word, and even the sacraments, alongside of the "presbyters," who in their office as "overseers" of the churches and of eucharistic celebrations would support or stand by them.

The Council of Trent had a decisive influence on the continued designation of the priesthood as a ministry of the Eucharist. Let us question a theologian, the French Dominican *A. Duval,* who is likewise a professor at the La Saulchoir College, whether this decisive influence should be understood in the exclusive sense, in which it is customarily understood.

Council documents indicate that the Tridentine fathers attributed great importance to the office of preaching, even if they did not include this office in their definition of the priesthood. It was not the intent of the council to issue an all-encompassing definition of the priesthood; it was solely concerned with providing proof of its sacramentality to rebut the deletions of Protestantism.

In particular, the Archbishop of Nicosia deplored the fact that the description of the various orders in their convergence on the Eucharist did not really make clear what the ecclesiastical hierarchy was. The Eucharist certainly dealt fully with the concept of sacrifice and the concomitant concept of priesthood, but not with the concept of the hierarchy. The bishops, however, were not in agreement about the concept of apostolic office, its transmission, or its differentiations. Therefore, no universal and complete definition was forthcoming:

> The decree of July 15, 1563 still leaves a great deal of empty space for the development of a doctrine on the priesthood, which would have to include all of the questionable elements in a comprehensive synthesis.

The description of the minor orders in relation to the priest as consecrator of the Eucharist—and not in relation to the bishop—was also hotly debated. "The theologians, or more accurately the Thomists, who alone are defending the viewpoint should rather be silent on this point!" cried out one bishop. The Dominican Duval specifically quotes in this matter several lines written by one of the Dominicans who was present there:

> One usually applies this classification of the Church's seven levels of orders only in relation to the sacrifice of the Eucharist. However, as a holy bishop from the previous century remarked very well, one can state more generally that the seven levels of orders were formerly used in reference to the bishop—they were to assist him not only in the [Eucharistic] sacrifice, but also with preaching (as those two functions which properly belonged to his office).

The council fathers actually did attempt to breathe renewed life into the minor orders and the diaconate, in that they once again attributed to them not only eucharistic, but also *kerygmatic* and administrative functions. The urgency of a response to the Protestants, who thought that the minor orders made no sense, led to an official announcement of their revival, but the various spheres of activity for them were never specifically enunciated. The council catechism was more specific in its descriptions, but it retained the old spheres of activity that had been handed on. The council even envisioned the creation of a new category of married clerics, sacristans, choristers, and so forth, who would fulfill minor functions in the event of a shortage of ordained clerics; they would be obligated to receive the tonsure and to wear clerical garb inside of church. In this instance, there would be a differentiation between the cleric in cultic service and the cleric preparing for the priesthood.

Observations: As with the ancient councils, the Tridentine Council also wanted to define that which was being threatened by emphatic denials, while it left open such disputed points as the function of the episcopacy and the sacramentality of the minor orders. Therefore, one cannot overly rely on it to define exclusively Christian priesthood as the function of eucharistic sacrifice. The Council of Trent also saw in minor orders and in the diaconate something other than just steps on the way to a higher priesthood. It would have liked to see all these orders exercised in the interest of building up the community, as well as to provide preparation for future orders. Its reform never reached a basic understanding on this point and was not pursued in any practical way. Furthermore, since the formation of the future priests took place in seminaries, it was practically impossible to exercise these functions. The formation of future priests occurred predominantly in the theoretical or theological sphere and was separated from the concrete life of the Church. No doubt the new method had its good effects, but it also had its disadvantages for the building up of communities, as well as for the practical side of pastoral formation. In our opinion, a serious investigation needs to be made into the old mode of formation for future priests and deacons, wherein the exercise of the minor offices and of the diaconate was part of the preparation for the priesthood. Such a serious study should focus on the advantages of practical training in a lay office or in the functions of a deacon, so as to improve upon the all too theoretical training of candidates for the priesthood.

We could track down a great deal more about the theology of the diaconate or about the lack thereof in theological literature dealing with the sacrament of orders. However, we believe that the thoughts presented in the foregoing do permit some conclusions, which it is hoped will contribute to a sharper delineation of the problem.

III. Conclusions

1. There is only a single sacrament of orders or of the hierarchical priesthood. According to the most ancient and most widely disseminated tradition, this sacrament is the episcopacy; according to the Scholastic tradition, it is the presbyterate or the *sacerdotium* [priesthood]. It is none other than the "apostolate" itself, which—according to the Council of Trent—the Lord instituted when he conferred upon the apostles and their successors the power to consecrate, offer and distribute his Body and his Blood, as well as to forgive or to retain sins.

It is, nevertheless, characteristic of the sacrament of orders or the priesthood that it permits lesser sacramental participations: the presbyterate and the diaconate, according to the most widely held opinion; the diaconate, the subdiaconate, and the minor orders, according to the Scholastic view. It seems to us, therefore, somewhat imprecise for some authors to say that the diaconate and the presbyterate—or in the Scholastic view, the episcopacy— according to the most current opinion are "sacraments." Without a doubt, the diaconate is "sacramental," but it is not an independent "sacrament" like baptism, confirmation, or marriage.

2. The sacrament of orders or the hierarchical priesthood with its various levels or degrees—whether one accepts the three degrees of diaconate, presbyterate, and episcopacy centered on the bishop; or the seven levels of porter, lector, exorcist, acolyte, subdeacon, deacon, and priest grouped around the priest and the eucharistic sacrifice—presents theology with a difficult problem, which gives rise to many diverse solutions. In order to solve this problem, one cannot proceed from just any favorite theory or theology but, rather, must begin with the facts, with tradition in its broadest sense, and with the practice of the Church.

It seems impossible to define the sacrament of orders on the basis of a general theory about sacraments, since one would first establish basic principles, to which the term *sacrament* must correspond, in order to align then the sacrament of orders with these principles. There are just too many dissimilarities between orders and the other sacraments, not to mention the dissimilarities among the various sacraments in general.

It also seems impossible to define the various levels of the sacrament of orders or of the priesthood using a generic term for orders, which is applied individually to this or to that order level. On the contrary, one must use as a point of departure the concrete function that this or that degree of orders—major or minor—at least originally exercised, as well as how this function was exercised or handed on liturgically. This is necessary to determine to what degree and in what way this order was consecrated or "sacramental" and its relationship to the Christian hierarchical priesthood (i.e., to the apostolate entrusted by Jesus to the Twelve), without further appeal to and in accordance with the pronouncements of the Council of Trent.

3. This is precisely the path followed by the Scholastics, as they proceeded from those facts and tenets known to them. Their synthesis of the priesthood as the power to consecrate, offer, and distribute the Eucharist is not lacking in clarity and coherence, since they identify no order that ranks higher than the one that confers this power, whereas direct or indirect service of the Eucharist is attributed to all of the lesser orders. This synthesis, at least initially, was confirmed by the Councils of Florence and Trent, as well as the *Code of Canon Law.*

The synthesis, however, which is based on the concrete situation of the Latin Church of the Middle Ages, contains more than one historical inconsistency. It proceeded from a too narrowly defined concept of Christian priesthood, which was understood solely, or at least primarily, as service of the Eucharist. Furthermore, it was based on a defective understanding of the ancient term *sacerdos,* which was used as a designation for the priest when, in reality, it was intended to designate the bishop. Finally, there was the erroneous belief in the apostolic origin of the subdiaconate and the other minor orders, at least to the extent that they were aggregated to the diaconate.

The Scholastic synthesis does not appear to be acknowledged today by anyone. All theologians acknowledge the sacramentality of the episcopacy and reject it with respect to the subdiaconate and minor orders. Nonetheless, this presents a problem that, in the opinion of Fr. Schillebeeckx, does not yet appear to have been resolved. The Scholastic position on orders, even if it has not been formally defined, has influenced the practice of the Latin Church for several centuries. If, generally speaking, one salvages the sacramentality of the episcopacy by reserving to it the power to confer the sacraments of confirmation and priestly orders, it then appears extremely difficult to disavow the belief of the Latin Church in the sacramental dignity of the subdiaconate and minor orders. Also, according to the Apostolic Constitution *Sacramentum ordinis,* one does not have the right to delete this belief with the stroke of a pen by simply pointing out that these levels of orders "according to the most widely held and most probable opinion" are actually not "sacramental." But it is precisely this that is being done by today's theologians, including the Thomists.

The only clear solution that we have found for this problem is that of C. Journet. He is also of the opinion that the subdiaconate and minor orders today should only be held to be sacramentals—with two reservations, however. First, according to St. Thomas, they actually *could* have been sacramental (even if they were instituted by the Church), and consequently, they *could* have been a fanning out of the divine powers of the diaconate; second, they probably had been truly sacramental in the earlier history of the Latin Church.

Meanwhile, several of the more current theologians appear to accept, without clearly stating it, an expanded authority of the Church over the participation of the lesser [orders] in the sacrament of orders. We would rather leave open the question of whether or not minor orders were truly sacramental in the earlier history of the Latin Church, as do both Fr. Schillebeeckx and the Apostolic Constitution *Sacramentum ordinis.*

4. In their desire to retain the essential aspects of the Thomistic position about orders or the priesthood as a sacramental service of eucharistic sacrifice, and to bring this position into harmony with the new and indisputable details of history, it appears to us that modern Scholastic theologians still overexag-

gerate the expanded authority of the Church with respect to differentiations and participation in this sacrament. In the same way, the sharp difference that they draw between orders and hierarchy, as well as between ordinational and jurisdictional power, in order thereby to justify the leadership authority of bishops and, above all, that of the pope (whose ordinational power, by the way, they restrict) is somewhat theoretical and contrived.

In this and many other cases, the theory that evolved from practice and is required for its justification and guidance to a certain degree went beyond the conditional assumptions of this practice or tradition. At that moment when the theory was proposed as law, it exerted dangerous influence on the exercise [of the office]. When contradicted by new facts, its proponents deemed it necessary to complicate its principles and theses, to split it up into parts and subdivide it in order to bring it into harmony with reality. By so doing, they went beyond their task. Their desire, on the one hand, to defend their *a priori* postulated theses about a little understood practice, and, on the other hand, their justification of a precisely delineated practice, whose scope these theses over-estimated, led these theologians unmistakably into a situation from which there was no way out. The fact that these theories were inappropriately applied to practices, to which they did not correspond, also contributed to these mistakes.

In this sense, the Apostolic Constitution of Pius XII, which makes reference to the three major and traditional degrees of orders—bishops, priests, and deacons—represents a fortuitous return to greater clarity and simplicity. If we call to mind what this same pope said about the difference between the hierarchy and the lay state anchored in divine law, and in particular the difference between the diaconate and the lay state, then we possess the major and simple, traditional lines of the *Constitution of the Church*. One must at all costs return to these major lines not only to find the real theological solution to the problem of the sacrament of orders or ecclesiastical hierarchy, but also so that the various sacramental or lay "states" can appropriately carry out their mission. This must be done so that the Church is no longer viewed by believers and nonbelievers as an inextricably juridical organism and can then clearly and articulately proclaim its message to today's world.

5. The episcopacy, presbyterate, and diaconate are recognized almost unanimously by theologians as sacramental and instituted by God. However, we want to correct emphatically a too one-sided view of things that would characterize these degrees of orders as three equal subspecies of one and the same genus, which corresponds to a certain number of equal characteristics. Generally speaking, one finds these representations in the manuals. The

differences between the various degrees of orders are too great and too significant to reduce them to a common denominator.

In reality, according to the most ancient and universal tradition, there is only a single order or one hierarchical priesthood—that of the bishop—and two lesser participations in this order or priesthood—the presbyterate and the diaconate. When the presbyterate or the diaconate or even the subdiaconate and the minor orders are called "orders," this should not irritate us or lead us to believe that this terminology implies a reference to sacramentality.

This designation, rather, goes back to the old Latin vocabulary, which used the term *ordo* to designate a specific class of citizens that was set apart via higher office from the *populus* (people) or the *plebs* (plebian class). Tertullian uses the terms *ordo* and *plebs* to differentiate between clergy and lay people, and in the Canon of the Mass, we still use the expression: "*nos servi tui sed et plebs tua sancta*" ("we your servants and your holy people"). Let us examine the phrase "*servi tui,*" because the "servant" etymologically— if not technically—is the "deacon." As far as the terms *populus* or *plebs* (which were used for the faithful) are concerned, these terms were replaced later on by the phrase "*ordo laicorum*" (lay order). Tertullian was already using the phrase *ordo sacerdotalis* (sacerdotal order) in his day. The phrase encompassed bishops, priests, and deacons and not only differentiates between them and the laity, but also between them and the clerics, who most probably exercised lay ecclesiastical functions.

Therefore, one can see at what point our body of terminology associated with the sacrament of orders and the various (priestly or nonpriestly) orders becomes ambiguous. As the *ordo monachorum* (monastic order) and, in its wake, all of the religious "states" are folded in, then the confusion becomes complete, and one can truly understand why the Lateran and Lyon Councils in the thirteenth century suppressed the establishment of new orders. All of this was hardly done to shed clear light on the importance of a Christian hierarchical order (i.e., on the apostolic priesthood of bishops).

6. The theologians, above all the Thomists, who understand the concept of priesthood entirely from the view of sacrament and the eucharistic sacrifice, encounter serious difficulties when it becomes necessary for them to differentiate between the episcopacy and the priesthood. In the final analysis, they can only paint themselves into a corner when they rely exclusively on the power reserved to the bishop to ordain other bishops. One really cannot figure out very well precisely where one should situate this difference, except on the jurisdictional plane, when one recalls the fact that our Lord instituted the

sacrament of orders by conferring on his apostles the power to consecrate his Body and to remit sins, and that the essence of priesthood is grounded in these powers. In this case, all those in the Church who hold the power to celebrate Mass and hear confessions are actually successors of the apostles.

It is very different with the diaconate. While in the above view, bishop and priest are so similar, there is a real gap between priest and deacon. It is no longer possible to see how the deacon with his extremely truncated, virtually nonexistent sacramental powers can still command a place in the *ordo sacerdotalis* or in the hierarchy. Even after the very clear words of Pope Prus XII about the renewal of the diaconate, one still hears the phrase "lay deacon"—an expression that is an oxymoron. It is certain, however, that there are two different aspects to the sacrament of orders or of the priesthood—one aspect of oversight and one of service—which in one and the same sacrament of orders are not mutually exclusive, but rather have found their sacramental expression in two different orders.

7. In order to resolve the difficulties, some theologians postulate that the difference between the various levels of the priesthood are not of direct divine origin, but rather of ecclesiastical origin. When the Council of Trent defined that in the Church there is a divinely instituted hierarchy consisting of bishops and priests and deacons (*ministri*), it did not emphasize the various *ministries,* but rather the institution of the hierarchy by God. Thus, the problem of determining which of these "servants" would be specifically instituted by God would solve itself, since it would apply to none of them directly, with the possible exception of the bishops as direct successors of the apostles.

The differentiation among bishops, priests, and deacons meanwhile appears to us to be so ancient, so universally widespread, and so confirmed by tradition that it cannot be characterized as traceable solely back to the Church, even if its divine origin was not formally defined by the council. As far as the borderline cases that are really difficult to assess are concerned, there is, in our opinion, no cause to make these into questions of principle nor with regard to their resolution to call everything into question. Such cases are to be found in all theories, thesis constructs, and systems.

Life and reality are never fully suited to the systematization to which we subject them, and it would not be considered very wise to drop a proven law only because some individual cases stubbornly defy their inclusion. One would, thereby, replace the simple and realistic law with harsh and increasingly complicated laws, which in addition would also prove to be far less beneficial. For every law or scientific schema—as "disinterested" as it might be—is in the final analysis still only intended to be beneficial. Even the most complicated of laws will only once again run up against new exceptions, which will make theologians or other scientists tear their hair out until the end of the world.

If one steadfastly sticks with the single episcopal or apostolic priesthood, then it would not be inadmissible to think that the Church—if not directly the bishops themselves—could on the basis of circumstances or needs expand or restrict the sacramental powers of both of the lesser degrees of orders that share in their priesthood. The Church has, by the way, already done this. Could her power, therefore, also be that far-reaching that she would suppress the participation of both [lesser degrees]? For example, could she permit the episcopacy and the presbyterate to merge and suppress the diaconate, which to some extent corresponds to the current status of our Western theology? On the other hand, could she confer on deacons the power to celebrate Mass, which viewed another way would result in the demise of the diaconate? This probably would not happen. Furthermore, we know of no instance where the Church has ever proceeded in a similar way.

8. In order to comprehend the hierarchical priesthood in its true and complete importance, one must in our opinion absolutely free himself from the overly juridical conception of our current theology and return to the perhaps less-settled and, therefore, more realistic and true-to-life concept of ancient tradition and even holy Scripture. There we find, naturally, neither our Scholastic definitions of sacramental character nor the difference between ordinational power and jurisdictional power, nor even that of the seven sacraments, individually or collectively. However, we do encounter there an intense and rich, multifaceted and glowing life that conforms to some universal laws, which represent the basis for that which Scholasticism would later conceptualize (unfortunately, not always in the best sense and with complete knowledge of the original contexts).

In our judgment, it is particularly necessary to go back to that time when the term *sacerdotium* was banned from the Christian vocabulary because it was too reminiscent of the image of the Jewish and pagan priesthoods, which in both instances were associated with ritual sacrifices. These priesthoods and the sacrifices as well were rendered invalid by the single priesthood and sacrifice of the Divine Master.

There is no doubt that the priesthood existed in that sense in which it was understood by later tradition: the Master conferred upon his apostles and their successors the power "to consecrate his Body," to "give it to eat," to preside at the eucharistic meal of the disciples, and there to speak the words that celebrated the memorial of his death and his resurrection, thereby ensuring his continuing "Real Presence" among them. He also handed on to them the power to forgive sins. But in addition, the Lord also conferred many other powers and commissioned offices and "services": to teach; to proclaim the Good News to the poor; to heal the sick; to drive out demons; to baptize; to serve your brothers; to strengthen them in their faith; to watch over my flock; and so forth.

In the most ancient communities and churches, the apostles passed on the office of missionary work, of proclamation, of oversight, of presiding, of administration, and of service to certain *persons* according to a specific *rite* that consisted of the laying on of hands while invoking the Holy Spirit. All of these offices were only intended to further the mission that the apostles had received from the Lord himself and to ensure its continuity for the future. It appears absurd and anachronistic to transplant into this our distinctions between orders and jurisdiction; between jurisdiction and magisterium; between the power to teach and the power to baptize; between presiding at the eucharistic assembly and leadership of that same faith community; between the work of charity and authorized instruction in the Master's commandments of love.

9. It was not until centuries later, when confronted with the significant problem of whether or not it was necessary to baptize or ordain a second time those who had abjured the faith or had been baptized or ordained in "separated" churches, that the Church became aware of the fact that originally and validly conferred baptism and ordination was permanently valid and impressed an "indelible mark" upon the person who received it. When the question arose about unworthy or heretical servants, the Church also recognized its right to deny to those individuals the exercise of their function—"jurisdiction"—even though she did not have the power to rescind the "ordination" originally conferred.

In the meantime, the Scholastics developed their theories about "sacramental character," the distinction between "orders" and "jurisdiction," about the hierarchy in both [spheres of] power, about sacraments and sacramentals. Since, however, they dissected the sacraments and the functions of the Church into terminological and juridical concepts, they significantly diminished their deeper relationship to life and their importance. When they attributed permanent sacramental powers to orders and those of proclamation and leadership to jurisdiction, and changed charity into a moral and theological virtue, they ripped apart that which should have remained united in the exercise of one and the same function. They, thereby, weakened considerably the primary sacramental principle of Christianity as a whole, and in particular that of the Church and of the episcopacy or Christian priesthood as service in building up the Body of Christ and as an expression and continuation of the salvific work of the Lord.

"*Sacerdotium*" in its total and traditional meaning is not solely the function of sacrifice and sacrament but also that of prayer and of cultic worship, of preaching and proclamation, of presiding and leadership, of service and of charity, and of the building up of the Body of Christ—from all points of view that may be associated with these efforts.

The sacramental aspect of the Church is, so to say, only making visible her deep inner unity from the inside out; it is the symbol or sign that both expresses and makes real this unity (effective sign). This aspect, however, loses its entire significance when the reality and the spiritual unity that it wants to signify are separated from it, no longer correspond to it, or are no longer comprehended. In this case, it still only represents a ritualism, and we fall back to the level of Jewish and pagan religion. With respect to the exaggerated separation between reality and the sacraments, between Christian love and the sacraments, one can understand the reaction of Protestantism and its opposition to the "sacraments" in general, and to the sacrament of orders in particular, or better still, to the all too juridical conception of them elaborated by the theology of the Middle Ages.

10. On the other hand, if we return the priesthood to the more universal and ancient plane of the mission of proclamation entrusted by Christ to the apostles and of the service of love, as well as of the building up of the Church as the Body of Christ, and do not restrict its external side or its sacramental expression, then we also comprehend the important role of the diaconate as a hierarchical mediating "service." This lesser service, which is really a *sacramentum-persona,* must give expression to and actualize the unity of the entire Body [of Christ] on a local basis. This is accomplished not only by administering the sacraments that make this unity visible and intelligible, but also in the daily life of the community or local church, in the organization of Christian charitable works, in prayer and in public or communal worship, in proclamation and in the catechumenate—in a word, in all those areas that prepare, foster, develop, and perfect the Christian life.

The deacon, divinely instituted, should be present everywhere in service to the priest or the bishop, who directly represents Christ, as well as in the service of the faithful or the catechumens, who are to meet Christ in his Church. As a mediator between the bishop and the Christian people, he occupies in the Body of Christ a principle place, which is indispensable for unity, proper order, and harmony, and for which his *person* and the ordination conferred upon him are intended to be the very *sacrament* itself. No less so than in the time of the apostles should it be necessary today that priests and bishops be held back by "waiting on tables" from their actual mission—from "service" of "prayer" and "Word" ("Word" is to be understood here in its broadest definition in the sense of the sacred or sacramental Word). Undoubtedly, they should have overall responsibility in the name of Christ, whom they represent, but they should not allow their sacred office to get lost in or be evaluated by a host of subordinate activities or even in the arbitration of daily legal disputes. This sphere of activity, which is also "service" in its own way, should be prepared, attended to, and alleviated by a "service" functioning as an "intermediary court." This "service" should retain, however, its capacity to continue to function in its own proper sphere, whereby its importance is emphasized and rendered "effective."

11. The ancient Church was not in the dark about this. She allotted to the diaconate the highest conceivable importance and entrusted it with the greatest number of most varied tasks—in the administering of the sacraments and leading of worship services, as well as in the regulation of those matters that concerned the temporal life of the Church, especially in the organization of works of charity. Even if they possibly did err by attributing the institution of the diaconate to the text from the Acts of the Apostles, it is still certain that this institution does go back to the Apostolic period, and at the very least, it does realize a thought so often expressed by the Lord—that of "service." Even if the power to preach and to baptize, with which deacons in the Latin Church theoretically had always been vested, was conferred upon them on the basis of an erroneous interpretation of this text, it is still an expression of the high regard accorded to this office by the Church. If, on the basis of this text, the number of deacons in a church had also been limited to seven—a limitation that had considerable consequences for the diaconate—then this indicates the respect shown for this number as the symbol of unity and wholeness and, in its own way, for the sacred or "sacramental" nature of this function.

On the other hand, if we ask ourselves wherein the "essence of Christianity" lies—and for this purpose, we consult Scripture, the Gospels, the writings of the apostles, as well as church history from its beginnings—it appears to us that the simplest and closest answer is that its essence is to be found in love, in divine as well as human love: in the Love, which is God himself; in the love of

Christ, which impels us; in the Love that is greatest of all. Can we, therefore, not say that when Christ instituted—at least *in genere*—the sacrament of love or service, the diaconate, he gave us the most beautiful of all the sacraments?

12. Now, let us engage in an anachronism of our own and transfer the ancient Christian vocabulary to today's ecclesiastical offices.

We have the *episcopacy*. It is responsible for missionary work and proclamation; it is a direct successor to the office of the apostles; leads and governs the local churches and is the guarantor of their internal unity and their unity with each other; is the link to the other apostles and bishops, especially to Peter and his successors, who according to ancient tradition stand at the head of the Roman Church.

We have the *presbyterate*. Its mission is to help the bishop to be effective in his responsibilities and to represent him; it presides over the local community, whose character will vary depending on local circumstances, the concrete makeup of the faithful or catechumens, and the different social, cultural, economic, or political conditions; it is the binding force among all these layers, guarantees union with the bishop and, above him, with the whole Church, and occupies an office that, on the sacramental plane, is actualized in presiding at the eucharistic meal and in administering the other sacraments that make visible and effective this union with the Church and, through her, with Christ.

Finally, we have the *diaconate*—and here our anchronism is complete, for the diaconate is prominent only by virtue of its absence. It is available to the bishop or priest for subordinate tasks (no longer as a delegate or representative), to which they can or should not directly devote themselves; it is charged with transforming the faithful and catchumens by word, example, deed, and love; under the direction of the bishop or priest, it is responsible for the preparation of sacramental or eucharistic services, as well as the leadership of the community participating in their concrete Christian life in this world. It is the bond of living union between everyday Christian life and sacramental life that gives expression to and actualizes this union—the bond of union among the faithful themselves in love and between them and their local leader or shepherd, who for his part is the link to the universal Church and to Christ, whom he represents directly.

13. What is the meaning of the tenets about sacramental character and the difference between orders and jurisdiction? Sacramental character reminds the faithful as well as the ministers about the permanent and basically indelible "character of the sacramental or ordinational gift," which God confers on certain persons when they enter the Church at baptism and confirmation, or

when they accept a special task in the Church through the diaconate, presbyterate, or episcopacy. It also reminds them in the same way about serious and decisive "character" of the personal commitment that accompanies the acceptance of this gift or the entrance into these orders.

The distinction between orders and jurisdiction reminds the faithful and office-bearers alike that the Church received from Christ, in the apostles and their successors, the power "to loose and to bind" on earth, and that Christ himself, glorified in heaven but present at all times in the Church through his Spirit, ratifies in heaven that which his Church on earth decides. The Church must watch over the retention of the true faith, sound morals, and unity. She can bind the consciences of her faithful and her shepherds by ecclesiastical regulations. As needs or circumstances warrant, she can limit, broaden, restrict, or combine the exercise of sacramentally conferred offices when unworthy or incompetent servants endanger her divine work.

All theologians agree that orders and jurisdiction should normally be joined together in one and the same person. In actuality, however, the differences and divisions between the spheres of power—orders without jurisdiction and jurisdiction without orders—have become so numerous and so varied that the one essential—*office* conferred by *ordination*—has almost lost its significance.

This sacramental significance, in which some contemporary theologians—rightly so, in our opinion—see the substance of the sacrament instituted by Christ, is barely visible anymore in the eyes of the simple faithful, not to mention the unbelievers. One needs a trained eye (that of a theologian) to be able to see past the brush (of countless ecclesiastical institutions) through to the real trees (divine institutions) that reach down into the earth (the foundation in Christ) and support the forest (the Church), if we may be permitted to use here this somewhat unique image.

We would like to illustrate this even more clearly by using some concrete, real-life examples. A priest is explaining to the faithful or even to some children what the sacrament of orders and its various levels in the Church are. He is immediately bombarded with questions: What is a Cardinal? an archbishop? an archimandrite? a patriarch? a metropolitan? an episcopal co-adjutor? a vicar general? an apostolic vicar? an apostolic prefect? a nuncio? a legate? an apostolic delegate? an archpriest? a cathedral rector? a dean? a pastor? a chaplain? a vicar? What is a father? a brother? a monk? a prior? a guardian? an abbot? a provinicial? a general? and last—but not least—a sister? a reverend mother?

Other examples: They explain to the faithful that the most important task of a priest consists in presiding at the eucharistic meal, where they would be with their Master, and in preparing them for worthy participation in this Meal (which is essentially a "communal" affair) by baptism, confirmation, religious and moral instruction, the forgiveness of sins, and so forth. Why then do they ordain priests and even bishops, whose only visible priestly role consists of the daily celebration of a eucharistic meal, at which they *alone* are the presiders, ministers, and table guests? When we approach such a priest or bishop to seek forgiveness for our sins, why do we receive the answer: Please forgive me, but I do not have jurisdiction . . .? Can one imagine the sometimes very unfriendly thoughts that the faithful have about these poor priests "without jurisdiction"?

Oh, this religious ignorance of the faithful! They do not even know how to differentiate between orders and office! They do not understand what orders are and what jurisdiction is! They do not see the difference between a sacrament and a power! One has to admit, however, that we really make the task very difficult for them. What is the meaning of orders, to which no office is assigned? On the other hand, how does one justify a legitimately important office that does not correspond to orders? Why are orders conferred without the power to exercise them? What sense does a sacrament make when it does not correspond to reality in concrete [everyday] life?

14. Fortunately—or unfortunately—for the diaconate this task is not as difficult. Most of the faithful do not even know that such an office—excuse me!—such an order exists!

Let us return to theological seriousness. The diaconate, we said, is a sacramental order; therefore, it is not an independent sacrament but, rather, the lesser participation in a single sacrament, in that of priestly or episcopal orders.

Does the diaconate imprint a sacramental character? Most theologians—at least implicitly—accept this. Not all however! Fr. Bouessé is of the opinion that the presbyterate alone (for him, according to the Thomistic view, the priesthood in the literal sense) imprints an indelible character; neither the diaconate nor the episcopacy can confer this character, since neither carries with it the essential function of the priesthood, the power over the eucharistic Body of Christ.

This strikes us as illogical. Even for St. Thomas, the lesser participation [minor orders] in the *sacerdotium-presbyteratus* imprints an indelible character. And when we consider the *sacerdotium-episcopatus,* in line with the ancient and traditional point of view, as office in the fullest sense, and view the presbyterate and diaconate as lesser sacramental participations in this office, then the illogicality is even greater. These offices are sacramentally conferred irrevocably, for life at least, and therefore, appear to impress upon their bearers an indelible character. In the opinions of E. Seiterich and Schillebeeckx, with whom we agree in this matter, the character of the deacon or priest is not an independent character anyway but, rather, a lesser participation in the priestly character of the bishop.

Does the order of deacon carry a jurisdiction with it? The only jurisdiction accorded to the deacon under current law is that of assisting the priest during the solemn celebration of Mass (a subdeacon must also be present, except in the missions) and that of singing the Gospel and the *"Ite missa est."* Furthermore, he also has the "restricted" jurisdiction to preach, to baptize, and to distribute communion (i.e., in order to exercise these rights, he needs special permission from the priest or the bishop). In this small example, one can gauge just how artificial and lifeless our sacramental theology and practices may have become.

What would the kind of jurisdiction be that would normally be associated with the office of an independent deacon? It would have to encompass all the mediating functions between bishops and priests on the one hand and the faithful on the other hand, as these functions devolve upon them in the liturgical sphere and in the concrete organization of the Christian community. Established along broad lines by a universal legislative framework, this jurisdiction should also be able to adjust flexibly to special conditions, as deemed necessary by local churches, bishops as well as priests, depending upon the special circumstances of different countries and epochs, civilizations, and mentalities.

For it appears evident to us that the jurisdiction of the deacon must always be subordinated to that of the bishop and even of the priest. In the past, some deacons exercised an inordinate jurisdiction (the archdeacon, the cardinal-deacon) that overshadowed that of the priests and even of some bishops. This is illogical. The fact, however, that the jurisdiction of the deacon has been reduced to practically zero makes no sense either.

15. How did it happen that the divinely instituted diaconate in the Latin Church lost at least its function and its significance, if not its place? There is here, to be sure, a theological admonition that cannot be suppressed by the nicest apologies and justifications of manifold ecclesiastical institutions.

The diaconate, which was so significant in the Church, was ever so slowly gnawed away from above and below, until all that was left of it was the ritual skeleton of a faded greatness. In this respect, it is to a certain degree a mirror image of our liturgy, with whose fate it is closely associated. When the Latin liturgy reached that stage in which it was prematurely viewed as completed and final, it could no longer adjust to the rhythm of the civilizations of the converted mission countries with their new linguistic, cultural, social, economic, and political circumstances. The liturgical role of the deacon, just like the liturgy itself, had stagnated in immobility.

However, the decline of the diaconate preceded that of the liturgy and affected, above all, its social or administrative function. According to St. Jerome, as early as the fourth century, the diaconate, even though lesser in orders than the priesthood, had become greater in dignity and wealth. The cardinal-deacon, the archdeacon, the apocrisiary or legate replaced the simple, subordinate mediating role of the deacon between priest and people. On the other hand, his function was gradually absorbed by others in similarly mediating functions—by the lector, psalmist, porter, subdeacon, grave-digger, acolyte, master of ceremonies, regular cleric or canon, religious, lay helper. The diaconate lost its significance, because it lost its function.

Later the various orders and religious congregations at least partially took over the caritative, *kerymatic,* or liturgical tasks of the diaconate. But these institutions settled in, so to speak, on the periphery of the Church, responded only to particular needs, and busied themselves primarily with "their" tasks. They no longer attended to the liturgical service of the deacon in the Church; nor did they see themselves as the link between active love of neighbor and the altar, which was the most significant and characteristic function of the diaconate. The missionary movement created other mediating functions: catechists and the various lay helpers (religious and nonreligious). Still later, the Catholic Action movements, as a countercurrent to what had become an all too individualistic Catholicism, founded their core circles and raised the theological problem of the "participation of the laity in the apostolate of hierarchy"—an obvious contradiction correctly rejected by Pius XII. The Liturgical Movement, for its part, created still other mediating offices in the justifiable desire to render eucharistic celebrations more lively and to convince the laity to participate more actively.

It occurred to none of these movements that their "new" creation replaced something that had been instituted by God himself: the diaconate. It took the chaos of the last war, the extreme shortage of priests, and the deep gulf between the clergy and the faithful before it was realized, at least in one country—in Germany—that a diaconate instituted by God still existed. It would be able to fill in these gaps, and the question should be asked about the possibility of awakening this ancient traditional institution to new life.

What should one conclude from this? The cardinalate, the archdiaconate, the nunciature, the canonicate, the minor orders, the religious orders and congregations, the core circles of Catholic Action and missionary activity, the liturgical mediating offices, in short, all ecclesiastical institutions, each in its own way and in its own time, skinned, thrashed, dispossessed, or replaced the diaconate—that singular divine institution that had been chosen to perform the "service" of mediation. Would not this be reason enough to ask ourselves whether or not we deserve, just a little, the same reproach that our Lord directed to the Jews: "You have a fine way of rejecting the commandment of God in order to keep your tradition"?

16. Should we risk further criticism of the ecclesiastical institutions? This would soon begin to resemble strongly that which the Reformers wrote in their day. But we believe along with H. Kung that a little criticism does no harm, and that its better to have this criticism come from within rather than from without. Now that the passions and interconfessional controversies have to a large extent subsided, perhaps there would be no better method of church reform than to read with a clear head the works of the Committee of the 100 (*Centuriatoren*) of Magdeburg and examine them in the light of the annals of church history. By doing so, we could ascertain if any of their criticisms contained correct ideas.

The fall of the diaconate remains an open question today. Ten, even a hundred ecclesiastical institutions have unfortunately displaced a divine institution. How do things stand with the other divine institutions and their functions?

Let us begin with ourselves, with the monks, so as not to arouse any indignation. Monks have assumed the responsibility of looking after one of the primary functions of the Church and of the hierarchy, the service of cultic worship and of prayer, and have converted it into a para-ecclesiastical institution. The service of the word was to be sure the first and most significant task of the hierarchical priesthood, which we equated with the episcopacy. One religious order has taken over an ancient title reserved to this episcopacy, that of the *ordo praedicatorum* [Order of Preachers], and transformed this office into an ecclesiastical institution. The *ordo presbyterorum* [order of presbyters] saw itself for its part relegated to a second-class status and stunted by an array of religious orders and priestly congregations, which called themselves "clerical orders" (a wonderful tautology!). Once again, these religious orders and congregations at the periphery of the Church and the hierarchy took over numerous priestly tasks and converted them into para-ecclesiastical institutions.

We do not need to discuss the diaconate any further. Its functions—once more on the periphery of the Church—have been confiscated by the canons regular, the Order of Friars Minor, the congregations and works of *Caritas,* the Catholic Action movements, and the new liturgical mediating offices. With that, there remains only one indisputably divine institution left: the laity, which is grounded in the Christian sacraments of baptism and confirmation. It, too, has been devalued by an impressive array of institutes, para-ecclesiastical congregations, by third orders, oblates, leagues, legions, vows, promises, actions, tasks, duties, and so forth. How can one possibly look through this forest of ecclesiastical (or better para-ecclesiastical) institutions to those simple and genuine "orders" of the Church, which were instituted by Christ: episcopacy, presbyterate, diaconate, and laity?

17. The apologists of Catholicism generally characterize all of these institutions as successful reforms of faltering institutions. This assertion appears to us to be very dangerous. If every "reform" has as its starting point the establishment of a new institution to replace or compete with existing institutions, as was the case in the past for all practical purposes, then it can no longer be foreseen where this movement will stop and what will finally be left of the original Christian institutions, which are indisputably of divine origin.

The many existing para-ecclesiastical movements, especially the religious institutes, generally behave as though they were continuing to care for and actualize the requisite function of "prophetic mission" in the Church. In the Church, there must always be a "prophetic mission," a "contradiction," or a "criticism." However, as soon as "prophetic mission" or "contradiction" creates its own existential framework, it forfeits *eo ipso* its prophetic function. This is so not only because their existence as discrete institutions weakens and overshadows the importance of much older institutions; once the prophetic enthusiasm has waned, these new forms established in place of or alongside of the old ones begin to manifest the same human shortcomings and weaknesses. Will new institutions endlessly be created to overcome the shortcomings of the old ones?

True prophetic mission and true contradiction produce their effects in the heart of the Church and do not create on the periphery new forms and institutions that, at first, may be beneficial but often also produce a goodly share of arrogance, presumptuousness, and human vanity. One has created "his own" work—but is it God's work? Genuine prophetic mission is always at work in the Church to animate the divine institutions—not to transform them, not to replace them with others, but rather to adapt them continually to the exigencies of the Church and of the world. Old Dollinger, who was largely responsible for the Old Catholic schism, always refused to join this movement, repeatedly confronting his old friends with this rejoinder: *reformatio fiat intra ecclesiam* [reform is accomplished *within* the Church]!

The Church received from Christ a specific limited number of institutions and means of salvation, which she must have ready for humankind, in order for them to be able to participate in his work of redemption. She is to transmit these genuine values, and not a whole lot of extraneous and incidental things, to all peoples according to the mission she was given. In so doing, she is not free to alter, suppress, or replace the means of salvation in their essential content or in their intended sense.

These means and institutions must, however, be translated into the languages of all peoples and adapted to the customs and cultures of all lands. The true prophetic mission must be preserved in this adaptation, and not in the endless creation of new systems and forms. In order to make this obvious, the hierarchical orders and the sacraments instituted by Christ must be given preeminence; they must carry out their God-given mission and must be reestablished in their true significance. The inevitable consequence thereof would be that all of those secondary institutions would have to be relentlessly set aside if and to that extent that they infringe upon these means of salvation, reduce their effectiveness, or complicate and cloud their significance.

18. One final conclusion, which concerns theology itself, needs to be mentioned here. Dollinger had hoped that theology in the Church would fulfill a prophetic mission, before which the hierarchy would constantly have to bow. There is some truth in that, to the extent that the hierarchy, comprised of fallible human beings, must also be reminded about their specific mission. The hierarchy, however, also cannot harass theology—in contrast to what Dollinger was trying to do—by creating a kind of public opinion that requires one to believe that everything that exists in the Church is justified, ordained, unchangeable, untouchable, and irreformable.

When we consider the huge number of folio volumes, encyclopedias, dissertations, manuals, collected works, and theological periodicals, we cannot suppress an uneasy feeling. Why are all these necessary? What practical use do they have for human life and for human institutions? What influence do they have if one considers them in light of their value with respect to Christian witness or their power to attract? What spirit of life is released by them? What syntheses, what principles, and what conclusions emerge from them?

When the "initiated" intrudes into this "secret region" and looks around a bit, then this feeling of uneasiness only increases. What a mess of subtleties, disputes, and tricky gimmicks of legal, historical, and archaeological scholarship! And again one asks the question: *Ad quid* [to what end]? What influence does all of this have on the concrete life of the Church, of believers, and of nonbelievers? Such an expenditure of effort should have indeed deserved a better objective!

This entire theology clings in confusion to a past, in which the common people have hopelessly little interest. Human beings live in a concrete present and think about the future. Over against this, this kind of theology seeks only to prove, justify, and defend a bunch of completely obsolete or barely supportable theses and institutions, with which humankind does not even know how to begin and which they, at best, humorously consider to be outmoded curiosities.

Does not theology have any other task to carry out? Did not Pope Pius XII also speak about public opinion? One hears everywhere that this public opinion is badly informed, yes even that people do not know the Church, its true mission, its goal, and the meaning of its dogmas and institutions. Could not theology exercise a little prophetic mission here?

All of the experts in the fields of warfare, politics, economics, social reform, and public life maintain—or, at least in practice, act according to the principle—that attack is the best defense. Do not the Church and theology have a battle to fight? Why do they hide behind a timid defense? behind constantly ill-fated, outdated apologetics? behind a paralyzing conservatism? That was not the behavior of the first Christians and the martyrs or true witnesses for Christ, or of the saints and genuine prophets of all times. They went, as their Master had told them to do, from house to house, from city to city, into the synagogues and into the public places; they preached on the rooftops. Should not theology in the same way climb down from its pedestal of Scholastic subtleties or historical scholarship and preach a little more "on the rooftops"?

As far as our war-like intentions are concerned, our "enemies" can rest easy. We have not targeted their pocketbook, their politics, economics, civilization, their technical progress, their philosophy, or their science. The only thing that we are emphatically pursuing is to bring to them the Good News of the Gospel. Even here, they are free in conscience to accept or reject this message. In the words of the Master, if they do not wish to listen to us, we are free to shake the dust off our shoes and to preach elsewhere.

This message, however, must be simply, clearly, and concretely understandable both within the Church as well as outside of it. Would it not be a nice "prophetic" task for theology to free the message of the Gospel and its simplicity from all of the historical, apologetic, legal, and scholastic stuff in which it has been buried, just for the fun of it, in order to make it unrecognizable and undiscoverable? Do we do theology a disservice when we assert that they have buried the pearl in a haystack, and that their most urgent task is to go look for it there again, so that it can once more shine before the eyes of everyone?

Let us return once more to our diaconate that tiny light, which has stood all too long beneath the basket but, fortunately, has not yet been extinguished! Could not theology see a very beautiful, very fitting, and—for the Church and for the world—a very beneficial task for itself in pointing out the greatness of this simple service of living love of neighbor? in emphasizing anew its divine origin? in accentuating its powerful effectiveness during the early centuries of Christianity? in confronting the abuses, negligence, and illegal usurpations that brought about its decline? To continue, theology could also facilitate the work of its restoration by not strangling it in a chaos of scholastic and legal terminology; by not constraining its unfolding right at the outset with emphasis on the danger of a possible deviation from true teaching or moral apprehensions; by not allowing this divine matter to be subordinated to the rights of human or ecclesiastical institutions; by clearing away all those outdated impediments that, while valid in their day, are no longer significant today; by emphasizing contemporary viewpoints of a service that fosters interpersonal contact between the faithful and pastors and sees therein the possibilities for building up a Christian community. Theology could recognize in the diaconate a service that would contrast the cold exercise of official charitable works or the paper statutes of lifeless organisms with the concrete reality of direct person-to-person contact in word and deed, in gift and sacrament; give clear expression to the sacramental significance of an inviolable degree of the ecclesiastical hierarchy; and, finally, connect this sacramental significance to the words, example, and mission of Him, who said: "I did not come to be served, but to serve."

On March 22, 1961, the renowned German theologian Karl Rahner, SJ, was named a consultor for the Second Vatican Council Preparatory Commission on the Administration of the Sacraments. Special attention was to be paid to questions concerning the diaconate, on which Rahner was considered to be an expert.

As reflected in the five articles in this volume that precede Rahner's work, the movement calling for the restoration of the permanent diaconate had generated considerable momentum in the two decades that preceded the Council, especially among those who had been associated with German Caritas, a church structure closely akin to our Catholic Charities. Rahner first came into contact with this movement in 1948. He was intrigued with the prospects that a renewed diaconate, opened to fathers of families, could offer to the Church and the renewal of the its ministry.

Rahner's contribution to the preparation of Lumen Gentium *has been considered by those who were on the scene to have been enormous. Deacons the world over will always remain in his debt for the construction of a theology of the diaconate that will endure among the foundational documents upon which the restoration and renewal of the diaconate as a lifetime ministry, opened to married men, has prospered.*

The three articles that follow were translated from the original German and first published in Theological Investigations.

Samuel M. Taub

The Theology of
the Restoration of the Diaconate

by Karl Rahner, SJ

The following systematic exposition of the doctrine of the diaconate in the Church—its meaning, its justification, and the reasons for advocating the restoration of the diaconate, including the manner in which this restoration might roughly be conceived—presupposes certain investigations on the diaconate from the point of view of biblical theology, history, and the

Magisterium and does not intend to repeat these here. It is, nevertheless, obvious (in the light of the essential methodology of Catholic theology) that systematic investigations in Catholic theology cannot be anything else but the systematization of what is known from historical revelation and, therefore, by means of the historical studies of theology and the doctrinal definitions of the Church's *Magisterium*. Should the reader, therefore, ask for proofs in the course of our explanation—proofs that are not explicitly given here—then we would refer him tacitly but emphatically to the other chapters of this book.

1. Concerning the Legitimacy of the Question about the Restoration of the Diaconate

(a) The problem of the legitimacy of the question about the restoration of the diaconate refers to the question as to whether it is in any way justifiable and has any sense in practice to make the possibility of the restoration of the diaconate in the Latin Church the subject of an investigation that is not purely theoretical and has some practical significance. For one might be of the opinion that the prevailing practice in the Latin Church today, and what the Church does and avoids as a result of it, is itself already a compelling argument for the view that this practice is not merely one among many possibles but is also the best possible one, since it has been formed by the experience of many centuries, and since its untroubled acceptance over many centuries has been considered something self-evident by the Church. It might seem, therefore, that it is no longer possible right from the start to pose any serious practical question regarding some other, opposed practice. This is the reason why this first Section will attempt to give a systematic explanation on this point of the legitimacy of posing our question at all.

(b) Presuppositions for the answer of this first question:

(i) The diaconate is a part of that office or *"ordo"* which Christ gave to the Church when he founded her; the diaconate as an ordination, or transmission of an office, belongs to those rites for the transmission of office, which Christ instituted in and for the Church by a proper *sacrament,* no matter how we may conceive this institution more exactly.[1] The sacramental nature of orders in general, and also the sacramental nature of the order of the diaconate in particular, can be presupposed here as proved from the positive sources and the doctrinal pronouncements made by the Church's *Magisterium.* As far as the sacramental nature of the diaconate is concerned, the present thesis is at least *"sententia certa et communis."*

(ii) The proposition concerning the sacramental nature of the diaconate refers to the ordination rite for this office (together with its powers and duties), an office which has been called the diaconate and has existed and been exercised under this name from the very beginning in the Church (i.e., from apostolic times) right up to the present time. It is indeed true that the more exact conception of the office going under this name, with its duties and its rights, shows quite considerable differences in various periods and regions of the Church. Yet anyone desirous of affirming not merely verbally but in very truth that the diaconate is a sacrament given to the Church by Christ will have to concede that all those who possessed this office in apostolic times and this for longer periods and in wider regions of the Church were real deacons, in spite of and with the greater or lesser differences in the office actually exercised by them; he will have to concede furthermore that those who held office under the name of deacons received their powers by a real sacramental ordination. The quite considerable differences in their official duties do not pose any real difficulty even as far as the unity and sacramental nature of this office and of its rite of transmission are concerned. For in spite of their differences, all these official duties coincide in the fact that, on the negative side, they do not include any rights pertaining to the real power of ruling in the Church and consequently also do not include the proper function of the priestly office which consists in the offering of the eucharistic sacrifice, while on the positive side they signify all those activities that assist the actual leaders of the Church in the fulfillment of their *own* office as such. In other words, the historically speaking very different functions of deacons are nevertheless of the one nature, *viz.* to help those who direct the Church, an assistance that does not usurp or replace the function of these leaders but supports its exercise by those who actually direct the Church herself. All assistance of this kind can basically be a factor in the office belonging to deacons and can, therefore, be rendered possible by that grace that is or can be given by the sacramental ordination of deacons. Even though in this way all such assistance falls both in the nature of things and as a matter of principle into the sphere of the diaconate, the Church can (as she actually did) lay special emphasis on one or other of these ways of assisting as the needs of the times may demand or take it out of the sphere of the powers of the diaconate given by the sacrament or leave it in that sphere—as it were—but keep it dormant (as she in fact did, for instance, in the case of certain powers of other grades of orders, such as a simple priest's power to confirm). All this leaves the nature of the diaconate intact, on the following three conditions: (1) There must remain the one function of assisting those who direct the Church in a task proper to these "directors," a task that consequently belongs to the officeholders in the

Church in contrast to the layman. (2) This office of assisting must basically and in itself be intended as a *permanent* task, since it would not be reasonable that a diaconate, whose sacramental nature and whose character cannot be lost, should of itself be given as a function conceived from the very start as something merely transitory. (3) This office of service and assistance must in fact be of fairly great importance since, according to the testimony of the history and practice of the Church in all ages, lesser degrees of such assistance have always been given in the Church, either permanently or in passing, by men who were neither called deacons in the strict sense of the word nor were appointed and equipped for such an assisting function by sacramental ordination.

(iii) The diaconate can indeed be a "step" by which someone ascends to the priesthood, at least in the *particular* sense that, as is proved especially by the teaching and practice of the Latin Church, the Church transmits a higher office to someone only after she has given him the lower office of the diaconate. This practice, however, is not essential but rather accidental to the diaconate; it is in principle based rather on the common human circumstance that the good exercise of a lower function often shows that the officeholder concerned is suitable for a higher function and thus can be called to this higher office. For the practice of the ancient Church proves that the diaconate was in no way merely regarded as a step on the way to the priesthood but rather that it was looked upon as a positively permanent office in the Church. This can also be seen from the very nature of things. If their characteristic function is properly understood, an office and a task that are necessary for a society and that are differentiated in this society from other offices are not just a step towards a higher office but can certainly be given to someone without thereby also transmitting to this office-bearer the capacity and the right of passing on to a higher office. Indeed, it may be that the nature of such an office is so different from that of another that the efficient exercise of the one does not yet prove to any appreciable extent that the holder is suitable for another higher office. It is in this light that we must interpret the proposition stating that the diaconate is the step by which one proceeds to the priesthood. If all this proposition is meant to state is that the Latin Church does not in fact ordain anyone to the priesthood unless she has first ordained him deacon, then this is a self-evident proposition. It would be an absolutely false proposition, however, if it is meant to imply that in the very nature of things the Church can ordain someone to the priesthood only after his ordination to the diaconate, as if the latter were a necessary presupposition for ordination to the priesthood (just as confirmation presupposes baptism), or that the diaconate is of its very essence the human testing of the moral and religious suitability of a candidate for the priesthood, or that someone can be suited for the diaconate only if he is also suited for and called to the priesthood. For the office of presbyter can be given validly even without previous ordination to the diaconate. This affirmation does not, of course, say anything against the present-day practice of the Church—a practice established in law—of only ordaining deacons to the priesthood. The hitherto existing practice of leaving only a very short interval of time between ordination to the diaconate and ordination to the priesthood does not give the impression that the diaconate is a means for testing the suitability of a candidate for the priesthood. The official duties of a deacon, properly and fully understood, are so different from those of a priest that suitability for the diaconate does not of itself signify any suitability for the priesthood, and thus this also need not be demanded of the deacon as such. To this extent, the diaconate does not have of its very nature the character of a step to the priesthood, except in the sense that (for reasons to be given later) the priesthood includes the powers of the diaconate *eminenter* and that, in fact, only those who are already deacons are ordained to the priesthood.

(c) The question about the restoration of the diaconate understood in this way (i.e., the question as to whether it is possible and advisable to restore the office and the transmission of the office of deacon in the Latin Church without the persons so ordained being ordained from the outset precisely as candidates for a later ordination to the priesthood) is a legitimate question for the following reasons:

(i) First of all, it would be wrong to maintain that the Church's present-day practice and legislation concerning the diaconate conceived merely as a step to the priesthood are absolutely universal. For the practice and legislation of the Latin Church does not by itself constitute the practice of the universal Church. In the Uniate Oriental churches there has been up to this day a diaconate that is more than merely a step to the priesthood. If one keeps this fact in mind and does full justice to it, then the practice of the Latin Church can at the most be taken as an argument for maintaining that at certain times in certain circumstances a diaconate considered merely as a step towards the priesthood was a possibility and perhaps also opportune. The Latin practice, however, proves neither that it is the only possible or lawful one, nor that it is and will remain the most opportune practice for all future ages and circumstances.

(ii) The fact that this practice endured for centuries likewise does not prove that it is to be advocated for the present age and for all future ages. As we know from church history, there have been many practices and customs in the Church which were fairly universal and of quite long duration without it being possible to conclude from this fact to their observance also in other and later ages and circumstances. The practice of admitting the laity only rarely to the Eucharist, and only under conditions unnecessarily difficult to fulfil, existed for centuries. For centuries during the patristic age, there was a practice and precept in the Latin Church by which certain sinners were admitted only once to sacramental ecclesiastical penance. For centuries there was a practice of granting indulgences for gifts of money to pious purposes. For many centuries it was not necessary for the validity of a marriage that it should be contracted in the presence of a priest. Furthermore, it must be borne in mind that the present-day practice concerning the diaconate has developed, without much thought and without any really explicit decisions, from historical conditions that no longer necessarily apply today. Basically, even within the present-day legislation of the Latin Church, a deacon need not be *ipso facto* debarred from the exercise of the powers and rights of his diaconate, if, after his ordination, he does not allow himself to be ordained to the priesthood; this fact is further proof that at best the present-day practice can be put forward only with extreme caution and many reservations when one is arguing about the best and most recommendable practice and legislation for the Church of today. Hence, even in practice it is really possible and legitimate to pose the question about the restoration of the diaconate in al seriousness.

2. Remarks about the Mutual Relationship between the Individual Offices in the Church

(a) As has already been said, we presuppose that positive theology has proved with regard to the diaconate that the ordination to the diaconate is a sacrament in the sense of being part of the sacrament of orders in the Church. This, however, does not as yet provide a sufficiently clear explanation of the relationship between the diaconate and the priesthood, a clarification that however is the necessary presupposition for any really adequate answer to many questions necessarily connected with the problem of the restoration of the diaconate. It is impossible, therefore, to avoid this question about the exact relationship between the priesthood and the diaconate completely, however much in this answer will remain uncertain and debatable for lack of magisterial pronouncements and on account of the obscurity of the history of the primitive Church.

(b) In view of the account of the election and constitution of the Seven (even if we want to or must understand them as deacons), and in order to do full justice to the considerable differences in structure of the "churches" in apostolic times, as well as for other reasons that cannot be explained here, it will be impossible to suppose that the tripartition of this office in the Church (i.e., the episcopal office, the sacerdotal office, and the office of deacon) goes back directly to the explicit will of the historical Jesus before or after the Resurrection. This does not deny the *ius divinum* of these three kinds or steps of this office. We will be perfectly free to suppose that Jesus instituted this office in the Church and gave it to her even with regard to these three steps *in the sense* that he gave the apostolic college with St. Peter at its head all those powers and faculties, duties and rights, which are either given necessarily (even without explicit declaration) together with the nature of the Church founded by him or which have also been explicitly declared to be such by him (e.g., with regard to the power of constituting certain sacraments); we will be quite free to suppose that with this institution of the Church as a perfect society, this office has also been given the right to transmit the power of office, to other later bearers of this office, in accordance with the practical needs of various places and times, either completely or merely to a certain limited degree.

The apostles obviously already made use of this possibility in the primitive Church, at least in the commission they gave to the Seven (who clearly were not given all the powers and responsibilities of the apostles themselves), in the commissioning of deacons who clearly did not possess all the powers proper to those who in this connection are called ἐπίσκοποι, and in the commissioning of a supreme collegial or monarchic authority in the individual "congregations" during the lifetime of the apostles, which supreme authority was obviously not given the fullness of the powers of an apostle in the proper sense. The variability of such partial transmissions of offices in the primitive Church surely shows that the apostles were conscious of the fact that they were not bound by any fixed stipulations made by Jesus regarding this distribution of the one total office present in and given to the Church by Christ in accordance with her nature, at least not by any stipulations beyond the appointment of the apostolic college with Peter at its head and the continued existence of this college through the authoritative transmission of its permanent powers. The same thing will then apply also to the official transmission rite of such an office. Basically, the transmission of an office in the Church is a sacrament at least where it concerns that office in its innermost being as sanctifying rather than sovereign power, and it remains sacramental, even if only part of this one office in the Church is transmitted, as long as the Church does not have a contrary intention in transmitting such a part-office of lesser extent (always under the general presuppositions, of course, which must necessarily be present for the existence of a sacrament, presuppositions arising either out of its own nature or out of the presuppositions of the intention in sacramental distribution as laid down by the Church herself). It is easy to see from this that, to start with, the consecration of a bishop must be regarded absolutely as a sacrament (in spite of the medieval attack on this proposition), presupposing of course that it is not to be supposed that all the *potestates ordinis* are already given by ordination to the priesthood but in a "tied up" form which is "untied" in a liturgical manner only by the sacramental of an episcopal consecration. It also becomes clear from the above consideration that the transmission of that part of the Church's office which is certainly the office of the priest communicates such an important part of that office in the Church that even this partial transmission of an office preserves the fundamental character of the Church's nature. This explains also why Tradition has always credited the ordination of a deacon with a sacramental nature. It makes us realize that the medieval theory of the sacramental nature of the subdiaconate and of the minor orders is not necessarily false, and that conversely the currently almost common conception of these orders can nevertheless be also correct, since it ultimately depends simply on the will of the Church whether or not she only associates a very modest part of her universal office, and the official rite of its transmission, with her will to administer a sacrament.

(c) What we have seen so far already enables us to make certain important statements with regard to the diaconate. In our apologetics concerning the restoration of the diaconate, we must first of all be careful (if what has just been said is true) not to proceed too simply and without sufficient qualifications from the fact that the diaconate as found in the Church is a sacrament. This thesis is indeed correct, insofar as the actually administered ordination to the diaconate is undoubtedly a sacrament. The diaconate is also certainly a sacrament willed by God *insofar as* the Church can give a separate transmission of the limited part of her office given in the diaconate and can transmit this part also by a sacrament. It is probably not absolutely certain, however, that the Church must always adopt such a tripartition of this office for all times, and so could not simply abolish the diaconate (i.e., could not transmit these official functions in such a way that they would always be given to a determined subject only together with the priestly powers). It is of course quite conceivable (and we have no intention of denying it here) that the tripartition of this office which was made by the apostles themselves during the apostolic age (even if it was not explicitly prescribed by Christ himself) nevertheless binds the later Church absolutely and that in this sense the diaconate is therefore *iuris divini* not only in content and possibility but also in its separate existence from the priesthood.[2] But since this cannot be maintained with absolute certainty, it is also impossible to state absolutely and categorically that the separate existence of the rights and duties of the diaconate in a separate office was laid down by Christ and thus binds the Church for always. It cannot be demanded categorically by this fact alone that the real diaconate should be restored, simply because the Latin Church is thought to be only fulfilling this obligation in appearances, as it were, by its particular form of diaconate as merely a fleeting step leading to the priesthood and not an office that endures and is really exercised in its own right. We will see later on that one can still appeal for the restoration of a really exercised and sacramentally administered diaconate even without using this oversimplified argument. Furthermore, we have already touched above on the fact that it is quite conceivable that at one time the official powers of the minor orders and of the subdiaconate used to be transmitted by a sacramental ordination, without it being necessary to hold for this reason alone that the constitution of these offices should still be a sacrament in the Church even today. It is impossible at least in principle clearly to exclude that possibility since there are also other similar cases that at least may be interpreted in this sense. For instance, the possibility of the Apostolic See giving a simple priest the faculty of confirming and perhaps even the faculty of ordaining priests can at least be interpreted in this way, without anything being essentially altered by the fact that in both cases it is presupposed at the very least that the subject invested extra-sacramentally with this new faculty must be an ordained priest. For it could equally well be conceived in other cases that baptism (or confirmation) are sufficient presuppositions for the possibility of a similar extra-sacramental transmission of the official powers of the minor orders and the subdiaconate, even though these can be given also by a sacramental rite; in short, it is quite conceivable that the manner of transmission depends to a certain extent on the will of the Church. We do in actual fact see that, particularly in the case of the diaconate, such a possibility must be taken into account. For it will hardly be possible to point to any function of the diaconate which the Church could not in any way bestow by an extra-sacramental authorization, and yet no one can dispute the fact that the ordination to the diaconate, by which such powers are actually conferred, is a sacrament. We must, therefore, basically recognize the fact that there can be offices in the Church that can indeed be conferred by a sacramental rite but which do not necessarily need to be conferred in this way, so that the exact manner of conferring them (whether it be sacramental or nonsacramental) depends on the will and the (implicit or explicit) intention of the Church. The recognition of this fact is not merely negatively significant for the question of the restoration of the diaconate by pointing out that one must not be *too* quick to conclude immediately from the possibility of a sacramental conferring of an office to an absolutely strict obligation on the Church to transmit the office concerned in a sacramental manner. Such an immediate inference is valid only for the totality of such transmissions of this office in the Church, in as much as one can certainly say with absolute certainty that the Church does not have the right to abolish altogether the sacramental transmission of an office (i.e., the sacrament of orders). But this is surely all we can conclude from the above. There is, however, also a positive side to this recognition that gives us an argument for the restoration of the diaconate. For if the above recognition is correct, then the way is absolutely open to us to reckon with the possibility that the office of deacon can exist also in a form in which it is not conferred in a sacramental manner. It is, in other words, the duty of theologians to have a look around the Church to see whether this office does not already actually exist and is not already actually exercised there as an office distinct from the priesthood, without it being also conferred for this reason alone by a sacramental rite. This is a genuine possibility especially because, according to what has been said previously, it cannot be postulated *a priori* that such an, as it were, anonymous deacon must already possess absolutely *all* those faculties that the Church grants at present to her already sacramentally ordained deacons (e.g., the right to administer solemn baptism and the right to distribute holy communion). For if, as we have said, the Church has the fundamental right to use her own discretion in giving someone a certain share in her universal office, then such a determinate participation can in certain circumstances still fulfil the nature of the diaconate even if certain particular powers are not included in this participation. It will soon become clear what exact significance these reflections have for our question concerning the restoration of the diaconate.

3. Questions concerning the Opportuneness of the Restoration of the Diaconate

(a) A more exact definition of the question.

It will be useful to make the question of the opportuneness of the diaconate more precise, since it can be posed in different ways, and since the precision given to this question here does not in any way suppose that it can be posed meaningfully *only* in the way it is posed *here*. It would be quite possible, for instance, to pose this question also with regard to the restoration of an independent but exclusively celibate diaconate, or with regard to the restoration of a diaconate with a predominantly liturgical task, or with regard to the restoration of a diaconate which equally refers from the outset to the whole Church. It is not our intention, however, to pose this question in any of these ways, since the point at which this whole problem touches most closely on life today demands that we pose the precise question we are going to ask here. This will become still clearer in the course of our later reflections about the opportuneness of the restoration of the diaconate. We are speaking, therefore, about a diaconate that: (i) is transmitted by the already familiar sacramental rite (i.e., the sacramental ordination to the diaconate) and (ii) is not merely a step to the priesthood.

The question about the restoration of the diaconate is posed in this respect in a positive but not exclusive sense. This means: we do not maintain that a permanent diaconate distinct from the priesthood is *alone* to be recommended and *alone* makes any sense, and that consequently any form of diaconate intended as a step towards the priesthood should be rejected. We therefore exclude right away the question as to whether or not the Church should also (even though not exclusively) keep to the present-day practice in her educational and sacramental commissioning of her priests of the Latin rite. It is reasonable to expect that the Latin Church will continue even in the future to ordain only deacons to the priesthood, and that she will also continue to maintain the previous canonical norms and obligations of the diaconate in those cases where the diaconate is conceived and accepted right from the start as a step to the priesthood. The question about the restoration of the diaconate does not at all concern itself with this other question, since we presuppose here from the very start that, side-by-side with a permanent office of deacon which is not to be thought of as a passage to the priesthood, there can also be—and it is sensible and advisable that there should be—a sacramental diaconate which serves as a step to the priesthood. For in this way, it will be impressed on the future priest that his office is not merely the office of the "elders" or of the director of a congregation, but also the office of the deacon, since the higher office in the Church also includes at least the obligation to do all in one's power to see to it that the office in the Church is given and exercised in all its fullness and in its fullest sense. Understood in this way, however, it includes also all those functions that are proper to the deacon. The point of the diaconate conceived as a stepping stone to the priesthood would also become clearer in such a case if the future priest were to exercise his diaconate for a longer period and in a really practical way, as a catechist, as a helper in the *Caritas* organization, etc., thus giving assistance to the ordinary care of souls and being really tested (at least to some extent) as to his suitability for the priesthood. But as stated, our question here concerns the restoration of a permanent diaconate that does not act as a step to the priesthood and takes this question in a positive yet not in an exclusive sense.

(iii) We are going to pose our question primarily as a question about a diaconate without any obligation of celibacy. In this respect, too, our limited but practical problem is meant in a positive and not in an exclusive sense. This means that we do not dispute the fact that the question of a sacramental and permanent diaconate can itself be posed meaningfully even if such a deacon were to be given the obligation of celibacy. It is also obvious that, if there can be and indeed should be married deacons in the Church, this does not exclude the possibility of deacons who have a proper obligation to celibacy and who are ordained deacons on this presumption; this refers not only to those deacons who receive the diaconate as a stage on the way to the priesthood but also to other cases. Why, for instance, should it not be just as possible for a member of a religious order or of a secular institute to be ordained deacon, as it is for a married man, given, of course, that the usual presuppositions for the reception of sacramental ordination to a permanent diaconate are fulfilled? If we pose the question about the restoration of a diaconate without obligation to celibacy, this not only leaves these questions quite open (or better, given an affirmative answer to the question of the possibility of a married diaconate, these other questions will *eo ipso* and *a fortiori* be answered in the affirmative), but also leaves it an open question under what precise conditions and presuppositions the Church may wish to and should confer the sacramental diaconate on a married man. It would also be conceivable, for instance, that the Latin Church might adopt a similar practice in this respect to the custom already existing in the Eastern Churches, with regard to the ordination of a secular priest; in other words, it is quite conceivable that she might be prepared to confer the diaconate on someone already married, but permit marriage to someone who was ordained deacon while still unmarried only on condition of his returning to the lay state, thus ensuring (if, for instance, a longer period is laid down between marriage and ordination to the diaconate) that only those will be admitted to the sacramental diaconate who have been sufficiently tried while still in the married to state. All these questions are left open here. The basic question concerns married deacons, however, since this is the only real way today of giving a sufficiently real meaning to this whole question. For it cannot be expected that the number of deacons would increase sufficiently for the accomplishment of the present-day mission of the Church, if the question about the restoration of the diaconate is not posed and positively solved as a question about the possibility of married ordained deacons.

(iv) When we pose the question about the opportuneness of restoring the diaconate, this does not implicitly presuppose that this opportuneness must necessarily be equally great in all parts of the Church, and that if this question of opportuneness is answered in the affirmative in principle the diaconate must therefore be restored in an equally real manner in every part of the Church. Even if we do affirm in principle that it is opportune, it still remains absolutely possible that in certain parts of the Church, where the social and pastoral conditions are simpler than elsewhere and where there is a sufficient number of priests, the old practice will continue. Such a difference in practice in the different parts of the Church is quite conceivable since such a difference actually already exists, if one does not simply identify the Catholic Church with the Latin part of the Church, and since there follows from the basic considerations already given the conclusion that the segmentation of the one office in the Church may be determined in its concrete realization by those concrete circumstances of the Church that in fact are not the same in the individual parts of the Church. Even supposing that the basic question is answered in the affirmative, it can easily be seen that the details of such a restoration in individual parts of the Church will have to be worked out by canon law, leaving it to the larger individual parts of the Church (such as, for instance, an ecclesiastical province or a national episcopal conference of larger countries) to decide whether or not (and to what extent) such a permanent diaconate should be restored in their part of the Church.

(b) The basic starting point for a correct answer of the question. If one wishes to pose this question correctly both in theory and in practice, and if one wishes to establish the presuppositions for a legitimate answer, then it must be borne in mind that as a matter of fact the office of deacon already exists in the Church. This is true even though in the Latin Church of the last few centuries this real and permanent office has not actually been conferred by a sacramental rite and perhaps does not contain all those powers that, according to current canon law, belong to a sacramentally ordained deacon and which would really be desirable for the actual office of a deacon. If we are to pose this question correctly, we must always remember the distinction and right relationship between the office and the sacramental transmission of this office. These are not identical entities, nor are they—as we have seen above—absolutely inseparable entities, at least in the case of the diaconate. They are mutually related realities in the sense that the sacramental rite of the transmission of the office receives its ultimate justification from the office and not vice versa. As stated above, no matter how true it may be that in certain circumstances there may be an office in the Church that can be, but is not necessarily, transmitted sacramentally, the ultimate reason for the opportuneness of a sacramental transmission of office will always be the opportuneness of the office itself. For a rite for the transmission of an office—a rite that is a sacrament—is not intended to be anything else than the sacramental conferring of the office itself and the sacramental distribution of the grace required for this office. Hence, of its very nature, the transmission of office finds its ultimate significance and reason for its opportuneness in the office itself. If, however, the question about the restoration of the sacramental ordination to the diaconate is to be posed legitimately and with any meaning at all, then it becomes necessary to consider the opportuneness of the office of the diaconate, since we must first of all clarify this question before there can be any real sense in posing the question about the opportuneness of a sacramental transmission of this office.

The question of the opportuneness of the office of the diaconate itself, however, can be posed in two ways. Either we ask about the opportuneness of an office that does not exist, or we answer the question about the opportuneness of the office by showing explicitly that this office does already exist, and that it exists precisely because it is useful and necessary in the Church. After that we can then proceed from this fact to bring out more clearly the special significance of a sacramental transmission of office. We can in fact adopt the second course. In other words, we proceed from the fact that the office of deacon actually exists to a sufficiently large extent in the Church or at least in many larger parts of the Church and thus shows itself to be meaningful, useful, and indeed necessary. It is quite easy to substantiate this statement in the light of the basic description of the nature of the office of deacon just given above (and as seen also in its history). It is certainly true that in the Latin Church only sacramentally ordained deacons possess the powers of administering solemn baptism and of distributing holy communion in the ordinary course of events. But it would be arbitrary and objectively unjustified to conceive these two powers as the real nature of the diaconate, as if this nature were present only when these powers are present. These two powers do not have any essential superiority over any others, if only because no one can dispute the fact that the Church could, if she wished, confer these two powers even without the sacramental ordination. The remaining duties of proclaiming God's word; of fulfilling important administrative functions as auxiliary organs of the bishop; of teaching Christian doctrine to the rising generation; duties of catechesis of adults; marriage instructions; even—in exceptional cases—of looking after a parish that is without a priest; duties of directing Christian organizations and clubs; and so forth, all these are certainly factors just as important in extent and depth for the total office and commission of the Church as are the specifically liturgical functions, which one may not indeed exclude from the basic elements of the office of deacon and yet must not raise either to the exaggerated position of the universal and most central essential element (even though the objective order and connection of the individual functions in the ideal nature of the diaconate may still remain completely open, and even though there can be no objection to the view that this ideal and full nature of the diaconate may in a certain respect be centered on the deacon's function at the altar).[3] The false emphasis laid on the liturgical functions of the deacon, which gives the impression that one can be a real deacon only by those functions and by them alone, probably stems from that strange and subconscious dread of a certain physical contact with the Eucharist, a dread that forgets that the ordinary Christian's contact with the Eucharist by his reception of it is no less in reality than the contact permitted to the deacon.

Keeping these considerations in mind, we need have no hesitation in making the following quite definite statements:

The office of the diaconate exists in the Church, and this even (if not almost exclusively in reality) outside the ranks of ordained deacons. For there are full-time, professional catechists and full-time, professional "welfare-workers" (in the widest sense of the word), who have taken on the full-time job of fulfilling the Church's mission of charity, who give lifelong service to the hierarchy, and who certainly think of the job for which they have been explicitly commissioned by the hierarchy as fulfilling an essential task for the Church. This is a task that belongs not only to the Church in general (so that it can be fulfilled from the outset and quite obviously even by lay people) but belongs quite peculiarly and specially to the office-bearers of the Church, to the hierarchy as such, so that this charitable work really possessed the formal nature of a real diaconate. There is in the Church a full-time, professional administration that represents a real auxiliary function for the fulfillment of the task of the hierarchy as such. We can speak of an office of deacon at least where these functions are exercised, to a fuller extent, by an explicit commission received from the hierarchy, under the immediate direction of the hierarchy and as a direct assistance to the task of the hierarchy, as a permanent and enduring function—even in those cases where this office has not been transmitted by sacramental ordination. This is true especially because this assertion does not deny that the determination, limitation, and exact organization of such offices could be undertaken in a more ideal fashion—in other words, that it would be quite consistent with the nature and meaning of such actually existing offices—if the Church, by her decrees, were to give them this or that further power which would clarify the significance and, for instance, the ultimate source of the already existing powers (i.e., their relationship to and ultimate connection with the altar). The starting point of our reflections on the opportuneness of the restoration of the diaconate is therefore to be found in the thesis that the concrete office of deacon which is to be restored already exists in the Church, even though only anonymously and without any exact canonical delimitation. This gives rise to the following conclusions:

Firstly, all that remains now to be asked concerns the opportuneness of a *sacramental* determination of these already existing offices; and secondly, this question is to be posed only where these offices exist or should exist in view of the requirements of the pastoral situation in a particular part of the Church. If we pose our question in this way, then it will be clear from the outset that the desire for the restoration of the diaconate is concerned only with those parts of the Church where, by reason of pastoral needs, this office exists or ought to exist; this desire does not demand a diaconate simply for the sake of having ordinations to the diaconate. Hence, we are not really concerned with introducing any new office, but only with the restoration of the sacramental conferring of an office that basically already exists though in an anonymous way. The precision thus given to our question is obviously not meant to dispute the fact that, by restoring the sacramental transmission of this office, the office itself can be made clearer and more permanent, and that the faithful can thereby be given an increased appreciation of this office and that the determination of the functions and powers of this office can thereby be widened. It is particularly important to stress this, since the reasons for the opportuneness of the sacramental conferring of the office can quite correctly be based on the needs discovered in pastoral theology (such as the lack of priests, the significance of this office, etc.) although these reasons do not directly prove the opportuneness and importance of the transmission of office but rather the opportuneness and importance of the office itself. Nevertheless, these pastoral reasons for the office, even where the office itself already exists, are also reasons for the opportuneness of the restoration of the sacramental transmission of the office, and this precisely because a sacramental transmission of office (as distinct from a nonsacramental transmission) can make the faithful more aware of the significance of the office itself, and can increase the attraction, propagation, and appreciation of the office itself for and among the faithful.

(c) The reasons for the opportuneness of the thus understood restoration of the diaconate:

(i) As already said above, there are many reasons that can be put forward for the restoration of the diaconate even in the sense defined here, and even though they prove directly the opportuneness of the office and only indirectly the opportuneness of the sacramental conferring of the office. Everything has really been said already about these reasons in many different ways and at different places in this book. Hence, all we really need to do here is just to say a few words about these reasons: the lack of priests, which forces us to transfer many of the functions previously exercised by priests to others who should nevertheless belong to the clergy; certain new needs of the care of souls growing out of the social and cultural situation, which cannot be supplied by the priests alone, even with the assistance of the specific apostolate of the laity (Apostolate of Catholics) and of Catholic Action in the strict sense; the dignity of certain offices existing in the Church which are not specifically sacerdotal offices but should nevertheless be recognized and honored by being given sacred orders; the possibility of winning a considerable number of men through a sacramental diaconate for the specific tasks of the Church's hierarchical office, men who do not feel themselves called to a celibacy based on spiritual reasons, without it being necessary to abolish the obligation of celibacy for priests; the possibility of relieving priests of many of the basics of the hierarchical (and not properly lay) apostolate which do indeed belong to the hierarchy as such and hence both theoretically and in practice cannot simply be delegated to lay people, and yet are of such a nature as to distract priests from a specifically priestly spiritual life and from a specifically priestly care of souls. As has been said, we do not intend to develop these various reasons further here since this has already been done elsewhere and also since they are not the real, ultimate dogmatic proof for the opportuneness of the restoration of the sacramental diaconate.

(ii) The decisive reason consists in the fact that (1) the office already exists; (2) a sacramental transmission of this office is possible; and (3) such a transmission, at least where the office exists, must be regarded basically and from the outset, if not as something necessary yet as something fitting and opportune. After what has already been said, the only point in this fundamental argument that really requires further explanation is the third one. God can certainly give the holder of an office the grace undoubtedly required for the carrying out of an existing office—a grace that, in such a case, is salvific not only for the office-bearer concerned but also for the Church herself—even if this office was not transmitted to the holder by a sacramental ordination. So much is self-evident, especially since according to the common opinion the highest office in the Church—the primacy of the pope—does not require any new sacramental ordination and yet undoubtedly requires the highest and most comprehensive grace of office, which in this case is not a sacramental grace even though it has sacramental roots, if you like, in the episcopal office of the pope. Whenever there exists an office in the Church that is necessary or useful to the Church, such an office necessarily participates in its own way, and of course to a different extent and in different degrees of urgency, in the assistance by grace, which God has promised to the Church for her continued existence and life. The assistance of grace must also take sufficient effect, by reason of the eschatologically indestructible character of the Church, even though this fact alone does not provide any absolute guarantee that this grace intended for the Church will become effective in a particular individual office-bearer. To this extent, the office in the Church—quite apart from whether or not it is conferred sacramentally—is itself already a tangible way in which God promises a grace of office, even if this office is not conferred sacramentally; the office itself is an element (if we may put it this way) of that proto-sacrament which is the Church herself, insofar as she herself is in her nature and existence the eschatologically final tangible form of God's salvific purpose for the world. Seen from this point of view, it is certainly true that we must not exaggerate the importance of a sacramental transmission of office (e.g., of the diaconate) for the holders of such an (explicit or anonymous) office of deacon. Seen in this light, it is also possible to find a certain justification for the Church's present practice in this matter which, in the light of what has just been said, need no longer be condemned as a totally regrettable and almost no longer explicable false development.

Yet it remains true to say that when the office and the divine assurance of the grace necessary for fulfilling the office can be given in a sacramental manner (and if this is meaningful and practicable), then they should be given in this way. This is certainly a governing principle of the Church's practical attitude in her sacramental practice in other respects. Theologians do not maintain, for instance, that confirmation or extreme unction, confession of devotion or frequent reception of the Eucharist are based on any absolute divine obligation for such sacramental actions. This implies, therefore, that absolutely speaking, the graces that can be received by such a reception of the sacraments can be received also in a nonsacramental way, since neither the increase of sanctifying grace nor the specifically sacramental graces must be conceived as if they could be obtained only by receiving the sacraments, and yet can be not merely very beneficial for salvation but in certain circumstances may even be necessary for salvation. Yet the practice and teaching of the Church in such cases is directed towards encouraging such a reception of the sacraments as something most salutary. It would be contrary to the Church's outlook, for instance, to discourage so-called confession of devotion on the basis that the graces given by it can be obtained just as well by some other means (such as prayer, examination of conscience, mortification, etc.). As far as is humanly possible and genuinely practicable, it is obvious that even those graces are to be given a sacramentally tangible form and presence in the life of the individual and of the Church, which are not bound up with a sacrament either by the nature of the grace concerned or by a divine ordinance (as in the case of baptism by water and of sacramental confession in the case of mortal sins) which imposes a positive obligation to receive the sacrament. All this follows simply from the basic structure of the Christian order of grace. This order is the order of the Word of God *become man,* the order of the Church, and of the eschatologically indissoluble union of the pneuma and the ecclesiological corporeality of the Spirit. The office and the grace of office belong together in the eschatological situation of the Church, in which the tangibility of the Church and of her possession of the Spirit in its totality can never be again torn apart; the grace of office, since it is the grace of God become man and the grace of the visible Church, always presses of its very nature towards some concrete tangible form and sign. Consequently, it can be said just as fundamentally that whenever the sacramental communication of grace is within the bounds of human possibilities and of what can reasonably be done, then it should be permitted to take place; in these circumstances, such a sacramental communication of grace is basically to be recommended and is opportune, and such a statement of its opportuneness cannot then be countered with the objection that one could after all receive these graces even without the sacrament.[4] Even though this statement regarding the possibility of obtaining the grace concerned may be perfectly correct, it simply cannot be used as an argument against the sensibleness and opportuneness of a sacramental communication of this grace. Otherwise, the *only* counter-argument against the arguments purporting to show that baptism by water is superfluous would be to appeal to an arbitrary, positive decree of God. We do not attribute any special force in this argumentation to the fact that the sacrament of the diaconate imparts an indelible sacramental character that cannot be received in any other way; after all, the significance and desirability of such a character *qua "sacramentum et res"* ultimately depends entirely on the significance and desirability both of the full power belonging to the office and of the grace of office, for which the character is a (positive but in our case not absolutely necessary) title.

Such an argumentation based on the nature of an office, of a grace of office and the possibility of the promise of such a grace by a sacrament, includes also the assertion that considerable existential effects will accrue from the facts and associations aimed at in this argumentation. This means that it is to be expected that someone who is given an office and God's promise of the grace of office in a sacramental manner will accept this office and grace of office in a much more radically existential manner, on account of the solemnity, uniqueness, and indestructible effects of such a sacramental transmission of office, than if he were given more or less the same office and grace in a different way. This is true especially because the grace of the sacrament is as such and of its very nature capable also of bringing about or deepening the personal acceptance of it in those who do not close themselves to it; in other words, given the necessary presuppositions, the sacramental grace itself extends and deepens the dispositions that are required for it.

In summary, it can be said quite simply that there exists in the Church a sacramental, grace-effecting rite of transmitting the office of the diaconate, at least as a possibility *iuris divini* in the Church; the office to which this sacramental rite of transmission is objectively adapted already exists in the Church to a sufficient extent and in a sufficient manner; there is a general law of the nature of the sacramental order of grace, which states that a sacramental rite that is possible should also be really applied to the communication of grace signified by it, wherever and whenever this communication is demanded; an office existing in the Church (even though to some extent only anonymously) requires the help of God's grace for its exercise, for the salvation of its holder, and for the benefit of the Church. It makes sense, therefore, to recommend that this existing office should also receive the grace necessary for it through the existing, sacramentally effective rite, and that the rite should not be employed simply for someone who either does not exercise this office or who (insofar as he does exercise it) receives the necessary grace for it from the order of the priesthood or who, as the holder of this office, tries to gain the necessary grace for his office in an exclusively extra-sacramental way. Hence, if a certain sacrament is possible in the Church, and perhaps even necessary (in the common opinion), then basically speaking all objections against the opportuneness of its existence on the basis that it has to be realized by ever new ordinations must be rejected as false and deceptive from the very start. Whether we presuppose that the Church must or merely can, according to Christ's will, establish the diaconate as an office separate from the combined office in the Church alters nothing as far as the stringency of this consideration is concerned. For if the diaconate taken as a "grade" of the combined office is a reality that must exist in the Church *iure divino,* then it is self-evident that the obligatory existence of this order is not fulfilled merely by the diaconate as it exists in the Latin Church today, where it is not very far removed from being a legal fiction, since in this part of the Church there is an ordination administered for an office which as such is almost never exercised in virtue of this ordination and which in this form has in any case no real significance in the Church. If the necessity and meaning of the sacramental transmission of an office must be justified by the office itself, then the office itself must have a significance in the Church which can really justify a sacramental rite; the diaconate which exists through the ordination actually administered in the Church today does not have this significance, and the actually existing and significant office of deacon in the Church lacks this ordination. Supposing, however, that the Church has the legal possibility but not the obligation *iuris divini* to give this sacramental ordination to the diaconate, then the right of not making use of this possibility can be explained and justified only if it can be proved that in present-day circumstances the Church can and does do without this separate office, and that she therefore is also quite right to omit the sacramental rite of the transmission of this office. But there is no possible proof for this. For the Church has actually got this (albeit unordained) office and this demonstrates its necessity. The real nonexistence of the diaconate in the Latin Church also cannot be remedied by simply obliging the future priests to exercise their diaconate for a somewhat longer period and in a more concrete manner before their ordination to the priesthood by helping as catechists, for instance, or as assistants in the parishes (by a "diaconate year" or "holiday diaconate"). For even so the order of the diaconate would still be regarded as a mere step toward the priesthood—and this is objectively false. Even under these circumstances, those who are actually engaged professionally and full-time in genuinely fulfilling the real tasks of the diaconate would still be deprived of the sacramental communication of the necessary grace of office; in other words, they would be deprived of a sacrament that of its nature is intended for them and does not really signify the sacramental communication of grace for the period during which someone is being tested as to his suitability for the priesthood. The simultaneous existence of a currently existing office and of the sacrament giving the grace primarily destined for this office (and which at the most is only secondarily intended also as a step to the priesthood) provides a basic argument for the opportuneness of the restoration of the diaconate as a sacrament. Fundamentally, therefore, it is not a question of comparing and weighing reasons for and against opportuneness; rather, as a result of a more profound theological insight into the nature of the diaconate both as an office and as a sacrament and into the historical conditions of the development that has led to an actual emptying-out of the sacrament of the diaconate, it is simply a question of squaring this with the basic fact that a possible and actually existing sacrament of ordination to an office must be given to those who have this office.

(iii) In any case, there are no serious objections to the opportuneness of such a restoration. After all, any fears of serious unsuitability will not arise on the grounds of the sacramental rite of the transmission of office but will at most be due to the office thus transmitted and existing in certain persons. This is really obvious and needs no further proof. The office of deacon does, however, already actually exist in the Church (even though without ordination) and its existence and the growth of its scope and of the numbers of those exercising it shows that the inconvenience, the harm, and danger which might give grounds for maintaining that the restoration of the diaconate is inopportune are not any greater in this case than is usual with any office administered by men. If such a good and useful office, which has not caused any inconveniences through its holders hitherto, comes now to be conferred by a sacramental rite of transmission of office, then this cannot bring about any hitherto unknown harm and dangers. One thing, of course, is true: a sacramental ordination to the diaconate makes the ordained office-bearer a member of the clergy, both from a dogmatic and a canonical point of view. But someone thus ordained is a cleric precisely to the extent of the function and power that he already possesses even now (prescinding from a few liturgical powers which do not make any essential difference here). Hence, if these powers and functions did not cause any inconvenience when invested in a noncleric, why should it be otherwise when they are invested in a cleric?

The question as to whether the existence of *married* clerics would give rise to difficulties and dangers in the Church will be treated separately.

(iv) Our basic argumentation proceeded from the fact that the office of deacon already exists in the Church and that the ordination to this office should be given precisely to this already existing office (or one which should be created by reason of the necessity of the office itself) since this also already existing ordination rite exists for this very purpose. This argumentation does not mean, however, that the opportuneness of such a restoration can be proved *only* under the presuppositions laid down by us. Even someone who is not prepared to admit that the office of a professional, lifelong catechist or of a social welfare worker, etc., is basically already the office of a deacon, can still prove that the restoration of the diaconate is justifiable. For even he can appreciate that, if the significance of one of Christ's sacraments in the Church is properly evaluated, it will be seen quite clearly that it was not instituted nor does it exist simply as a (very unreal) prelude for those who will be ordained priests a few months later and who after that do not exercise this office as such any longer (an office for which they received a sacred order) to any great extent and in any explicitly realized way. If one presupposes the existence of this sacrament in this way (as we have also done, of course, in our basic argument), then it also becomes clear that we can confine ourselves in all our considerations here regarding the restoration of the diaconate to the question of the male holders of such offices, which we regard as belonging fundamentally to the diaconate. The question as to whether and why sacramental orders are reserved to the male sex—and this even in their lowest "grades" and in spite of the existence of an institution of deaconesses in the early Church—does not need to occupy us here, since the only problem concerning us here is to determine to whom in the Church it makes any sense to give that sacrament which already exists at the present time and which as such is given to men only.

4. Diaconate and Celibacy[5]

We have already stated above that the question about the restoration of the diaconate is really practical and significant only if it also at least includes the question of the restoration of a sacramental diaconate for married men. For many, the latter question contains the strongest emotional and practical difficulties against the desire for such a restoration. In order to get a clear idea of this question, it must first of all be pointed out once more that the question of celibacy or noncelibacy must not be regarded in view of the sacramental ordination to the office, but in view of the office itself. Wherever celibacy is thought to be necessary or most desirable, the demand for celibacy must be deduced either from its intrinsic significance for the Church or from a consideration of the office as such with which celibacy is to be associated. That celibacy has an intrinsic significance for the Church, is neither disputable nor does it require any further explanation and proof here. A celibacy that is immediately and of itself alone significant for the celibate and for the Church (as lived in the communities that practice the Evangelical Counsels) is from the very outset excluded from our discussion. In our present context, it can only be a question of determining whether the office of the deacon, like the priestly office, has such an inner affinity with celibacy that, as in the case of the Latin priestly and episcopal office, the Church deems it advisable and feels it justifiable to demand celibacy also of the deacons (no matter how precisely this mutual affinity is to be interpreted; whether it be by the nature of celibacy itself or by pastoral consideration or in view of the service of the altar, etc.). If one bears the distinction of office and of the rite of the transmission of office clearly in mind—and if one is quite clear in one's mind about the fact that in the very nature of things a rite of the transmission of office can "demand" celibacy only if the office to be transmitted demands it—then it will be easy to answer the question with which we are now concerned. For the Church shows by her practice that she does not see any very close and necessary connection between the office of deacon and celibacy. For this office exists and is transmitted in the Church without celibacy being demanded. For, those men and office-bearers in the Church in whose case the desirability of a sacramental transmission of office is indicated here are *de facto* for the most part married men, and neither the official Church nor people in the Church have ever maintained or felt any incompatibility or inconvenience in the coexistence of this office and marriage in recent centuries or at the present time.

Thus, if properly posed, this question does not inquire whether, in contrast to previous practice, one should from now on stop imposing the obligation of celibacy on anyone who is to be ordained a deacon. For the candidate for ordination with whom we are concerned here is not someone who wants to become a priest and someone on whom—basically for this and no other reason—the Church already imposes the obligation of celibacy at the time of his ordination to the subdiaconate; he is a candidate to whom the Church is to give the sacramental ordination for an office that he already has as a married person, which has been transmitted to him and which he exercises as a married person. Hence, from an objective and not merely verbal point of view, there is no question here of annulling any previous law existing in the Church today; for, the deacon who exercises his own particular office as a permanent job in the Church no longer exists—and has not existed for a long time now—in the Church (or at the most exists only *per accidens, viz.* when someone, in accordance with canon 973 §2, advances no further than the diaconate on his way to the priesthood, and yet is not laicized). The answer to the question as to the fundamental necessity of imposing the obligation of celibacy must be sought by asking whether these deacons, who exist in as far as the nature and the office of the diaconate are concerned even though they are not ordained deacons, should have the obligation of celibacy newly imposed on them, contrary to the previous practice of the Church, who up till now has given what in fact is the office of the diaconate to married people. Once this question is put properly in this way, it immediately becomes evident that it must be answered in the negative. Marriage has a greater inner affinity with the office of deacon than has celibacy, since the deacon in his specific, official function is quite clearly the link between the clergy and the altar, on the one hand, and the world with its Christian task, on the other; up till now the Church has not demanded celibacy for this office, and such a demand also does not follow from ordination. Why should there then be a demand for it now, a demand that in practice would to a large extent prevent the new realization of the diaconate, since in this case most of those who are deacons in fact would, and would have to, give up any claim to the official ordination which is due to them, and the few among them who already live a celibate life for other reasons (especially in religious communities) would not be able to supply that additional number of real deacons which the present-day pastoral situation of the Church demands? It must always be borne in mind in this connection that in a true theology of marriage, marriage must really and truly not be regarded as a mere concession to human weakness (a conception attempted over and over again by an almost manichaean intellectual undercurrent in the Church) but must be seen to have an absolutely positive and essential function, not only in the private Christian life of certain individuals but also in the Church. Marriage, understood as a sacramentally consecrated union, is both in and for the Church the concrete and real representation and living example of the mystery of Christ's union with the Church. Hence, marriage fulfills an absolutely necessary function in the Church and for the Church herself. How, then, should marriage be less advisable for the office of deacon? A deacon may see his marriage rather as an essential factor for his duties as a deacon, since a Christian marriage has precisely this function of testifying to the powerful influences of grace for the Church. Since, in the case of the ordained diaconate being retained also as a step to the office of the priesthood, the formation and task of the deacons going on to the priesthood and of those who remain deacons will be different and separate from the outset, and since both these different kinds of deacon and the faithful will be clearly conscious of this very difference, it cannot seriously be feared that we might arouse opposition to the celibacy of the diaconate as leading to the priesthood by appealing for married deacons. Nor need we be afraid that the position of these married deacons might be used to relax or attack priestly celibacy. If there were any danger of this happening, then the existence of married priests in the Eastern Uniate Churches should also be a danger to the celibacy of the priests in the Latin Church, or serious difficulties should arise from the coexistence of celibate bishops and married priests in the Eastern Churches. Furthermore, none of the faithful in the Latin Church has any difficulty in seeing that celibacy has a special affinity with the priesthood as such, and they certainly distinguish the duty and dignity of deacons so clearly from the duties and the dignity of the priest that they will neither get the feeling that if deacons married, then the priest should also be allowed to marry, nor that deacons should be celibate because the priest is celibate. Certain emotional restraints and difficulties (as, for instance, in the case of receiving communion from a married deacon) have no real objective basis and will quickly disappear when people get used to things, just as certain emotional qualms about a reception of communion not preceded by a longer period of eucharistic fast have disappeared.

That the Church's feelings too have always made a distinction in this question between the priest and the deacon is shown by the fact that the right to marry has been restored in many cases and with comparatively little difficulty to deacons who have been laicized, whereas the laicized priest is usually refused this permission. Although the permission to marry will certainly avoid considerable difficulties and burdens for the deacon, difficulties and burdens that would occur if celibacy were demanded of him, it need not be denied that marriage also presents certain difficulties and dangers for the exercise of a diaconate worthy of this office. Nevertheless, in view of the specific function of the deacon which directs him to go out into the world, these difficulties and dangers are certainly considerably less than if celibacy were demanded. These difficulties and the danger of harmful results for the Church could be lessened even further if canon law were to offer a fairly wide and practicable possibility of laicization for deacons, to be given either at the request of the deacon himself or at the instigation of the bishop. As has already been emphasized, the recommendation of a diaconate together with marriage is naturally not meant to suggest that *only* married deacons should be bearers of an independent and permanent office. There is nothing to stop the Church from ordaining to the diaconate even those who either have already taken the obligation of religious celibacy upon themselves for some other reason (as, for instance, in religious communities) or who undertake this obligation in connection with their ordination to the diaconate and by an explicit declaration before the Church. It has also been stated already that one might consider the possibility of combining ordination to the diaconate with marriage only in the case of those who are already married and who have already proved themselves by their Christian married life and their previously exercised functions of the diaconate to be suitable candidates for the reception of this ordination. Only, in such a case, one ought not to drag out this testing period for too long; considering the professional character of the diaconate, this period could no doubt be fixed approximately in accordance with what is demanded in this respect from candidates for the priesthood. For even the ordination to the diaconate is not, after all, a reward for a diaconate already exercised for almost a whole lifetime, but is the communicating of grace for the exercise of an office that is still to be carried out.

5. Office and Grace of Office

It will be useful to give a few further systematic reflections about the office and the grace attached to the office, both separately and in their relations to one another.

(a) It is clear from history and also from the declarations of the Church's *Magisterium* and canon law how widespread and intrinsically diversified the office of deacon is. It has also become clear from history that the conception of what actually is the very heart of the essence of the diaconate has been, and has remained to this day, comparatively fluctuating and contradictory. It is probably not to be expected that the Church herself will make any real declarations in the coming Council about the question of a basic, unified essential structure of the office of deacon. This question will presumably always remain a disputed question among theologians. Nevertheless, it will surely be possible to base oneself on the fact that, judging by the declarations of current canon law, the liturgical function will not be lacking even in the essential picture of the future deacon, however much it must be left an open question to what extent in individual cases and details the regulations (which perhaps will not necessarily be uniform in all parts of the Church) will or will not draw on the future holders of a permanent diaconate for the carrying out of liturgical functions (e.g., for assisting at marriages, distributing holy communion). In the same way, one will have to hold it to be an indisputable fact that this future ordained diaconate will not be limited to these liturgical functions but will have wider and important tasks and powers in the Church and in her pastoral practice. Given these two presuppositions, there then arises the speculative question about the mutual relationships between these many different liturgical and extra-liturgical functions which are all part of the one diaconate.

To begin with, it is (naturally) obvious from the history of the diaconate, from the similar practice of the Church with regard to the priesthood, and from the basic possibility (explained above) of dividing and accentuating the different parts of the collective office in the Church, that there can be different types or distinct forms of the one complete diaconate. This means in practice that, without prejudice to the unity and uniformity of the office of the diaconate, the focal point of the task of a deacon may at different times lie in different directions, and that on this account the candidates for such an ordained diaconate may also be able to approach this one office and calling in the Church from comparatively very different directions. In other words, even in any future practice and legislation of the Church, there will presumably be no deacons who would—in principle and permanently—want to exclude the liturgical commission and obligation, although it can be left an open question as to whether or not such an intention and legal determination on the part of the Church would nevertheless be in itself possible. This does not, however, exclude the possibility that the focal point of the life of such a deacon might lie in the work of the Church's *Caritas* movement or in the administrative sphere of the Church. And in principle there are many other conceivable functions part from those just mentioned, functions that determine the concrete form of the diaconate (without it being necessary or possible to enumerate them here) provided only that these functions are part of the Church's official functions as such, and that in the service and diaconia of the episcopal and sacerdotal office there is fulfilled the task belonging to the hierarchy as distinct from the laity in the Church. It will moreover be possible to say that one can quite properly center all these different tasks on the altar, if we may express the referred to connection and inner unity of these many-sided tasks of the diaconate in this way. It will not be necessary to say that the liturgical function of the deacon is the real, proper function of his office, whereas all his other functions are just secondary, "part-time" functions. Such a statement surely contradicts the early history of the diaconate; it would surely bring us back again to that conception that has led to reducing the scope of this office, the very thing we should be trying to overcome today; it would also be wrong for the very reason that these liturgical functions do not in practice and in the concrete presuppose ordination with any greater necessity than do the rest of the deacon's functions (or do so at most only *iure humano* in canon law).

On the other hand, the equally necessary character of the *kerygmatic,* charitable, and administrative functions of the deacon for the essence of the diaconate does not prevent us from regarding them as functions that basically are really already given together with his duties connected with the central mystery of the Church, which is the Eucharist. For the Eucharist is not only the sacrifice of Christ offered to God and the sacrament of the individual encounter with Christ and of private satisfaction; rather, it is the event in which the nature of the Church itself comes to be realized actually in the most intensive way, the event in which the Church becomes herself and comes to be present in her most profound actuality at a certain point in space and time.[6] Here in the anamnesis of the death of Christ is the effective pronouncement of the Word of God, which at best can really only be interpreted when proclaimed and taught.[7] Here the unity of the Church is achieved in its most intensive way in the sacramental symbol and the love of Christ. Hence, if the deacon shares in a special way in the Eucharist understood as the central self-realization of the Church, and if he does this as the helper of the episcopal or priestly representative of Christ, who is the Head of the Church, and as the representative of the people and as the interpreter of the sacred mystery for the people and all this as a permanent function—then the deacon cannot in principle withdraw from those functions of the Church by which she gives an exposition, in her sacred teaching, of the anamnesis of the Redemption and by which her unity in faith, hope, and charity, celebrated in the Eucharist, is spread by her—through the direction of the faithful and through Christian charity— over the whole of man's life. Seen in this light, it becomes understandable how these different basic functions of the deacon, however distinct they may appear at first, form a unity among themselves, and proceed from and return to the central mystery of the Eucharist. This also makes it understandable that the old controversy about whether the diaconate is a more spiritual or a more profane office in the Church is really due to a misunderstanding. The proclamation of the word and the realization of love which are sacramentally present in the Eucharist are not profane realities in life, but are a self-realization and an actualization of the holy Church, insofar as she is holy in the actual reality of life in which man's salvation must be effected.

(b) It is not easy to delimit the task of the deacon from the tasks and possibilities a layman possesses in the Church by his lay apostolate and his participation in Catholic Action.[8] This is difficult even from a purely extrinsic point of view, since it is really impossible—from a purely material point of view—to mention any function of the deacon that even an "unordained" layman could not fulfill, provided merely that he has been given the necessary authorization by the Church. This is true even of the deacon's liturgical functions. Yet this fact is not really surprising and does not represent any real problem peculiar to the diaconate as such; it is a question already raised by the Church's official functions as a whole. One can, of course, say that there are certain individual powers and tasks belonging *iure divino* only to ordained office-bearers (the power of consecrating in the celebration of the Eucharist, the power to ordain priests, the power to administer confirmation and the anointing of the sick, the giving of priestly absolution). It would be completely wrong, however, to try to say in principle that these tasks and powers alone characterize the Church's office and that everything else (prescinding perhaps from strictly jurisdictional acts) is *eo ipso* a merely lay task and power. Rather, the hierarchical office includes the power of proclaiming the Gospel and also the exercise of Christian *caritas* in a way specific to this office as such, even though—on a superficial viewing—the material realization of such hierarchical tasks may not appear to be very much different from the words and deeds of a layman witnessing to Christ's Gospel and love. Even though this formal distinction may not be immediately clear, it nevertheless exists. The layman's task as such, for instance, will be to bear witness to the truth and love of Christ by his words and deeds only in *that* situation of his life which is proper to him by reason of his human natural existence. The holder of hierarchic powers and tasks, on the other hand, will have to bear witness to and proclaim the Gospel even outside his proper "place" determined by his human and natural exist-ence. He will in a real sense be an "ambassador," who by his divine mission is sent out of his own personal situation in order to carry the Gospel "in season and out of season" into strange places (which is just as possible and necessary in the "home missions" as it is in the "foreign missions"). Similarly, the attestation of the *Caritas Christi* will be a task of the Church's official function in the measure, urgency, and concrete manner by which this *caritas* appears as the direct act of the "visible Church" as such and no longer merely as the fulfillment of the general Christian duty of Christian love of neighbor. We do not claim that by these few allusions we have made a sufficiently clear and exhaustive distinction between the characteristics of these tasks of the official element of the Church and those of the laity in the Church which may—materially speaking—appear to be almost identical. But this difference does exist, because there is a difference *iure divino* between the hierarchy and the people of the Church (in spite of the universal priesthood of all believers) and because this difference cannot be confined to the few powers of the potestas ordinis which we have actually mentioned or to the *potestas iurisdictionis* in the strictest sense.

If this difference exists then this means, however, that all the tasks and powers of a deacon are characterized by the general characteristics of the tasks and powers of the Church's hierarchical office as distinct from the tasks and powers of lay people. That this fact is not very evident in the practical administration and consciousness of the Church today is due to the fact that nowadays certain tasks and powers are fulfilled by lay people as a lifelong profession (and not merely as a spare-time job and by reason of a passing, accidental need), tasks and powers that basically belong to the hierarchy as such and as a whole and which in the past, if they had been performed professionally and permanently, would have stamped those performing them as members of the clergy, so that the Church would also have confirmed this membership by ordination. Hence, the circumstance that—to the superficial observer—most of what this future "absolute" deacon will be doing could also be done by laymen, does not, on closer analysis of this activity, speak for its truly lay character, but rather for the demand that such an office-bearer ought to be given that ecclesiastical and, in certain circumstances, sacramental ordination which exists or existed in the Church precisely for these offices. The fact that the boundary between a lay task and a hierarchical one is somewhat vague (in the "downward" direction) is due to the nature of things and merely proves the inner unity of the official element and the people in the Church relative to the task of the Church, which after all is one and the same in its concern for the kingdom of God. Empirically speaking and in practice, it can always be said, however, that whenever someone performs a task permanently and professionally, and whenever this is a task that the higher office (i.e., the bishop and the priests) recognizes and exercises as an intrinsic element of its own task or as an indispensable, direct, and in itself significant auxiliary function of that task, this person is in principle performing a clerical office.[9] On this basis, it is absolutely feasible to draw a basic distinction between the office of the deacon and the task of the lay apostle and to prove the demand for the restoration of the ordination to the diaconate.

(c) In this connection, we must also say a word about the relationship of the diaconate to the priesthood and consequently of the deacon to the priest. Here, too, there are certain obscurities in the traditional conception. It sometimes looks as if the diaconate and the simple priesthood are two coexisting extensions of the one episcopal office (even though they are not simply of the same rank and of equal dignity), so that the deacon cannot really appear as an auxiliary to the simple priest; at other times—and this is probably the clearer and more widespread view—there appears the conception that the deacon is simply the helper of the priest, and this in such a way that even the simple priesthood possesses *eminenter* all the rights and powers of the diaconate and the diaconate can only be regarded as an extension and auxiliary organ of the simple priesthood. If our reflections in no. 2 above were correct, then the question as to which of these two conceptions is in fact the right one (which is sometimes more than a purely theoretical question) can really be decided only by an actual decision of the Church, in the knowledge that the Church could in certain circumstances have decided differently. For if the Church can, under the necessary presuppositions, divide her collective office according to the concrete pastoral needs in the Church at any particular time, then she can in principle do this by separating two coexisting offices from her collective office, so that then neither of these offices would possess the powers of the other, or she can separate a higher and a lower office in such a way that the higher would include the powers of the lower. It is sometimes not so easy to tell which of these two possibilities has in fact been realized in the consciousness and intention of the Church. We have already pointed out, for instance, that one may possibly suppose that even the simple priesthood may of itself include the powers of confirming and of ordaining priests in its *potestas ordinis* (although these will in most cases be present only in a "dormant" state), powers that are certainly contained in the episcopal office. One should also consider the question as to whether a deacon, who is consecrated a bishop *"per saltum"* without previous ordination to the priesthood, also receives the priestly powers solely by this episcopal consecration. On the basis of these and similar reflections, it should be possible to draw the conclusion that many, if not all, things regarding the constitution of the scope of an office depend on the actual will of the Church. Hence, given that certain powers are different of their very nature, they may indeed be conferred separately, but they need not be. Consequently, the answer to the real question about the relationship of the diaconate to the priesthood cannot be simply deduced from the abstract nature of these two realities but only from the question as to which powers the Church in fact wishes to confer by this or that ordination and which not. If, however, the question is posed in this way, then it will be impossible to doubt that in her ordination to the priesthood the Church does not presuppose the ordained to possess the powers of the diaconate in such a way that, if he did not already possess them on account of his ordination to the diaconate then he would not receive them by this ordination to the priesthood. This follows, as has been said, not only because it is not easy to see, from what has just been shown under (a), why a priest should not already be commissioned and obliged to the self-realization of the Church in teaching and in charity by his duties at the altar, since these tasks seem to result of themselves from the full nature of the eucharistic celebration, but it follows also from the Church's own free intention which, in the case of an ordination to the priesthood *per saltum,* has never yet maintained that such a priest is incapable of exercising the powers of the diaconate. Even so, such a consideration may not be absolutely compelling on the purely speculative level, for one cannot assert that the powers of the diaconate can be conferred only by a sacramental ordination; yet, when looked at in the whole setting of real life, the above fact nevertheless shows the intention of the Church outlined above, since the Church has never appealed to her right to transmit the diaconate extra-sacramentally when it was a question of the possibility of a priest's exercise of the functions of the diaconate without actual ordination to the diaconate; instead, the Church has always explained her conception and intention regarding this fact by maintaining that the priest can do *eminenter* what the deacon is capable of doing. Hence, it will have to be said that by the priestly ordination actually dispensed by her, the Church intends to constitute a priest who is always also, at least *eminenter,* a deacon, whether or not he has been specially ordained deacon beforehand.

This, however, does not yet provide a clear explanation of the relationship between priest and deacon which is in question here. All that it tells us is that every priest is also a deacon, but this does not as yet really tell us anything clearly about the intrinsic relationship between the specific powers of the deacon and the specifically priestly powers. We also cannot simply presume with regard to this question that the different functions and powers of the diaconate must all have the same relationship to the specific nature of the priesthood. It may be true, for example, that the priest *qua* priest, and hence *qua* mystagogue of the celebration of the mysteries of the Church, has a more essential and a closer relationship to the task of teaching than to the charitable task. This would be true particularly if it were conceivable in the nature of things that the Church either confers priestly powers on a priest without thereby obliging him to a different form of *caritas* than that to which any Christian is obliged, or entrusts a deacon with the performance of charitable works which as such are an obligation of the hierarchical Church; in other words, even when such a separation is not undertaken, the emphasis within a commission which in itself embraces several powers, may nevertheless be very different. Consequently, and in spite of what has been said up till now, it is not absolutely impossible that a deacon may, for instance, be the organ of the collective episcopal power with regard to the charitable works of the Church with an emphasis and explicitness that are not present in the actual office of an individual priest in the service of the bishop. For the rest, it will in practice depend on the actual will of the bishop whether he associates a deacon and his task more directly with himself or whether he wishes to see the task of the deacon as a direct help for the simple priest (the parish priest). The fact that the ordaining Church recognizes that the powers of the deacon are also contained in the priesthood as such and intends to confer them by the priesthood does not in practice exclude the possibility of associating the deacon directly to the bishop as his helper.

(d) There is not much to be said here about the grace of office of the diaconate. The powers given by an office and the grace attached to an office for the exercise of the office—an exercise that sanctifies the office-bearer himself—are certainly realities distinct from each other yet mutually related to one another. The ordination itself naturally cannot directly—by the very act of ordination—give the grace of office demanded by a lifelong exercise of this office. The ordination must be understood rather as the divine (sacramentally tangible) promise of the help of grace which, by reason of this promise, God is ready to give in the course of the life of the office-bearer, and which he will give to the extent in which the office-bearer opens his soul more and more to this grace by trying to do justice to his office with the help of divine grace. As regards the grace of office itself, everything to be said about the effect of divine

171

grace in general applies also to this grace in particular. Furthermore, whatever applies to all the sacraments that have in any way a constituting character (i.e., baptism, confirmation, holy orders, and matrimony) applies also in this case: it is possible to allow for their graces to revive, and it is possible to deepen these graces.

6. Full-Time and Part-Time Diaconate

Any discussion of the restoration of the diaconate will have to consider also the question as to whether these deacons (especially the married ones) would be meant to practice their diaconate as a full-time occupation—in other words, as priests and bishops do in normal circumstances—or whether this ordained diaconate should be a kind of part-time job for men who for the rest of the time follow a normal secular occupation and, as it were, conceive their diaconate as an intensified activity of the lay apostolate or of Catholic Action, which has been given a special character by ordination. If we are to expect any kind of clear answer to this question, which undoubtedly is also of practical importance, then we must first of all distinguish our concepts. For, as far as the concept of "vocation" is concerned, we must distinguish between a vocation in a metaphysical and theological sense and a vocation in the ordinary economic sense. St. Paul, for instance, was a tentmaker in the ordinary economic sense (i.e., he was forced to devote a great deal of his time to this trade in order to give himself an economic basis for existence). By his inner attitude, however, he was an apostle and nothing else, that is, his apostolic vocation and task was the only real, personal motive force of his whole life; it formed his life; it was the only guiding line of his actions, everything else was subordinated to it; and even his economic vocation, by which he earned his bread, served this other vocation and nothing else, no matter how time-consuming it may have been. His apostolate, if we may put it this way, was not a spare-time job; it was not merely a hobby or just an additional though extremely ideal occupation transforming his life, but the real existential, formative principle of his life, even though it may of necessity have taken up less of his time sometimes than his trade of tentmaking. A religious task and purpose does not *eo ipso* become the life-giving formative principle of a vocation in the metaphysico-theological sense, simply because it is objectively on a higher level than what constitutes a secular, economic vocation. Someone who, for example, is a research chemist by the whole inner inclination of his personality can nevertheless be an extremely zealous worker in Catholic Action as a lay apostle; he can in certain cases play an important role in a parish; he may indeed recognize and acknowledge the purely objectively higher value of his religious purpose as compared with the ideals of his vocation as a chemist; nevertheless, he will be a chemist by profession even in a metaphysico-theological sense, and not an apostle. For, in spite of everything and having regard to the whole of his personal life, his job as a chemist is the essential law of his life (understanding, of course, that this does not refer to the general formative principles valid for every human being and every Christian, but to his professionally specifying formative principles). Conversely, a member of a secular institute, for instance, if he understands his life according to the Evangelical Counsels properly, will have to interpret his secular occupation as a means of realizing those specifically religious and apostolic purposes that are proper to such a secular institute; in a metaphysico-theological sense, such a member (even if he is a research worker) will, therefore, have a spiritual and not a worldly vocation, even when—in a secular, sociological sense—he does a secular job. Of course, it also follows from what has been said that the transition from one of these notions to the other will be quite vague in the hard realities of life. It is clear that in the individual concrete case, it will perhaps be difficult to determine the boundary. Indeed, in the history of a particular life, a part-time occupation may become a real vocation in the theological and existential sense, and what was previously a vocation in the metaphysico-theological sense may deteriorate to being a job in a merely economic or perhaps secular sense (i.e., to being a "job by which one gains one's living").

If one makes this fundamental distinction, then one will presumably be able to say: Only where the diaconate is a vocation in the theological and existential sense in the life of a certain person should the Church ordain that person by the sacrament of the diaconate; where, on the other hand, in spite of the inner understanding and serious idealism with which they are exercised, the functions of the diaconate are merely something like an idealistic spare-time occupation, which does not really constitute the inner structural principle of a person's life, such a person performing the activities of the diaconate should not be ordained deacon by the Church. This principle surely follows from the fact that an ordination, especially by the character given by it, is meant to stamp a person permanently and completely and should claim the whole person, with all his internal and external powers, for such a permanent commission and authorization of service in the Church. If this principle were to be basically disputed, then it would also be no longer possible to explain why the Church does not normally want the priest to be burdened with some other civil job but wants him to live by the altar. In view of this fact, the ordained deacon must fundamentally be someone who normally receives his livelihood from the Church in basically the same way and with basically the same "titles" as canon law envisages for the priest. Of course this does not tell us anything about the extent to which this normal case will be realized at a particular time and in a particular country. It does not determine whether the exceptional cases (as was already true at the time of St. Paul) will not sometimes become the "normal" practice (i.e., whether ordained deacons, as well as priests, must not in certain conditions work for their living by a bread-winning job). Yet even in this case they would be, and would have to be, men whose personal life is completely formed by their vocation as deacons, their vocation in the theological sense. In other words, ordination to the diaconate cannot be given as a kind of reward or decoration for a zealous apostolate. This again does not mean, however, that it is inconceivable that in certain economic and social conditions, where those who are anxious to do creative work can and do leave their bread-earning jobs in good time, there will be a noticeable increase in the number of those who regard and choose the diaconate as a genuine vocation in the theological sense. The mere fact of more advanced age is no real obstacle to this.

7. Remarks about Certain Practical Norms for the Restoration of the Diaconate

We intend merely to indicate these norms here insofar as they more or less represent self-evident conclusions from our previous fundamental reflections; in this way, we should be in a position to show to some extent that even in practice such a restoration of the diaconate is not really as revolutionary a measure as might be thought at first. It must be understood, of course, that such norms can have legal validity only if they are laid down by the ecclesiastical authorities.

(a) The canonical and liturgical laws regarding those deacons who accept their office and ordination with the declared intention of becoming priests can quite easily remain as they have been up till now. It is not the task of these reflections to examine whether a practical, longer interval between the time of ordination to the diaconate and ordination to the priesthood would be advisable and practicable for the training and testing of candidates for the priesthood. Since in the Latin Church the candidate for the priestly office makes a sworn declaration before reception of the subdiaconate, to the effect that he knows the obligation of celibacy and wishes to take it freely upon himself, there can be no doubt about which of the two classes of deacon someone belongs to, especially since the candidates for the priesthood who become deacons receive a religious and theological training that is completely different in content, place, and so forth, from the training of the "absolute" deacons (to coin a phrase). If one leaves the diaconate as a step in orders towards the priesthood, then nothing at all needs to be changed in the canonical legislation for the priesthood, and the candidate for the priesthood is made to realize with sacramental clearness that his office, too, since it includes the diaconate, is a service and not a lording it over others. It becomes clear to him in this way also that he must regard the "absolute" deacons as his true brothers in the spirit, appointed for the same unique task of the Church as his.

(b) All our previous reflections started from and were directed to the fact that the sacramental transmission of the office of the diaconate should be used whenever this office already exists more or less explicitly (even though perhaps not in all its functions and powers) and that we should not create more or less artificial offices, which are not demanded by the needs of the care of souls but are created simply in order to be able to confer an ordination to the diaconate. It cannot be doubted, however, that the offices presupposed for the restoration of the ordination of deacons do not exist to the same extent, with equal significance and in equal numbers in different parts of the Church. And furthermore where they do not exist, they are presumably nonexistent partly because they are not really required (since there are, for instance, sufficient priests who can easily and without special difficulty fulfill the tasks of the diaconate together with their own); on the other hand, these offices may indeed be absent partly also on account of a certain atrophy in the Church's pastoral care which really requires these offices but simply has not yet developed them to a sufficient extent. Such a situation certainly makes it desirable that the centralized, universal ecclesiastical legislation concerning the restoration of the diaconate should be merely a skeleton legislation making it possible to administer such ordinations where the actual existence of these offices would make such a procedure reasonable and desirable. Such a legislation should advise and facilitate the establishment of such offices where the situation of the care of souls demands it and where the possibility of an ordination to an office would make it easier to give these offices to suitable candidates. It should be legislation, finally, that does not make the restoration of the diaconate an obligation for regions where the situation does not warrant it and where this restoration would have no real meaning if it were carried through. A merely skeleton legislation, which would leave room for a genuine differentiation in the Church in accordance with the religious, pastoral, cultural, and historical situation, would reasonably and homogeneously fit into that general tendency in the Church (in accordance with the principle of subsidiary functions valid also for the Church) that desires to introduce a certain decentralization in the Church wherever the objectively existing or desirable difference

175

of the individual parts of the Church obviously calls for such decentralization. The most suitable subjects for such differentiated and independent practices with regard to the ordination and utilization of deacons presumably would not be so much individual dioceses but rather certain wider ecclesiastical configurations, such as an ecclesiastical province or the totality of dioceses in a country, so that a metropolitan or a national conference of bishops would be the proper legislator (with the approval of the Apostolic See) for such particular regulations.

(c) Such a skeleton legislation issued by Rome could give the holders of particular rights in the Church (perhaps with certain conditions to be worked out in more detail) the right to ordain men to the diaconate without obligation to celibacy, provided they have proved themselves by a Christian life put to the test and by a "professional" exercise (cf. no. 6) of an important part of those tasks which, according to the Church's tradition, constitute the office of deacon (i.e., liturgical, teaching, charitable, administrative functions, in which connection it should be noted that such a candidate of an ordained diaconate need not have exercised all these functions in actual fact, but may have specialized in one of them as his main task). Before ordaining anyone, the bishop must be convinced that the candidate for ordination to the diaconate has the desire and firm purpose to exercise this office for life, as a member of the clergy but without a desire to become a priest, and that he has the necessary physical, mental, and religious qualifications for this. If the candidate is already married, then the bishop must of course also take his Christian conduct of marriage into consideration when judging his suitability. It will probably also have to be part of this skeleton legislation to decide whether the ordination of an "absolute" deacon should be administered to someone already married (if he has not accepted the obligation or celibacy by ordination or by membership of a religious institute) or whether ordination to the diaconate can be given even to a suitable candidate who is still unmarried but does not wish to renounce the right to marry. Perhaps the question is not so urgent in practice because it can be expected in general that a candidate for ordination to the diaconate who has already been tested for a longer period (which is necessary) and who is likely to think about getting married will be already married by the time the longer trial period of his training and testing in the exercise of his vocation is over, a period that must be demanded in any case. Certainly, it has been said elsewhere that this trial period should also not be stretched out *too* long, if we are not to contradict the whole meaning of such an ordination. No matter what may be the exact details of this skeleton legislation, a certain elasticity in its application to territorial and personal circumstances will be advisable, in the same way as it has already been done in the case of the legislation regarding the priesthood (dispensation from the statutory age for ordination, etc.). This skeleton legislation will have to incorporate also some general rules about the possibility and manner of laicization of such ordained deacons. It will be advisable, for various practical reasons, not to make withdrawal from *this* clerical station too difficult, whether the first move be made by the deacon himself or by the bishop (both of which must be open possibilities). This outline-legislation must naturally also occupy itself with the celibate "absolute" deacon, since he too is a possibility. With regard to the obligation to celibacy in this case, the legislation will either have to state what is already (or perhaps will be) the canonical rule with regard to the celibacy of deacons going on to the priesthood, or what is right where there is some other reason for the celibacy of such a deacon, *viz.* on the grounds of his obligation as a member of a religious society or secular institute. To this extent, it will be quite easy to lay down rules for the celibacy of such a deacon.

(d) The deacon thus ordained will surely also have the right, at least basically, to exercise those liturgical functions that belong to him according to canons 741; 845 §2; 1147 §4; 1342 §1 of the *Code of Canon Law,* and will have this explicit and unreserved right even if he is married. It must be left to the Church's legislative activity and presumably to her universal legislation to decide whether these liturgical powers should be extended still further and should be made more precise by a universal ecclesiastical legislation (whether they should be extended, for instance, to the right of assisting at marriages, to wider powers for blessings for all things permitted to the priest, to the power of giving benediction). The diaconate will, however, gain in significance, in estimation and pastoral usefulness, if the legislation is magnanimous and broadminded in this respect. After all, even this skeleton legislation can make provision for the individual ordinary to promulgate more exact regulations regarding the use of these liturgical powers, even though in certain cases this may mean limiting these powers to some extent in practice. It is taken for granted that in these liturgical functions the deacons will be bound by the liturgical laws (e.g., with regard to liturgical dress) just as the rest of the clergy.

(e) An elastic, general legislation of universal canon law will probably not be able to go further in its decrees about the exercise of the office, about dress, and about the married deacons' way of life, than stating that they must in all these respects follow the directions of their ordinary. But with regard to these directions to be given by the ordinary, we will once more have to remind ourselves of the fundamental principle that it is the *office* and not the ordination to the office which must be the basic norm for all these directives. Hence, the manner of life which up till now has been recognized and encouraged by the Church authorities as corresponding to the office must also correspond to this office even after ordination. This applies also, for instance, to the question of lay dress of such an officeholder according to the customs of the particular country. These ordinances must therefore not be an external and mechanical transference of the laws applicable to the conduct of the bearers of higher orders.

(f) The canonical obedience towards his bishop, to which the ordained deacon is obliged as a member of the clergy, embraces:

(i) The obligation to exercise his office as perfectly as possible on the lines laid down by the bishop (i.e., that office which the person concerned exercised in the service of the Church even before his ordination to the diaconate and which was meant to be sanctified and perfected by this ordination). This canonical obedience at least need not contain the obligation to exercise a totally different kind of diaconate from the one for which the person concerned was trained and in which and for which he was ordained;

(ii) The obligation to exercise the liturgical functions of a deacon, when and in the measure to which the bishop deems this necessary for an ordered and fruitful care of souls;

(iii) The obligation to lead a life in keeping with his ecclesiastical office and ordination. For the rest, the norms of this canonical obedience will have to be conceived analogously to those of the canonical obedience of the priest, with obvious modifications that will be necessary in the nature of things.

(g) The livelihood of a deacon in the service of the Church (again in accordance with our basic reflections) will first of all be that which the Church (the bishop or the parish) had already given and was obliged to give to such a deacon on account of the office he exercised even before his ordination. It is clear that the Church's obligation to see to the deacon's maintenance is increased by ordination and by the fact that the ordained belongs to the clergy. The formally juridical part of the Church's obligation to look after the maintenance of the deacon can be carried out in accordance with the *"titulus canonicus"* of the other orders. It is understood that this maintenance, which the Church owes to her ordained deacons within the limits of her possibilities, includes also the maintenance of the deacon's family in accordance with what is fitting for the station and purpose of his vocation.

(h) The training of an "absolute" deacon. The general, skeleton legislation will no doubt have to lay down certain guiding lines also for the training of "absolute" deacons, without thereby doing violence to the great difference of conditions in different countries and hence of the actual characteristics of the deacon's service in these different countries. In this sense, it would have to be demanded that the formation of such deacons correspond to the following principles:

— The deacon must receive a general religious education corresponding to what is customary and possible in the case of an educated Christian layman in a particular region.

— He must receive the schooling and formation demanded by the needs and possibilities of the particular region for the carrying out of the office he exercises or should exercise even apart from ordination to the diaconate (e.g., the office of welfare worker, social worker, catechist, ecclesiastical administrator). It is not necessary, therefore, that this professional training should be the same for all deacons. On the contrary, it will be desirable that this formation should be very specialized but thorough so that as a result of this formation the later professional activity of such a deacon will vindicate itself on its own merits and not merely by the ordained character of the person concerned. It follows from this that at least this part of the general formation of a deacon will demand different training schools and cannot be given uniformly to all deacons. This will not necessitate the establishment of a very complicated, new training machinery, since no new offices and hence no new training institutes need be created; it will be quite sufficient to utilize and eventually adapt to one's higher purpose those training facilities which even now serve the purpose of preparing candidates for their different occupations. If the future ordained deacon is to engage mostly in catechetical tasks in the Church, then he must of course be given a thorough theological training, a training that must more or less correspond to the training demanded of a priest engaged in the care of souls (according to the rules and customs of the particular country). A more detailed treatment of this question will be found elsewhere in this book. The general schooling (e.g., secondary school), demanded and sufficient in the institutions concerned with this vocational training, should also be demanded and suffice for ordination to the diaconate.

— This formation of the deacon will also have to include a fairly long period of exercising his particular office in the service of the Church before ordination. It would perhaps be more desirable to determine the age for ordination of the absolute deacon on this basis, rather than simply demanding systematically a certain fixed age for this. If, for instance, someone has exercised his diaconate outstandingly well for three to five years after thorough training (and has thereby automatically reached the age at which the Church confers even ordination to the priesthood), then there should be no reason for not conferring ordination to the diaconate.

— Finally, there should be an additional, brief but thorough period of instruction and practice in the liturgical functions which are part of the deacon's duty. The question as to whether it would be possible and desirable to train all the different categories of deacons in common as far as this part of their training is concerned is something that will have to be decided in accordance with the different conditions in different countries. During the whole training (i.e., both the more vocational and the liturgical training), the corresponding religious and spiritual instruction and formation of the candidates for the diaconate must also be looked after. This part of the training could be conceived analogously to the formation given to candidates for the priesthood by the spiritual director.

(i) Since presumably any skeleton legislation issued by Rome could say very little about the actual life of ordained deacons both "on duty" and privately, it will be the task of the bishop to help the ordained deacons by suitable norms and recommendations to ensure that their personal, human, and religious life will correspond to their spiritual station and their office in the Church; that marriage may harmoniously fit into, and positively advance, the mission given to them by the Church; and that they may foster that unity and cooperation among deacons and with the priestly pastors of souls which are so necessary both for the fulfillment of their task, and to ensure that the unity and cooperation between deacons and priests are made evident and the characteristics of the office of the deacon come to be distinguished clearly from the priestly office. Above all, it will have to be recommended that the deacon should assist at the daily celebration of the eucharistic sacrifice and that he should make a regular habit of meditative reading of the Scriptures.

(j) In accordance with the proper nature of the different orders in the Church, it seems less suitable—and indeed superfluous—to demand reception of the minor orders as a condition for ordination to the diaconate in the case of "absolute" deacons.

Notes

1. Cf. K. Rahner, *Kirche und Sakramente* (Freiburg, 1960), pp. 85-95. (English translation: *The Church and the Sacraments, Quaestiones Disputatae* IX [Edinburgh/London, 1963].)

2. Cf. on this difficult question, my Essay in the jubilee volume for Erik Wolf (Frankfurt, 1961): "*Uber das ius divinum in der Kirche*" (p. 277 in this volume).

3. Cf. my Essay "*Priesterliche Existenz*" in *Schriften zur Theologie* III (Einsiedeln, 1960), pp. 285-312. This Essay works out the connection between the priesthood and the sacramental, liturgical function and shows also the function of the prophetic as a factor on which the existence of the priesthood is founded. This could be applied analogously to the connection and difference of the functions of the diaconate. No matter how much the ligturgical function, properly and fully understood, may be the starting point and source for the whole nature of the diaconate, the charitable and *kerygmatic* task of the deacon too, in their unfolding of the total content of the Mystery of the Altar, are not merely secondary consequences of this essential basis but are themselves essential factors of the diaconate on which its existence is based. (*Theological Investigations* III [London/Baltimore, 1966]).

4. Cf. on this my Essay "Personal and Sacramental Piety" in *Theological Investiagations* III (London, 1963), pp. 109-133, where what has been said here in thesis is developed more in detail.

5. It is not our intention here to treat all the aspects of this question. This question is discussed more fully in A. Auer's contribution to the collective work, *Diaconia in Christo,* edited by K. Rahner and H. Vorgrimler (Freiburg, 1962), pp. 325-339.

6. Cf. K. Rahner, "*Zur Theologie der Pfarre,*" in H. Rahner, *Die Pfarre* (Freiburg, 1960), pp. 27-39.

7. A more detailed exposition of this will be found in my Essay "*Wort und Eucharistie,*" in *Schriften zur Theologie* IV (Einsiedeln, 1960), pp. 315-355.

8. This question is taken up once more in P. Winninger's chapter with special reference to the situation in France and the very active Catholic Action in that country: *Diaconia in Christo* (Freiburg, 1962), pp. 380-388.

9. Cf. for this my Essays on the subject of the layman in the Church, indicated by the chapter "*Laie und Ordensleben,*" in Sendung und Gnade (Innsbruck, 1961), pp. 364-396.

The Teaching of
the Second Vatican Council on
the Diaconate

by Karl Rahner, SJ

The subject that I have been asked to examine here is concerned with the teaching of the Second Vatican Council on the diaconate and the restoration of this.[1] So far as I know, in the various documents of this Council three texts in particular treat this subject. The most important of these is, of course, article 29 of the third chapter of the Constitution *Lumen Gentium.* In addition to this, two further texts have to be taken into consideration, namely, a passage that falls under no. 16 of the "Scheme on the Missionary Activity of the Church," a scheme on which there is still some little work to be done. Here, the restoration of the diaconate is treated from the point of view of the necessity of such a restoration in the missions. A further brief reference to this restoration is to be found in article 17 of the *Decree on the Oriental Catholic Churches,* which has already been promulgated. Here, it is stated that where the institution of the diaconate as a permanent state has ceased to be the practice it should be introduced once more.

First let us concentrate upon the principal of these passages, that which occurs in *Lumen Gentium.* It is not possible for me here to set forth the history leading up to this passage. Here, I would only recall the fact that this question is numbered among the five so-called test questions that were laid before the Council on October 3, 1963. The fifth question asked whether the fathers were agreed on the point that mention should be made in the *Constitution on the Church* of the diaconate and the necessity for its restoration. To this general question, which was intended merely to provide a general direction for a further working out of this decree, an affirmative answer was given, 1,588 of the fathers voting in favor of it, with 525 against. It was, therefore, a notable majority. The work of the theological commission went forward along the lines indicated by this vote, with the result that that text was produced which—apart from a few small alterations—we now read in the Constitution.

In a vote taken on September 28, 1964, the radical necessity for, and possibility of a restoration of the diaconate as a permanent state in the Church was accepted by an overwhelming majority. On September 29, the precise points of detail involved were laid before the fathers of the Council. These agreed by a comfortable two-thirds majority that even married men of mature age could be admitted to the order of deacon. On the same day, in the aula of the Council, the fathers rejected—by a majority the extent of which is not known, but which was substantial—the idea that younger men too could be admitted to the diaconate without any obligation to remain celibate. This must be sufficient here with regard to the history of the text. For the time appropriate to a brief lecture does not admit of entering any further into the manner in which these documents emerged and acquired their existing form. Let us turn our attention to the actual *texts* themselves. In this we shall, normally speaking, be referring to the Constitution *Lumen Gentium*. But where it is a question of entering into the reasons that the Second Vatican Council had for believing that the diaconate should be restored, we must also refer to the "Scheme on the Missionary Activity of the Church," which was prepared because—in my opinion—the reasons are set forth more clearly and more profoundly there than in the *Constitution on the Church* itself. I shall be saying a few words more on this point at a later stage.

I.

The first point to be made with regard to the teaching of the Second Vatican Council on the diaconate is concerned with the question of the essence of this as a permanent official state and as a sacrament in the Church. In this teaching, it is laid down first that the hierarchy of orders in the Church does in fact include, or at least could include, a state which, though subordinate, does constitute a genuine and permanent degree of the sacrament of order. In spite of this, according to the teaching and practice of the Western—as opposed to the Eastern—Church, the diaconate has come to be regarded ever since the Middle Ages (apart from a few isolated cases, which we cannot enter into here) merely as a necessary stage in the process of being raised to the priesthood. Now in the teaching of the Council, which is in conformity with the earliest and most universal teaching, it is expressly laid down that there is—or at least there could be—a degree in the hierarchy of orders, genuine, permanent, and sacramental, which is something more than a mere stage on the way to priestly ordination. It is one which could be, and under certain circumstances actually ought to be, recognized as a state and a degree in the hierarchy of orders, albeit a lower one, which has a genuine and essential function of its own distinct from that of the order of priest. From this point of view, therefore, the nature of the diaconate is such that it belongs in very truth to the hierarchy of order in the Church herself. It is not a lay state, but belongs to the three official states or degrees in the hierarchy of order itself, so that in all truth and reality deacons belong to the officially instituted and sacred orders which Christ founded in his Church. When, therefore, we distinguish between laymen on the one hand and the hierarchy of the Church on the other, we should certainly not assign the deacons to the lay state, nor should the diaconate itself be understood as in some sense designating the status of outstanding lay functionaries in the Church. On the contrary, the diaconate is, in very truth, a degree, albeit a subordinate one, in the hierarchy of order itself. Now with regard to the tasks that are, in practice, attached to this order of deacon, the passage with which we are concerned distinguishes between these various tasks of the diaconate in almost the same way as in its presentation of the official functions of bishops and priests. A new division has been introduced here according to which three general official functions are envisaged: the function of teaching; the function of sanctifying; and the function of leading. It is true that with regard to the third function certain more precise distinctions and provisos have been introduced. But it is still quite evident that in the *Constitution on the Church* these three general official functions, which apply to every official state in the hierarchy of the Church, are attributed to the office of deacon also.

This appears from what is said here about the function of preaching the word. It is stated that the deacon's part in this is to read the Sacred Scriptures to the faithful and to instruct and exhort the people. In other words, the function of preaching the Gospel is attributed to the deacon too, though of course in union and cooperation with the Church under the direction of the bishop and, in some respects, of the priest too. Thus with regard to the first function, which is attributed to all those who have been officially ordained in the Church, this applies to the deacon too. In the passage under consideration here the function of sanctifying is likewise attributed to the deacon clearly enough. In fact it is stated that it is his task solemnly to confer baptism; to have custody of and to distribute the Eucharist; to assist at and to bless marriages in the Church's name; to carry the Viaticum to the dying; to preside in the liturgy and prayers of the faithful; to dispense the sacraments; and to conduct the rites of burial. Again with regard to the function of guiding and leading, we can find something in our text that has reference to the deacon. For in it, the task of directing and administering is explicitly adduced. Now it is true that this task of the deacon belongs to the service of the Church and not, strictly speaking, to the guiding of her, this being, in a certain sense, confined to the bishops alone. Nevertheless, the deacon does, in a certain sense, share in this task, and it actually belongs to the very nature of diaconate itself to the extent that explicit mention is made of the task of administration. Of course, this is expressed only very briefly and in a few words. On the other hand, the task of charitable activity receives just as brief a mention even though this does undoubtedly belong, according to the very earliest traditions of the Church and with a firm basis in holy Scripture, to the office of deacon.

Nevertheless, we are compelled to say in all honesty that the text itself does not supply much information on this question. Perhaps, on the other hand, the scheme on the missions, *Ad Gentes Divinitus,* can help us for these official functions of the deacon are likewise mentioned here. The function of preaching the word is expressly mentioned. It is said that in the missions deacons have the duty of preaching the word of God as catechists. The function of sanctifying receives slighter mention in that particular scheme. But to compensate for this, it is expressed all the more clearly that the activity of deacons can, in a certain respect, be understood as a function of providing official guidance and leadership, or at least a sharing in this. This is what is meant when it is said that it is the task of the deacons in the missions to act in the name of the parish priest or the bishop in giving guidance to the widespread communities. Again the official function of performing works of charity is expressly mentioned here. It is said that it is the deacon's responsibility actively to engage himself in works expressive of love in the form of social and charitable activities. In this scheme, therefore, this aspect is developed on a broader basis than in *De Ecclesia* itself.

Now with regard to the essence of this order of deacon, the essential point—and one that finds expression in all the texts we have mentioned—is the sacramentality of the diaconate. On this point, the documents leave no room for doubt. What is in question here is a sacrament, a genuinely sacramental consecration, a sacramental grace that is imparted through the laying on of hands.

II.

The topic that is being treated in the main text—and also in the texts on the Eastern Churches and on the missions—is the restoration of the diaconate. In article 29 of the Constitution *Lumen Gentium,* two sections are devoted to this. The first concerns the theology of the diaconate; the second speaks explicitly of the restoration of the diaconate on which we shall now have something more to say.

This restoration is characterized in the "Scheme on the Church's Missionary Activity" as useful and to be recommended, and in the *Decree on the Catholic Eastern Churches,* it is urgently advocated. The reasons which the texts adduce for this deserve to be considered first. The presentation of these reasons appear, as I have already indicated at the beginning of this article, to have brought about a salutary development between the Constitution *Lumen Gentium* and the scheme *Ad Gentes Divinitus.* In the *Constitution on the Church,* it is stated that the tasks of the deacon as enumerated here are certainly supremely necessary for the life of the Church, and that even though, in the current administration of the Latin Church, there are many areas in which these tasks can only be performed with difficulty, still in the future the diaconate can be restored as a special order in the Church's hierarchy, existing as such in its own right. The reason adduced in the Constitution, therefore, is to be sought primarily in the difficulties of the concrete situation. It is said that there can be no question that these tasks are necessary: baptizing, preaching, the works of charity, and so forth. And it is further stated that the restoration of the deacon is necessary because, owing to the lack of priests today, it has become extremely difficult to fulfill these tasks. The scheme on the missions has not yet achieved final completion. But the reasons put forward here, while they do not run counter to this text in the *Constitution on the Church,* still differ from it nevertheless in certain notable respects. For this scheme treats of those individuals who already, in effect, are actually performing the official functions of the deacon by acting as catechists and so preaching the word of God; by acting in the name of the parish priest or the bishop to guide and administer the scattered Christian communities; or by performing the works of charity in social or philanthropic activities. Such individuals, the scheme states, should be fortified by the laying on of hands, as handed down from the apostles, so that they may be able more effectively to perform their diaconal functions through the grace of the sacrament. Here, therefore, it is not any actual difficulty—for instance, the lack of priests, etc.—which is adduced, rather it is asserted that the official functions appropriate to deacons already in practice exist in the Church. Now it is assumed as self-evident and actually asserted that since these individuals are actually performing these official functions, which already in practice exist in the Church, they should, as a matter of necessity or at least of suitability, be further fortified with that sacramental grace which according to the doctrine of the Church, is truly designed precisely for these official functions. In other words, it is simply stated: "The official functions already exist. We know from revelation that the diaconate also has a sacramental status. Why, therefore, should those individuals who already exercise these official functions of the deacon be deprived of that grace which does *de facto* exist in the Church as a sacramental grace?" The scheme on the work of the missions, therefore, abstracts from the question of whether or not the external circumstances and difficulties—the lack of priests, etc.—are so great that fresh resources are necessary to come to the help of the Church's priests and hierarchically ordained ministers in their work. It is simply stated that these official functions are actually in existence in practice and in effect, and that those who perform them should do so in that specifically sacramental power with which Christ has *de facto* endowed his Church.

Now with regard to the restoration of the diaconate itself, the authority appropriate to this is mentioned in both texts. It is said that the conferences of bishops, instituted in various forms and over different areas, can undertake this restoration. Similarly, in the scheme on the missions it is said that the appropriate conferences of bishops who have regarded the restoration of the diaconate as beneficial must be the ones to put it into practice. We must, therefore, lay down clearly and unequivocally that according to both texts the proper authority to act in this matter is not the pope but the conferences of bishops. It is to these conferences in themselves, here taken as the bodies from which such action must appropriately proceed, that power is ascribed to decide in this question as to whether it is opportune to bring about such a restoration in the different areas. Of course, this must take place, as is also explicitly laid down, in full agreement with the pope or with his assent. Nevertheless, it is the bishops who have to take the initiative in this matter, and who therefore have the responsibility of examining and judging as to whether it is opportune to bring about such a restoration in the different territories. It would be mistaken, therefore, for the bishops to suppose that the initiative has to come from the Holy See. On the contrary, the task with which we are here concerned is not directly that of the actual restoration itself, but rather of investigating and judging whether restoration is opportune. And this task is assigned, by the passages from *Lumen Gentium* dealing with the missions, to the bishops. Now once such an authorization has been given there can be no doubt that, for all the difficulties, a manifest duty exists to act upon it also. I do not say that there is a duty to bring about a renewal of the diaconate, but rather a duty to take all possible pains to examine and to judge whether or not this is opportune in a given area.

In the light of this, it also becomes clear what is being laid down in these passages with regard to the manner in which the restoration should take place. With regard to the territorial spheres, it is immediately evident that these passages do not presuppose that the restoration must necessarily take place everywhere in the world at the same time. There can be no doubt that a given conference of bishops can arrive at the judgment that in their particular area such a restoration of the diaconate is necessary and would be extremely beneficial, whereas another conference of bishops may arrive at the opposite judgment so far as its area is concerned. We have seen that the authorized bodies who have the power to bring about this restoration are the various conferences of bishops. And to this extent, it is obvious that it need not necessarily be expedient for a uniform restoration to take place simultaneously throughout the entire Catholic Church. But no conference of bishops can say, "Since our colleagues in another country are not restoring the diaconate, we too can peaceably abide by the practice which has been customary up to the present." Right from the outset and of set purpose, the text itself provides for the possibility of the restoration of the diaconate being confined to a particular region. But since this is within the power not of the individual bishops but of the bishops' conferences and territorial assemblies of bishops, there is no doubt that in a given country or in a greater area a certain uniformity is necessarily required. I do not believe that an individual bishop can set himself up in opposition to such a restoration against the majority decision of his colleagues who belong to the same conference of bishops. Otherwise, it would not in fact have been stated that it is for the conference of bishops to judge of the expediency of this restoration. The idea that this question is within the competence of an individual bishop to decide is certainly contrary to the spirit and the letter of the passages concerned.

After prolonged discussions, the decree decides that in any such restoration the diaconate can be conferred upon more mature men as well, and even when they are married. On the other hand, it is explicitly laid down that younger men too, when they are suitable, can be raised to the order of deacon, though in this case they are bound to celibacy. In view of this, it is evident that the text with which we are concerned itself envisages various classes of deacons. Naturally, this now opens the way to further and more far-reaching discussions, the subject matter of which no doubt presents difficulties of its own. Nevertheless, we must accept the text as it stands and recognize that in any such restoration at least two classes are envisaged: younger deacons who are bound to celibacy; and others who are of more mature age and married, upon whom this sacramental ordination can likewise be conferred. Surely, no one will deny that the diaconate as conferred upon these more mature men will, in practice and in the concrete, have a greater significance and more influence from the pastoral point of view in the life of the Church than the other case, which is likewise envisaged in the text concerned.

III.

We must now briefly enter into certain further questions that are still left open by the texts themselves. First, the question surely arises of who these men of more mature age are. What actual age is envisaged here? The actual terms of the text are extremely general and somewhat vague, and probably this is deliberate, because in this field, after all, there is need for a little further experience in deciding how old married men should be in order to be ordained deacons. Next, a further question arises as to what conferences of bishops or regional assemblies of bishops of various kinds the texts intend to refer to. Here too the answer is not easy. The conferences of bishops are so different from one another in respect of the number of their members, their status, the extent of the regions they represent, that in this respect many questions can suggest themselves. On the other hand, even this difficulty could, without great effort, be removed because even after they have come to their judgment as to whether a restoration of the diaconate is opportune, it is only with the agreement and assent of the pope himself that this restoration actually takes place.

The text says nothing about the kind o*f formation* that the future deacons should undergo. Here too there is much that still needs to be considered and examined in greater detail. Nevertheless, I believe that in view of the fact that the scheme on the missions envisages men who are already performing the tasks appropriate to deacons, we should regard this in itself as an indication of what kind of formation is required. Those individuals ought to be put forward for ordination who have already *de facto* acquired sufficient formation and experience in the Church's work, and who are already performing the official functions of deacons. On this view, not so very many difficulties will arise in our considerations of what sort of formation deacons should undergo as might otherwise be expected. *De facto* such individuals already exist. *De facto*, therefore, they are already to a large extent formed and prepared for their diaconal functions and experienced in them. The form and manner of formation, therefore, which has hitherto been considered sufficient for the formation of such individuals will also to a large extent be no less adequate for the formation of the future deacons. Otherwise, those who already perform the official functions of deacons would, in fact, have been unable to perform them at all.

A further question that has been left open in the texts with which we are concerned is that of the diaconate as a "lower" *degree* of order. One statement that has a certain relevance here is that passage in the *Constitution on the Church* which states that deacons would be ordained not as a preliminary to the priesthood but for a ministry of their own. Nevertheless, with regard to this "lower degree," several theological questions still remain unanswered. It is stated that the deacon exercises his ministry in union with the bishop and his priests. But what, in more precise terms, is the relationship that the deacon bears to the bishop or to the priest or to both together? How can we define more precisely the reasons for representing the order of deacon as a "lower" degree of order? Much in the way of theological exploration and examination is still needed in order to establish this. Of course, it is true that the deacon does not have those functions that, according to the official teaching of the Church and especially that of the Council of Trent, belong only to the priest, as for instance the administration of the sacrament of penance and the consecration at the eucharistic mystery. And to this extent, there is a palpable and easily comprehensible difference between the diaconate and the priesthood. From this basis, therefore, we can easily go on to say that the status of the deacon is lower as compared with that of the priest. Nevertheless, this does not necessarily or *ipso facto* imply that the diaconate is simply a "lower" degree from every point of view. When we think of the ministry on behalf of the poor, and of many other tasks that belong primarily to the deacon, it is no longer easy to perceive how the diaconate could be designated in this connection as a lower degree. Moreover, a point that we should particularly notice is that the Constitution *Lumen Gentium* carefully avoids saying that the episcopate (*munus episcopali*) is a "higher" degree, above that of the priesthood. On the contrary, it regards the episcopate as constituting, of its essence, the plenitude of an order that is, though hierarchically structured, integrally one, and that exists in the Church in virtue of a divine institution. Now if we make this way of regarding the matter our own, then we can consider the diaconate too as constituting in its own right an authentic and special mode of participation in this one integral order in the Church. From this it follows that, on the one hand, we both can and must say that the diaconate is a lower or more restricted mode of participation in this order than the priesthood. But at the same time, we do not necessarily have to say that this is the case in every respect. My belief is that the bishop has the most solemn duty of making the love of Christ present in the world in relation to all who toil and suffer, who are poor and weak, who have to bear persecution, and so forth. Now if this task belongs, in a quite primary sense, to the bishop himself, the deacon has no less vital a share in it than any priest. I have decided to mention this one point alone in order to show that the text with which we are concerned still leaves many questions open, both for further theological investigation and also so far as the Church's practice is concerned.

In conclusion, perhaps it will be appropriate to return once more to something that has already been said in order to enlarge upon it a little further. When we look more closely into the texts relating to deacons in the *Constitution on the Church* and the *Decree on the Church's Missionary Activity,* we find that it is not permissible, theologically speaking, to say that the tasks there ascribed to the future deacons can also be performed by laymen, or perhaps by those who, at some point in the future are to be equipped with the lower orders. In my opinion, any such conception would be, from all points of view, quite untheological. In the sacrament of order a threefold division exists both in the sacrament itself and in the official functions that go with it, and no one can deny that from apostolic times onwards the Church has been aware of, has recognized, and has actually exercised her God-given right to impose this division. Now if, and to the extent that, this is true—and it cannot be denied by anyone without danger of heresy—then, in my opinion, a further point manifestly follows, one that is clearly stated in the *Decree on the Church's Missionary Activity*. It is that when certain individuals in the Church are in fact fulfilling certain specific functions, then the Church herself must supplement this by conferring on them that grace which our Lord specially instituted precisely for these functions, and which he gave his Church authority to confer in sacramental form. This is the fundamental point for consideration in this whole question of the restoration of the diaconate. It is not some arbitrary question of what functions can or cannot be exercised by whom. It is not some kind of romantic revival that is in question here, of a reality that did in fact exist in the early Church. Rather, what we are asking here is whether in our Church of the present day the office of deacon is *de facto* being performed. If, and to the extent that we have to answer this question in the affirmative, or if and to the extent that we have to say that it is absolutely necessary for there to be such an office, given the circumstances of the present day, then this office is to be set up. And if an individual is already suitable for this office, then it seems to me to be necessary on theological grounds that grace should be conferred upon him, which does exist in the Church precisely for the official functions that he is *de facto* performing. Moreover, it appears that all other considerations are, from the outset, excluded from this genuinely theological one. We are not in the least concerned with the question of whether absolutely speaking it is possible for laymen too to give holy communion to others. No one will deny that this is possible. But the question that is being asked here is whether the Church really needs individuals who will have the duty of doing this and much else besides as part of their official and permanent functions, and as part of the normal life of the Church. If such individuals are needed, if such a permanent office, together with its functions, can be provided for in the Church, or if, indeed, it actually already exists, then the matter is already decided. The Church already has, in her possession, that sacramental grace which is designed for this office, which is already present and being exercised in her. And this sacramental grace must be conferred on those individuals. Theologically speaking, no other factors enter into the question. This may suffice by way of introduction. Since other theologians will be exploring the nature of the case from the theological point of view, I have been able to confine myself to certain aspects that have, of their very nature, been raised by the relevant conciliar documents.[2]

Notes

1. For the concrete occasion in view of which this lecture was composed, cf. the list of sources at the end of *Theological Investigations* X, Writings of 1965-1967 (New York: Herder and Herder, 1973). Translation copyright 1973 by Darton, Longman & Todd, Ltd., London, England.

2. For a fuller treatment of this, cf. the conference report entitled *"Le diacre dans l'eglise et le monde d'aujourd'hui,"* P. Winniger and Y. Congar, eds. in *Unam Sanctam* 59 (Paris, 1966). The concrete occasion for which this lecture was composed was such that it was not possible to enter into the new prescriptions for the diaconate set forth in the *Motu Proprio "Sancrorum Diaconatus Ordinem"* (cf. *L'Osservatore Romano*, June 28, 1967, p. 1). For a more detailed interpretation of this document, I may draw attention to the edition with commentary that is to be brought out by Herbert Vorgrimler and publihsed by the Paulinus-Verlag, Trier (*Nachkonziliare Dokumentation*, No. 9). On the situation in Germany, cf. K. Rahner, H. Vorgrimler, J. Kramer, *"Zur Erneuerung des Diakonats in Deutschland,"* in *Stimmen der Zeit* 180 (1967), pp. 145-153. For further information on the current movements, attention may be drawn to a series of documents entitled *Diakonia*, and produced by the *Internationale Diakonatskreis* at Freiburg im Breisgau.

On the Diaconate

by Karl Rahner, SJ

Such far-reaching and rapid developments have taken place in the theology and the practice of the permanent diaconate[1] that even twenty years ago it would have been quite impossible to guess at them. Certain theological movements in the last few years before the Council, the Council itself, and certain impulses arising from it have all undoubtedly contributed to this. In our present consideration, however, we have no intention of reopening in any direct sense the discussion of this conciliar theology of the diaconate and the practical effects deriving from this. We must begin by taking all this as already recognized and valid.[2] Since the Council, however, and without any direct dependence upon it, the development of the diaconate has received a quite fresh impetus, and it is this that we shall be concerned with here. For in the light of this fresh impetus, which we are on the point of describing, the question of the content, the significance, the usefulness, or even the necessity of the permanent diaconate will be presented from an aspect that is quite different from those that have formerly been discussed, and different even from those that were considered in the Council. The new stimulus to develop a theology, and concomitant with this new practical applications too, of the diaconate stems from the new theology of the priestly office. This is something that, in its current developments, was still not envisaged at all in the Council, or at any rate, if it was so, the statements in which it was referred to did not attract any attention. This new development of the theology of the priestly office, which is of the utmost importance for the diaconate, generates its own forward impulse, and this from two different directions: from the standpoint of the biblical theology of "office" in the Church, and from the situation both within the Church herself and in secular society in which the priestly office is placed today. Although we must begin by speaking of the fresh problems raised by the theology of the priestly office, our treatment of this must necessarily be extremely brief, and we shall only discuss these problems insofar as they throw some light upon the theology of the diaconate itself.

The first point to be clearly recognized in the New Testament theology[3] of "office" in the Church concerns the division of this into the office of priest and bishop. Insofar as we can discern this division at all in the New Testament, it certainly does not consist in any clear line of demarcation drawn between the office of priest and bishop. Moreover, it is clear that that which constitutes the essence of this office does not consist in any immediately apprehensible sense in sacramental powers of a specifically sacerdotal kind or, more precisely still, in any special powers exercised in the community's celebration of the Eucharist. Insofar as we can discern any special office in the Christian community as portrayed in the New Testament, with its universal priesthood, it is characterized primarily by a special mission to preach the word and by the function of leading and directing a Christian community, and in this connection the question of the relationship and at the same time the distinction between these two functions represents a further special problem in its own right. Of course we can say, and objectively speaking we are certainly justified in saying, that any official preaching of the word or leadership of the community achieves its supreme point in that proclamation of the death of the Lord, which takes place in the liturgy of the community. And it is in this liturgy that the community itself achieves the fullness of its own nature in a form that is sacramentally most intense. In this sense, we can certainly establish a rational connection between the traditional and sacerdotal concept of the priestly office, which is also that sanctioned by the Council of Trent, and the conception of office that we find in the New Testament, which is not in any direct sense defined in specifically priestly (i.e., cultic and sacerdotal) terms. But even if we recognize this, still the question of the nature of the priestly office is presented in a fresh form by the New Testament and needs to be answered afresh by working out a fresh way of organizing the manifold elements belonging to the priestly office based upon the Bible itself.

To this a second point must be added, which also derives from the present-day biblical theology of "office" in the Church. In the light of the New Testament, it is surely possible to conceive of official functions within the society of the Church that are quite different from those that spontaneously occur to our minds today when we speak of "office" in the Church and go on straightway to divide this into the offices of bishop, priest, and deacon in the conviction that these three hierarchical degrees can be easily and unambiguously distinguished from one another, and that these alone, when taken together, represent the single totality of "office" in the Church. It is true that the three terms do occur already in the New Testament: *bishop, presbyter, diakon*. But even if it appears in the Pastoral Epistles that by the end of the apostolic age the bishop as an individual already possesses a well-defined function of leadership in the local community reserved to him alone, still this in itself is not enough to supply any unambiguous distinction between the three concepts or to assign any unambiguous content to each of the three. In other words, in terms of the New Testament there is indeed an "office" in the Church, and this is ultimately one. But it can be subdivided into various functions according to the concrete needs of any given community. These functions as distributed in this sense between various s will certainly also have to be thought of as hierarchically arranged. But the element of "office" in the Church is certainly still fluid. Various sociological patterns can be employed in determining the concrete forms that it assumes and the variations that it undergoes, and moreover no very clear lines of demarcation are to be found in the New Testament marking it off from other charisms contributing to the well-being of the community, which cannot be regarded as official or institutional in any proper sense. In passing, a further point must also be emphasized: the fact that in the New Testament the Church's "office" is still fluid in this sense, and that variation is still possible in the way in which its different functions are distributed between different s, according to the concrete circumstances and requirements in any given case, does not gainsay the sacramentality of the three hierarchical degrees of order recognized in our own times. In other words, these factors in the New Testament cannot be contested on the ground of the dogmatic teaching of the sacramentality of order as it exists in the present day. There is a further question of what the reasons are, in more precise terms, for ascribing a sacramental force to the juridical act of conferring "office" in the Church. But this question need not concern us for our immediate purposes. In any case, the teaching of dogmatic theology demonstrates the fact that the single sacrament of *ordo,* even though it really is single (otherwise, there would be more than seven sacraments), can be subdivided into different degrees, and this teaching also demonstrates the fact that at least as late as the high Middle Ages the theologians uncompromisingly taught that the truly sacramental element in order was further subdivided into very minor and insignificant official posts in the Church. And they also taught uncompromisingly that the conferring of a share in the single "office" of the Church allowed for a far greater variation and modification of content among the official posts that the Church recognized than we are nowadays accustomed to accept as either possible or actual. What all this implies for the diaconate can be explained only at a later stage.

We must first consider the fresh impetus which the theology and practical application of the priestly office implies for the diaconate from yet another aspect. The problems entailed in the situation of the present-day priest, both within the society of the Church and within secular society, must briefly be touched upon.[4]

Formerly, in virtue of his priestly office, it was taken for granted that the priest has a specific and well-defined position in secular society. In virtue of his priestly office, he had also a calling in the worldly sense, a "firm position" even at the secular level, a plain and recognized "role" in the body politic. Today this is no longer so obvious. The question is raised, for instance, whether a priest should not follow a secular calling as well in order to achieve an indisputable position in the world, and one which provides him with economic support, so that he may bear an effective witness to the Gospel precisely from this well-recognized position. In fact, there are here and there in the secular institutes priests who side-by-side with their priestly tasks follow a worldly calling. This, together with the phenomenon of the worker-priests, demonstrates the fact that we have already reached a stage that is beyond that of purely academic speculation.

There is a further question, namely, whether in view of the dangerous lack of priests today there should not be individuals who, in addition to their priestly office, also follow a worldly calling as a "full-time job." These would exercise their priestly functions on Sunday or in the evening as a "part-time job." This question points in the same direction. An additional factor is that, even regarded from within the Church, those who hold the priestly office in the Church at least to some extent have gathered to themselves and exercised functions in the Church which are both very intensive and very numerous, even though—if we take the traditional conception of the priesthood as our starting-point—we cannot really see why such functions should be exercised precisely by priests. The phenomenon of the lay religious instructor, the so-called lay theologian, and many others besides show that even this question which is interior to the society of the Church is no mere theoretical problem. These are findings that both at the theological and the practical levels have, properly speaking, only been realized in their full relevance since the Council, and it is in the light of these that the question of the diaconate too must be viewed today. Although the factor of "office" in the Church is ultimately one, in respect of its functions and its distribution among various of its holders,[5] it is far more elastic, flexible, and fluid—if we may so express it—than has been realized in the last few centuries. We have no intention here of drawing from this the conclusion that we should *ipso facto* call in question or seek to revise the threefold division of the single office of the Church into bishop, priest, and deacon, which had already become classic and canonical at the beginning of the post-apostolic age. At the same time, it should not be forgotten that the great theologians of the Middle Ages still counted the so-called minor orders as well—in other words, those belonging to quite unimportant s in the Church—as to be included also among those degrees of office that are sacramentally conferred. Moreover, even to this day, the Church has not produced any official doctrinal decision that rules out such a theory.

But even when we simply take for granted the three degrees in the hierarchical division of ecclesiastical office, still it must at least be concluded from the evidence, which we have mentioned both in terms of biblical theology and of the state of contemporary society, that it is possible freely to reconsider in more precise terms both the content of the three offices in the Church and the lines of demarcation between them. Moreover, this reappraisal needs to be something more than merely an affair of the reason engaging in theological speculation so as to establish what is the case. Also, and more than this, it must at least to some extent be capable of leading to an alteration in the content of these offices and to the establishing of new and real lines of demarcation between them. (That this is not impossible from the outset is indeed also demonstrated by the fact that, for instance, it cannot be asserted in any very precise terms whether the power of conferring the sacrament of confirmation belongs to the episcopal or the priestly office. This is something that on any showing needs, from this aspect, to be determined once and for all as a matter of positive law by the Church).

On this basis, it would be theologically justified to say that the function and tasks of the renewed and permanent diaconate enumerated by the Council do not restrict our scope for working out a more profound and also a fresh and creative theology of the diaconate. These functions adduced in the Council vary greatly in their significance. Taken in isolation any one of them can also be conferred upon one who is not a deacon, although on any right under-standing of the single complex "office" in the Church this does not tell against the significance and the sacramentality of the diaconate itself. These functions enumerated by the Council are not coordinated among themselves by it so as to constitute the diaconate as a unified whole in which all these functions and tasks are manifestly interconnected. And finally, it is by no means certain that in the diaconate in its contemporary form, in contrast, and also as an alternative to these historical functions of the diaconate, quite other functions may be present that will characterize the diaconate of the future far more decisively than these former ones. In this theological situation, in which the question of what a deacon is and what he should be in the future is still, to a very great extent, an open one; in this situation, in which it is possible to work out a new definition of what the diaconate shall mean, not merely at the speculative but at the practical level as well, it seems to me that, properly speaking, only the following fixed points can be regarded as established: the deacon receives his office together with the powers and duties appropriate to it. The conferring of this office on the part of the episcopate has a sacramental character and, because of this, must take place in the manner required for a sacramental act performed in public, something that is perfectly reconcilable with a considerable breadth of choice in the form which this conferring of the office of deacon is to assume. It is not normal (i.e., legitimate in the ordinary circumstances prevailing in a Christian community) for the deacon to have the power of presiding at the eucharistic liturgy. For while it is true that this does not simply constitute in itself alone the content of the priestly office or the basic theological starting-point for defining its nature, still this power is, after all, proper to the priestly office and will surely remain so in the future, although it still does not carry with it any absolute, fixed, or unalterable connection with the official preaching of the word of God and the direction of the community (taking these in turn as constituting a unity). It seems to me, however, that these three specifications of the diaconate constitute at the same time the sole three invariable factors that can be attributed with certainty to the diaconate.

All that has been said up to this point has been intended to convey in barest outline the insight that we cannot, properly speaking, define the meaning and content of the diaconate of the future on the basis of the New Testament, the ancient practice of the Western Church, or of course on the basis of the Eastern Church's conception of the diaconate either,[6] although at the same time the three invariable factors mentioned above have to be respected. Today, therefore, what is properly in question is not a restoration of the diaconate in its ancient form, but a creative conception of the diaconate of the future. Ancient models of the diaconate can provide stimuli for this new specification of it. Nevertheless, in this new and creative specification, what is involved is not merely a restructuring of the traditional functions of the ancient diaconate at the level of speculative theology. But how is this new specification of the nature (i.e., the specific function) of the diaconate of the future to be arrived at? This is the difficult question with which the Church has to cope today, the moment she has resolved upon a renewal of the diaconate of this kind. Two points should be self-evident from the outset in this quest for a new conception of the diaconate:

1. Any such creatively new conception cannot be worked out exclusively at the conference table of rational theological speculation, because in principle and in all cases no concrete decisions can be arrived at solely and exclusively by a process of theological reasoning. Practical and concrete experimentation is required. All kinds of attempts have to be made, even though they do not lead immediately, or in all cases, to results that are serviceable or permanent, and even

though, conversely, such attempts have to be undertake only with theological speculation as their concomitant, and with an attitude of realism and prudence.

2. It can readily be accepted from the outset that the diaconate of the future as it is realized in the concrete will admit of a quite considerable number of variations of form. This is surely something that we should expect both with regard to the concrete functions attached to an office of this kind and with regard to the various holders of this office. For even an office that, as a matter of theological principle, is conceived of very much as a unity certainly demands considerable variations in the forms it assumes in the situation that exists today both in the Church and also in secular society, with all its extreme complexities and variations. In fact, it can be the case that it will only be from a fairly wide variety of concrete forms assumed by the diaconate (forms that have been prompted by the situation of the Church and her concrete practice, and which have almost been forced upon her) that we shall gradually come to recognize the single theological essence common to all these various forms and underlying them, and constituting the ministry of the diaconate as an office of the Church.

Now if I am to attempt to say anything with regard to this content and nature of the diaconate of the future, I would like to begin by drawing attention to the fact that probably the best treatment that has been accorded to this theme up to the present is that of H. Vorgrimler in the *Handbuch der Pastoraltheologie* IV.[7] In what follows, I shall be relying very much on this study, but I would like to present what I have to say in my own words and on my own responsibility.

In order to find an answer to our question concerning the nature and function (which is the same thing) of the future diaconate, certain preliminary methodological remarks must first be made, and then certain negative boundary lines must be drawn, and, finally, an attempt must be made to state in positive terms what the future diaconate will be.

First, a few preliminary methodological remarks. In the days of the Council, the line of argument that I customarily followed in support of the restoration and renewal of the permanent diaconate was as follows: the diaconate already exists *de facto* in an anonymous form in the Church of today. In these circumstances, it is right that those who are already vested with this anonymous diaconate should also have the sacramental commission conferred upon them, because in principle it is possible for there to be a sacramental diaconate in the Church, and such a sacramental commission is reasonable and productive of grace.[8]

This line of argument was, and still is in principle, not unjustified. Today, however, it is no longer adequate, for first in asserting that *de facto* the function of the diaconate was already being exercised in the Church, albeit in anonymous form and without any sacramental commission, we allowed ourselves to be influenced too much by the model of the earlier form of the diaconate,[9] although this in itself did not simply make our assertion false. It was not possible on these grounds to define more precisely what form the diaconate is to assume in the future in terms of its functions and activities. With regard to the functions already *de facto* existing in the Church, it could not easily be explained which ones would be conferred by means of a sacramental commissioning and which would not. In the "institutional Church" in the future, even though it is certain that in the future too there will be functions of this kind pertaining to the administrative practice of the Church such as not merely can be, but actually should be exercised by laymen, even so it will remain to some extent a question of practical judgment to decide where to draw the borderline in the concrete between this type of function and the other type. There is a further point to be noticed pertaining to methodology. The diaconate of the future will remain an integral part of the official ministry of the Church, as hierarchically organized. On the one hand, therefore, it must certainly manifestly be seen to be a subdivision of this official ministry and its functions, deriving from the very nature of the official ministry itself. On the other hand, however, this subdivision can and must be conditioned by the concrete situation in which the Church fulfills her task through her official ministry. It follows that whatever authentic basis we find for instituting the diaconate of the future in its distinctive form, it must be such that it does not in any sense depend upon the postulate that this concrete form of the diaconate as conceived of in the present must have been in existence all along and of necessity, and must continue to exist for all time. This means that the concrete situation of the Church is an essential element in this line of argument. This does not invalidate the *jus divinum* of the diaconate (and, as the concomitant of this, its sacramentality too) for this *jus divinum* simply implies that the Church's official institutions belong essentially to the Church herself, that they are communicated sacramentally as such, and that this special quality inherent in them also extends to the concrete subdivisions of these institutions whenever the process of subdividing the single institution of order is demanded by the concrete situation of the Church or is, at any rate, reasonable in view of it.

There is one final point that has to be taken into account from the outset with regard to this basic flexibility and adaptability of the single institution of order in the Church and the forms into which it is subdivided. It is that any specific subdivision of this order is itself in turn capable of appearing in various concrete forms as demanded by the concrete circumstances and tasks of the Church, and that in such subordinate manifestations of it various aspects may be particularly emphasized at various times. In seeking a theological basis for the future diaconate, therefore, we do not need to make it our aim to evolve any absolutely univocal and uniform type of deacon. The priesthood, itself is subject to a wide range of variations, even though it is conceived of as consisting essentially in the authoritative preaching of the Gospel in the name of the Church, and in guiding and directing the community (both functions being thought of as a unity), and this in itself is enough to make it apparent that the diaconate does not necessarily have to be univocal and uniform in the sense indicated. Admittedly, it is necessary that a single basic essence of the diaconate, deriving from the very nature of order itself and from the concrete situation of the Church (for it is this that demands that the single institution of order shall be subdivided in this way) shall be common to all these variations of type, which the diaconate may assume in the concrete, and shall be recognizable as such in them all. But all that we can demand is that it shall continue to be sufficiently intelligible why this particular subdivision of order is called the diaconate, and how it is adequately to be distinguished in terms of theology from those other "official" functions that are present in the Church as institutions, and which are both distinct from the priestly office and at the same time not to be conceived of as pertaining to the diaconate. In this respect, it is inevitable that in the process of drawing the lines of division certain points will remain unclarified. The reason is first that in view of the variations in the way in which the single institution of order the Church is subdivided it is quite impossible wholly to avoid such points of obscurity; we have simply to accept them and make due allowance for them. Second, it is perfectly possible that the future situation of the Church will make it necessary, and will actually bring it about that new and hitherto unfamiliar ways of subdividing the institution of order will be introduced, and that concerning these it will not always be easy to say *a priori* whether they constitute a variant form of the diaconate or a subdivision of order which cannot be subsumed under this concept of the diaconate.

Now let us turn to certain negative demarcations of the diaconate. In order to be in a position to define these, the following preliminary points have to be made: the Church as a whole, and therefore all her members—including, therefore the so-called laity—have been entrusted with a ministry towards man to work for his salvation. This universal ministry has an individual and a social dimension affecting both those entrusted with it and those to whom it is directed. This universal Christian *diakonia*, binding in the same way upon clergy and lay people alike, is a Christian duty that no one individual can transfer to the rest. In this universal *diakonia*, each has a responsibility towards all, and each Christian has a responsibility not only towards his fellow Christians but essentially towards every man as well. But not withstanding this, the concrete form in which this universal *diakonia* or ministry is realized in the individual Christian life, and in which each individual discharges his personal responsibility varies according to the concrete circumstances of those involved, both those vested with this ministry and those to whom it is directed. Now without prejudice to this universal *diakonia,* there is a special *diakonia* proper to those who are officially ordained. The reason for this is twofold: First, ordination considered as an official institution too can be understood only as conferring the authorization, the duty, and the equipment to minister to other Christians and individuals. Second, in the community of Christians called the Church, which is of necessity constituted as a society with institutions, there is need for a special office with special functions and the powers entailed in these attached to it, with a particular part to play (we shall not be describing or justifying this in any more precise detail here) within this universal *diakonia*. On the basis of these prior considerations, we can now lay down the following negative lines of demarcation with regard to the diaconate in the special and restricted sense as part of the official institution of order in the Church, with special functions of its own. Its specific nature cannot, in any proper sense, be regarded as consisting in the function of leadership as such. For this is proper to the episcopal and priestly office. In some cases, as in the missions or communities deprived of priests, the deacon is entrusted with leadership functions of this kind, and this is perfectly possible chiefly in virtue of the fact that he belongs to the ranks of those who are officially ordained. But all such cases are secondary and do not imply that this leadership function belongs specifically to his particular office. Nor does the office of deacon imply that the laity are deprived of their mission and duty to exercise the universal diaconate or that these can transfer their mission to the officially ordained deacon. Again the officially ordained deacon is not, properly speaking, a mediator between clergy and lay people in the Church, for, at least in principle, there is no need for any such mediation even though it may be conceded that in specific sociological situations in the Church the deacon does perform a useful secondary function of this kind. In principle, however, this function does not constitute the very nature of his office, and the very fact that he himself belongs to the ranks of those who have been officially ordained—in other words, to the clergy—is in itself enough to show that this is not the case. Again the true nature of the diaconate cannot be defined in terms of specific cultic powers, even though *de facto* he may exercise powers of this kind, such as baptizing, conferring Christian burial, giving communion, performing the sacramentals, and so forth; at least, provided the official Church gives a certain authorization for them, such specifically sacral functions can also be assumed by any baptized layman, and even though this fact does not in itself alone in principle exclude the possibility of empowering the individual sacramentally to exercise a whole complex of such sacral functions, still at least today—in the present situation of the Church and the concrete possibilities thereby entailed—such functions should be left to laymen and should be regarded as functions that are not so important in themselves that they need to constitute a specific office in the Church of today. Nor does the office of deacon, in the proper sense, imply that bishops and priests should be able to transfer the specifically diaconal functions entailed in the institution of order in the Church in general to the deacon in the strict sense in such a way that they themselves would have nothing more to do with such diaconal functions. The institution of order is ultimately one, and any subdivisions introduced into it do not in fact imply that the various ways in which this single office is shared are simply set alongside one another as so many separate compartments. The significance of the episcopal office at least is such that the institution of order in general in the Church must be present in it in its fullness, and in view of this, those who hold it cannot transfer the specifically diaconal functions contained in it (which we shall have to define more precisely at a later stage) in such a way that they no longer remain the responsibility of the bishop himself. And the same applies analogously to the priestly office to the extent that this too involves leading a community constituted by a particular locality or class, analogous in structure to the Church presided over by the bishop. The fact that an office is subdivided does not in fact imply that single official institution is *a priori* split up into totally different functions. Rather, it signifies a graded participation which is made necessary *a posteriori* by the concrete situation, because the technical work, material conditions, etc., involved are such that in practice no one individual can perform by himself everything that is absolutely speaking required of his office.

After applying these negative lines of demarcation to the office of deacon, we must now attempt to define its nature in positive terms. Once more, we have to emphasize that this process of defining the nature of the office of deacon cannot be deduced solely from any one abstract concept of the nature of officially constituted order in the Church. Rather, we have to take into account the concrete situation prevailing today in which this official institution has to fulfil its function.[10]

The office of order in the Church has the function of building up the Church herself, forming the community. Now this function of forming the community implies not merely a function of the kind that might be contrasted with the function of mediating personal salvation to the individual as such. On the contrary, this function of forming the community also and precisely implies that in human and Christian terms a place is assigned to the individual, as such, in the community such that in it he finds a position in the ecclesiastical and social life of the Church from which he can live out his own individual human and Christian life so as to achieve his salvation. This function of forming the community, which also and essentially involves certain prior conditions simply at the human level, and which also implies an integration of the individual into the community (something that is itself different from any totalitarian subjugation of the individual on the part of an ecclesiastical society) is confronted today, in the conditions of secular human life, with special difficulties entailed in the contemporary state of society. Hence, those officially vested with the task of forming the community, in this sense are required to become specialists in their own right, to learn special kinds of knowledge and skills such as cannot be either presupposed as already present or capable of being acquired by every ordained individual.

In earlier times, secular society itself was so constituted as to ensure that men were integrated to a greater or lesser degree, but in any case in sufficient measure, into secular society. Right from the first, they had in it that role that best fitted them and sufficient stability and security at the human level. The ecclesiastical community could from the outset presuppose a society at the secular level that was sufficiently integrated to provide due scope for the life of the individual, and did not need to make any special provision for this social integration of the individual into secular society.

Today, all this has changed. The individual man lives in a society that is in a state of great disintegration—and therefore in a state of insecurity as to his proper role—and this also implies a lack of the natural human substrate for a Christian life on the individuals' part, and for his incorporation into the Christian community as such. Of course, secular society itself has the task of striving ever anew to achieve this integration of society. But precisely in virtue of the institutional factors, which it creates for this purpose, it in turn introduces new forms of disintegration. Now what we have to bear in mind in the case of these individuals who are socially disintegrated in this sense is not merely those who, from the economical aspect, are very poor and oppressed, not merely the conflicts between the social classes in the usual sense of the term. There are other such forms of disintegration also. There are the lonely, those who are in various ways cast aside by secular society, deprived of any secure place or any role in society to give them stability and free them from burdens of care. There are also those who while they are still young and immature have to be integrated into society.

This task of integration is primarily a human one, one from which the Church even as such cannot withdraw herself if she is to serve humanity as such. It is a task for the Church even though in this respect she cannot claim any monopoly in discharging this task in human society. Furthermore, this task is a specifically ecclesiastical one to the extent that the integration of the individual at the human level into the human community and society is the necessary prior condition for the forming of an ecclesiastical community, while conversely any such process of forming an ecclesiastical community or of providing a permanent place for the individual in the community of the Church always also has repercussions upon the formation of the human community and the humanization of secular society.

This task, then, of integrating the individual both into a humanized secular society and at the same time, in particular, into the community of the Church is, from these various points of view, a function of the Church. And it is a function of such a kind that it presupposes specialist equipment and human qualities that can neither be possessed nor acquired by every one of the Church's official functionaries. But if this task, which we may surely describe with justice as a diaconal task in a specific sense, is a task for the *official* Church as such, and if today it cannot adequately be discharged by every one of the Church's officials for want of specialist equipment at the material and human level, then it follows that the Church today must institute a special subdivision within the single institution of order,[11] which can be called the diaconate in the specific sense and in the sense that we have defined. And it is precisely this that constitutes the diaconate as it must be today, regardless of whether the earlier diaconate did or did not have this specific content. This is not to dispute the fact that this diaconate of the future as understood in this sense does still continue to have a sufficient connection with the earlier diaconate to make it legitimate for us to apply the old name *diaconate* to it.[12]

The position is, then, that on the one hand, one of the tasks of the Church's official ministers is to build up the Christian community by integrating man into the civic and ecclesiastical community when he exists today in a state that is, to a large extent, disintegrated from a religious and social point of view, while on the other, this task cannot be fulfilled unless those charged with it have specialized formation of the most varied kind at their command, such as bishops and priests cannot possess. It is this position, therefore, that makes it necessary to have the diaconate as a special official institution.

We have now explained the starting-point for determining the nature of the future diaconate on the basis of the nature of the institution of order itself and of the contemporary situation of the Church in the concrete. But even though we have done this, many questions still remain open with regard to the forms in which it is to be developed in the concrete. It is, in a true sense, evident in the light of our basic position that even in respect of the sphere allotted to him from the very nature of the diaconate itself the future deacon cannot be an "all-round" deacon but must, rather, be himself in turn a specialist even within this sphere. The question of which specialized tasks pertaining to this diaconal ministry have to be discharged in a particular branch of the Church or local community by such a specialist holder of the office depends of course on the concrete circumstances of the particular branch of the Church or local community concerned. With regard to these specialist deacons, we should not seek to deduce too much *a priori*. For uniformity within the individual groupings within the Church is far from being an aim to be striven for. At this level, the particular and special forms of the diaconate that are developed should be arrived at on the basis of the concrete needs and requirements of the Church's life. A deacon may be working in a factory or trade, he may be running a community home, he may be a welfare worker, an assistant in pastoral work, a specialist in marriage counseling, engaged in preventing suicides, or in similar tasks. All these are perfectly possible concrete forms of the diaconate that may be developed, although it is clear that those engaged in them should have a minimum of specifically religious powers and duties and, by actively engaging in the celebration of the eucharist on Sundays, should give expression to the fact that the diaconate, as the spirit of fraternity put into practice, finds its starting-point and its supreme sacramental realization in the sacrament of unity. It seems to me that, with regard to these concrete forms of the diaconate that are developed, the question of the teacher of religion in primary and secondary schools represents a special problem. Perhaps, it is not necessary to conclude without further ado that the function of the "teacher" who is not a priest in the Church, the function of the "lay theologian" in the Church, should be subsumed under the diaconate as understood here. The "teacher" (*didaskalos*) in the Church already figures prominently in the New Testament, and it must be remembered first that he does not necessarily have to be identified with the priestly leader of the community, and second that it cannot simply be taken for granted that the only possible role for such a teacher in the Church of the future will be as a teacher of religious doctrine to immature schoolchildren. These facts in themselves are enough to show that the role of "teacher" in the Church does not necessarily have to be subsumed under the diaconate as understood here. But at least certain concrete roles that will be developed for the "teachers" in the Church (i.e., those in which the teaching given to adults is designed to introduce these to the Christian life, and so into the Christian community) can perfectly well be understood as a specialized form of the diaconate.

The theological nature of the diaconate has nothing in it that decides the question beforehand of whether a deacon should work as a "full-time" deacon (i.e., engage himself in this ministry as his chief calling in the secular sense) or whether he should exercise his office on what is, from the point of view of the state, a "part-time basis." The theological nature of the diaconate does not predetermine from the outset the question of whether a combination of ecclesiastical office and secular calling of this kind constitutes simply the *de facto* combination of two roles that do not have much to do with one another or whether, as in the case of the worker-priests properly so called, these two tasks compenetrate one another. The theological essence of the diaconate does not predetermine from the outset whether deacons should be drawn from the ranks of younger men or from the class of those who have been prematurely relegated to retirement by contemporary society because their physical powers have been somewhat reduced even though they have reached the full maturity of their experience of life. All these possibilities are given, and which of them are to be realized in practice is a question that must be decided in the light of the concrete circumstances involved. The same applies to the question of whether a deacon should work as an individual in isolation or in a team made up of several deacons; whether he should work directly under the bishop in the fulfillment of his task or should be assigned to one particular parish priest.

In any doctrinal review of the nature of the diaconate, one thing further must also be said concerning the sacramental grace that is imparted through this sacrament. A sacramental grace that is ritually communicated by the conferring of a given office in the Church has, in virtue of that fact in itself, a quite peculiar character. The reason that it is imparted by means of a ritual conferment of office is because this office can only be exercised in accordance with its true nature if it is fulfilled in faith, hope, and love. The reason is that while the absence of any personal or "existential" engagement on the part of the individual (i.e., in the case supposed, an engagement that is sustained by grace) certainly does not simply "invalidate" the ways in which this office is fulfilled, still it is contrary to the nature of the office itself and, hence, something that is indeed conceivable in individual holders of office, but not in the Church as a whole. For in her, the dimension of her social and historical reality can never totally and definitively be separated from her endowment with the Spirit. Any conferment of office by the Church and in her, therefore, always also constitutes the offering and the promise of that grace which alone really makes the fulfillment of this office an ecclesiastical fulfillment in the full sense. Any such "grace of office," therefore, is given precisely in order that the individual holder of the office may fulfil his ministry for the other members of the Church in accordance with its true nature. It "sanctifies" the holder of the office precisely inasmuch as it equips him not to seek his own sanctification in an "egoistical" manner, but rather, by directing his gaze away from himself and forgetting himself, to serve his neighbor in the Church.

It is in this that the very essence of every charisma of office, every "grace of office" consists. It "sanctifies" the individual on whom it is conferred precisely in virtue of the fact that he forgets himself in the service of his neighbor. Hence, it is that on any true understanding of the nature of the Church as a society and as pneumatic at the same time the grace of office is not, properly speaking, something that is supplementary, that fills out the basic equipment that is given when an office is conferred within her, but rather actually constitutes this basic equipment of office in itself. This in itself *ipso facto* implies the further point that this grace of office is not something that takes place solely at that particular point in time when the office is sacramentally conferred and actually constitutes that point, but rather implies the promise of God to support with his grace the whole conduct of office on the part of the ordained individual in his life, a promise which, therefore, is constantly achieving fresh actualization in the life of the deacon. Once we recognize that to be appointed to the diaconal function in the Church is something abiding and ultimately irrevocable, and recognize too that the promise entailed in this of the assistance of the Spirit of the Church for the fulfillment of this task as something that is likewise abiding, we have *ipso facto* also achieved an understanding of that which in tradition and in the teaching of the Council of Trent is called sacramental character, something that is present in every "degree" of the single sacrament of order in the manner appropriate to each degree. It is really superfluous to embark on any lofty speculations over and above what has already been said concerning this "character *indelebilis*" inherent in the sacrament of order. Such speculations would merely give rise to ideas that are inessential or else would state in other terms something that is, in the very nature of the case, entailed in the enduring nature precisely of this specific ministerial task and the abiding nature of the offer of grace inherent in it.

Now if we are to give any adequate account of the sacramental grace of the diaconate, we must now consider this event of grace from yet a further aspect. For this purpose, we must undertake a consideration that touches upon the relationship that exists between grace and sacrament in general. Any shortsightedness in theology or any excessively naive piety constantly entails the danger of unconsciously falling into the position of regarding the sacraments exclusively as *the* events of grace alone (even though this is in contradiction to other firmly held theological positions). Such a position, however, is false. He who seeks God in a spirit of faith, love, and hope is *ipso facto* justified—a child of God and a temple of the Spirit even before he has received the baptism of water—though of course even in any such "subjective" attitude the will to receive baptism is implicitly and unconsciously included. At least in normal cases, he who comes to the sacrament of penance as a repentant sinner comes as one who has already been justified and whose sins have already been forgiven. The prayer of the *confiteor* before Mass, if it is uttered with a sincere heart, is not merely the desire addressed to God for the forgiveness of some sin, a desire emanating solely from the individual himself. Rather, it is an event of grace which God himself brings about in the individual and through his act. The question of why, without prejudice to these obvious points, the sacraments are, nevertheless, meaningful and, under certain circumstances necessary is one that cannot explicitly be discussed here. The reasonableness of and necessity for the sacraments arises ultimately from the nature of man as a physical person and from the "incarnatorial" dynamism of grace itself. For as the grace precisely of *Christ,* this seeks to project itself beyond the source and center of human living as endowed with grace and to achieve a dimension of historical concretion in space and time. For it is in this alone that even grace achieves its full effectiveness and power over all dimensions of human existence.

Let us, therefore, apply these points which we recognize as evidence to the diaconate. First, it is clear that there can be powers in the social dimension of the Church that, in order to exist at all and to be validly applied, presuppose in the society concerned a specific conferment of office achieved in a manner that is juridically defined. Speaking quite in general, it is also perfectly conceivable that such official functions in a society can be conferred in various ways. Now it has already been said that the particular functions inherent in the diaconate, however they are to be thought of in more precise terms in their particular details, and whatever possible new forms are to be conceived of for them, are "in themselves" also within the power of a "layman" and can be exercised by him even though this fact does not call in question the reasonableness of such a complex of tasks and powers as are involved in the diaconate, and therefore of the diaconate itself as an office in the Church. If we consider this point in conjunction with what has been said above with regard to extra-sacramental and pre-sacramental grace, then we can freely arrive at the following conclusion: that amalgam of functions that is or can be unified and sacramentally conferred in the diaconate already exists independently of any such sacramental conferring of office, and this complex amalgam of functions is exercised in its "lay" practitioners (provided the necessary conditions are present for grace to become effective) with a grace that is, in its effects, the same grace directed towards the service of neighbor, which is manifested and conferred *"ex opere operato"* in a sacramental mode in the sacramental order of the diaconate. We say this for the "consolation" of those who, in virtue of the functions that they do *de facto* exercise in the Church are striving to attain to the diaconate as a sacrament, but have not yet had it conferred upon them through the imposition of hands. In a Church that is permeated by the Holy Spirit even such a ministry as this cannot be "devoid of the Spirit." Conversely, however, it follows from the same radical connection between sacrament (sacramental sign) and grace that the fact that the lay "deacon" is endowed with the Spirit does not invalidate the reasonableness and relative necessity of the sacramental diaconate. Precisely this extra- and pre-sacramental grace enjoyed by the lay "deacon" demands, in virtue of its incarnatorial dynamism, to achieve its due sacramental manifestation in the Church in which this grace in itself finds the full realization of its essence. So true is this, indeed, that conversely this "incarnation" of it becomes the sign that effects the grace itself. This is true just as it is also the case that, when diaconal functions are exercised in the Church, and when these are entrusted in a more or less informal way to individuals, there is a tendency for them to become recognized and entrusted to those individuals in that more formal manner in which the recognition and the conferring of them can be called a sacrament in the proper sense, appointing the individuals concerned to the office of deacon.

Notes

1. In this study is the text of a lecture which the author gave on December 7, 1968 in Freiburg, on the occation of a conference on the diaconate. For the purposes of publication, a few notes have been added to it.

2. On the state of the discussion at the Council itself, cf. the commentary on article 29 of the Decree *Lumen Gentium*, by H. Vorgrimler, *LTK* Suppl. I (Freiburg, 1966), pp. 256-259; cf. also idem., *"Erneuerung des Diakonats nach dem Konzil,"* in *Der Seelsorger* 35 (1965), pp. 102-115; K. Rahner, "The Teaching of the Second Vatican Council on the Diaconate," *Theological Investigations* X (London/New York, 1973), pp. 222-234 [also published in this present volume]; also H. Vorgrimler, *"Sur Theologie des Diakonats. Thesen,"* *Der Diakon heute*, edited by the Cathedral School, *Akademie für Erwachsenenbildung der Diözese Würzburg,* 1969), pp. 39-43; idem., *"Der theologische Ort des Diakonats,"* *Handbuch der Pastoraltheologie* IV (Freiburg, 1969), pp. 417ff.

3. On this, cf. H. Schürmann, *"Neutestamentliche Marginalien zur Frage der Entsakralisierung,"* I/II, *Der Seelsorger* 38 (1968), pp. 38-40, 89-104; J. Blank, *"Der Priester im Lichte der Bibel,"* ibid., pp. 155-164. But see also, H. Schlier, *"Grundelemente des priesterlichen Amtes im Neuen Testament,"* *Theologie und Philosophie* 44 (1969), pp. 161-180.

4. There is a constantly increasing body of literature on this subject, which it is quite impossible to present here. For this reason, reference will only be made to the address which the author delivered on September 4, 1968, at the Conference of German Catholics in Essen: *"Dogmatische Grundlagen des priesterlichen Selbstverständnisses,"* *Mitten in dieser Welt*, edited by the Central Committee of German Catholics (Paderborn, 1968), pp. 96-115. Reference may also be made to the following articles: "The Point of Departure in Theology for Determining the Nature of the Priestly Office," in *Theological Investigations* XII (London/New York), pp. 31-38; "Theological Reflections upon the Priestly Image of Today and Tomorrow," in *Theological Investigations* XII (London/New York), pp. 39-60.

5. On this, cf. the author's article, *"Die Aufgleiderung des einen Amtes der Kirche"* in *Handbuch der Pastoral-theologie* I (Freiburg, 1964; 2nd ed. 1970), pp. 160-167, together with the chapters that follow. On the concept of office in general, reference may be made to the author's commentary on the third chapter of *Lumen Gentium* as found in *LTK* Suppl. I (Freiburg, 1966), pp. 210-246. On the question of whether it is possible for a way of subdividing the institution of order to be developed *juris divini* within Christian history, cf. also the author's article, "Reflection on the Concept of

Ius Divinum" in Catholic Thought's *Theological Investigations* V (London/Baltimore, 1966), pp. 219-243.

6. This also becomes clear in view of the very different motives adduced at the Council as arguments in favor of restoring the diaconate. In the *Decree on the Church,* the motive adduced is the importance of specific functions (no. 29); in the *Decree for the Eastern Churches,* the motive is the ancient discipline of the sacrament of order (no. 17); and in the *Decree on the Missions,* the fact that the diaconal ministry is already being exercised in practice (no. 16).

7. On this, cf. note 5, above.

8. On this, cf. my article, "The Theology of the Restoration of the Diaconate," in *Theologial Investigations* V (London/Baltimore, 1966), pp. 268-3143.

9. Up to the present, the best general presentation is still to be found in K. Rahner, H. Vorgrimler, ed., *Diakonia in Christo, Questiones Disputatae* 15/16 (Freiburg, 1962).

10. So far as the present author is concerned, cf. on this requirement the considerations put forward at the scientific and speculative level in *Handbuch der Pastoral-theologie* II/1 (Freiburg, 1966), pp. 181-188, and further "Practical Theology within the Totality of Theological Disciplines," in *Theological Investigations* IX (London/New York, 1972), pp. 101-115.

11. On this, cf. also the section in *Handbuch der Pastoral-theologie* adduced in note 5, above.

12. On this, cf. also the author's "Practical Theology and Social Work in the Church," in *Theological Investigations* X (London/New York, 1972), pp. 349-370.